Informal Logic

Critical Thinking

Custom Edition

Sinnott Armstrong/Fogelin

CENGAGE
Learning·

Australia • Brazil • Japan • Korea • Mexico • Singapore • Spain • United Kingdom • United States

CENGAGE
Learning·

Informal Logic: Critical Thinking, Custom Edition

Cengage Advantage Books: Understanding Arguments: An Introduction to Informal Logic, 9th Edition
Walter Sinnott-Armstrong | Robert J. Fogelin

© 2015, 2010, 2005, 2001 Cengage Learning. All rights reserved.

Senior Manager, Student Engagement:

Linda deStefano

Janey Moeller

Manager, Student Engagement:

Julie Dierig

Marketing Manager:

Rachael Kloos

Manager, Production Editorial:

Kim Fry

Manager, Intellectual Property Project Manager:

Brian Methe

Senior Manager, Production and Manufacturing:

Donna M. Brown

Manager, Production:

Terri Daley

ALL RIGHTS RESERVED. No part of this work covered by the copyright herein may be reproduced, transmitted, stored or used in any form or by any means graphic, electronic, or mechanical, including but not limited to photocopying, recording, scanning, digitizing, taping, Web distribution, information networks, or information storage and retrieval systems, except as permitted under Section 107 or 108 of the 1976 United States Copyright Act, without the prior written permission of the publisher.

For product information and technology assistance, contact us at
Cengage Learning Customer & Sales Support, 1-800-354-9706
For permission to use material from this text or product,
submit all requests online at **cengage.com/permissions**
Further permissions questions can be emailed to
permissionrequest@cengage.com

This book contains select works from existing Cengage Learning resources and was produced by Cengage Learning Custom Solutions for collegiate use. As such, those adopting and/or contributing to this work are responsible for editorial content accuracy, continuity and completeness.

Compilation © 2014 Cengage Learning

ISBN-13: 978-1-305-30815-2

ISBN-10: 1-305-30815-8

WCN: 01-100-101

Cengage Learning

5191 Natorp Boulevard
Mason, Ohio 45040
USA

Cengage Learning is a leading provider of customized learning solutions with office locations around the globe, including Singapore, the United Kingdom, Australia, Mexico, Brazil, and Japan. Locate your local office at:
international.cengage.com/region.

Cengage Learning products are represented in Canada by Nelson Education, Ltd.
For your lifelong learning solutions, visit **www.cengage.com/custom.**
Visit our corporate website at **www.cengage.com.**

Printed in the United States of America

Brief Contents

Uses of Arguments

What are arguments? In our view, arguments are tools, so the first step toward understanding arguments is to ask what they are used for—what people are trying to accomplish when they give arguments. This brief chapter will propose a definition of arguments and then explore two main purposes of arguments: justification and explanation. Both justifications and explanations try to provide reasons, but reasons of different kinds. Justifications are supposed to give reasons to believe their conclusions, whereas explanations are supposed to give reasons why their conclusions are true. Each of these purposes is more complicated and fascinating than is usually assumed.

WHAT ARGUMENTS ARE

The word "argument" may suggest quarrels or squabbles. That is what a child means when she reports that her parents are having an argument. Arguments of that sort often include abuse, name-calling, and yelling. That is not what this book is about. The goal here is not to teach you to yell louder, to be more abusive, or to beat your opponents into submission.

Our topic is the kind of argument defined by Monty Python in their justly famous "Argument Clinic." In this skit, a client enters a clinic and pays for an argument. In the first room, however, all he gets is abuse, which is not argument. When he finally finds the right room to get an argument, the person who is supposed to give him an argument simply denies whatever the client says, so the client complains that mere denial is different from argument, because "an argument is a connected series of statements to establish a definite proposition." This definition is almost correct. As we will see, the purpose of an argument need not always be to "establish" its conclusion, both because some conclusions were established in advance and because many reasons are inconclusive. Nonetheless, Monty Python's definition needs to be modified only a little in order to arrive at an adequate definition:

> An argument is a connected series of sentences, statements, or propositions
> (called "premises") that are intended to give a reason of some kind for a sentence,
> statement, or proposition (called the "conclusion").

This definition does not pretend to be precise, but it does tell us what arguments are made of (sentences, statements, or propositions) and what their purpose is (to give reasons).

Another virtue of this definition is that it is flexible enough to cover the wide variety of arguments that people actually give. Different arguments are intended to give reasons of very different sorts. These reasons might be justificatory reasons to believe or to disbelieve some claim. They might, instead, be explanatory reasons why something happened. They might even be practical reasons to do some act. Because reasons come in so many kinds, arguments are useful in a great variety of situations in daily life. Trying to determine why your computer crashed, why your friend acted the way she did, and whether it will rain tomorrow as well as trying to decide which political candidate to vote for, which play to use at a crucial point in a football game, where to go to college, and whether to support or oppose capital punishment—all involve weighing and evaluating reasons.

It is inaccurate, therefore, to think of arguments as serving only one single, simple purpose. People often assume that you always use every argument to make other people believe what you believe and what they did not believe before hearing or reading the argument. Actually, however, some arguments are used for that purpose, but others are not. To fully understand arguments in all their glory, then, we need to distinguish different uses of argument. In particular, we will focus on two exemplary purposes: justification and explanation.

JUSTIFICATIONS

One of the most prominent uses of arguments is to justify a disputed claim. For example, if I claim that September 11, 2001, was a Tuesday, and you deny this or simply express some doubt, then we might look for a calendar. But suppose we don't have a calendar for 2001. Luckily, we do find a calendar for 2002. Now I can justify my claim to you by presenting this argument: The calendar shows that September 11 was on Wednesday in 2002; 2002 was not a leap year, since 2002 is not divisible by 4; nonleap years have 365 days, which is 1 more day than 52 weeks; so September 11 must have been on Tuesday in 2001. You should now be convinced.

What have I done? My utterance of this argument has the *effect* of changing your mind by getting you to believe a conclusion that you did not believe before. Of course, I might also be able to change your mind by hypnotizing you. But normally I do not want to use hypnosis. I also do not want to change your mind by manufacturing a fake calendar for 2002 with the wrong dates or by fooling you with a bad argument. Such tricks would not satisfy my goals fully. This shows that changing your mind is not all that I am trying to accomplish. I want more than simply to *persuade* you or *convince* you. What else do I want? My additional aim is to show you that you *should* change your mind, and why. I want my argument to be *good* and to give you a *good reason* to change your mind. I want my argument not only to persuade you but also to make you *justified* in believing my conclusion.

The above example is typical of one kind of justification, but there are other patterns. Suppose that I share your doubts about which day of the week it was on September 11, 2001. Then I might use the same argument to justify my belief as well as yours. Indeed, you don't even need to be present. If I am all alone, and I just want to figure out which day of the week it was on September 11, 2001, then I might think in terms of this same argument. Here the goal is not to convince anybody else, but the argument is still used to find a good reason to believe the conclusion.

In cases like these, we can say that the argument is used for *impersonal normative justification*. The justification is normative because the goal is to find a reason that is a good reason. It is impersonal because what is sought is a reason that is or should be accepted as a good reason by everyone capable of grasping this argument, regardless of who they are. The purpose is to show that there *is* a reason to believe the conclusion, regardless of who *has* a reason to believe it. Other arguments, in contrast, are aimed at specific people, and the goal is to show that those particular people are committed to the conclusion or have a reason to believe the conclusion. Such individualized uses of arguments seek what can be called *personal justification*.

There should be nothing surprising about different people having different reasons. I might climb a mountain to appreciate the view at the top, whereas you climb it to get exercise, and your friend climbs it to be able to talk to you while you climb it. Different people can have different reasons for the same action. Similarly, different people can have different reasons to believe the same conclusion. Suppose that someone is murdered in the ballroom with a revolver. I might have good reason to believe that Miss Peacock did not commit the murder, because I saw her in the library at the time the murder was committed. You might not trust me when I tell you that I saw her, but you still might have good reason to believe that she is innocent, because you believe that Colonel Mustard did it alone. Even if I doubt that Colonel Mustard did it, we still each have our own reasons to agree that Miss Peacock is innocent.

When different people with different beliefs are involved, we need to ask who is supposed to accept the reason that is given in an argument. A speaker might give an argument to show a listener that the speaker has a reason to believe something, even though the speaker knows that the audience does not and need not accept that reason. Suppose that you are an atheist, but I am an evangelical Christian, and you ask me why I believe that Jesus rose from the dead. I might respond that the Bible says that Jesus rose from the dead, and what the Bible says must be true, so Jesus rose from the dead. This argument tells you what *my* reasons are for believing what I believe, even if *you* do not accept those reasons. My argument can be used to show you that

I have reasons and what my reasons are, regardless of whether you believe that my reasons are good ones and also regardless of whether my reasons really are good ones.

The reverse can also happen. A speaker might give an argument to show a listener that the listener has a reason to believe something, even though the speaker does not accept that reason. Suppose that you often throw loud parties late into the night close to my bedroom. I want to convince you to stop or at least quiet down. Fortunately, you think that every citizen ought to obey the law. I disagree, for I am an anarchist bent on undermining all governments and laws. Still, I want to get a good night's sleep before the protest tomorrow, so I might argue that it is illegal to make that much noise so late, and you ought to obey the law, so you ought to stop throwing such loud parties. This argument can show you that *you* are committed to its conclusion, even if *I* believe that its premises are false.

Of course, whether I succeed in showing my audience that they have a reason to believe my conclusion depends on who my audience is. My argument won't work against loud neighbors who don't care about the law. Consequently, we need to know who the audience is and what they believe in order to be able to show them what reason they have to believe a conclusion.

In all of these cases, arguments are used to show that someone has a reason to believe the conclusion of the argument. That is why all of these uses can be seen as providing different kinds of justification. The differences become crucial when we try to evaluate such arguments. If my goal is to show you that you have a reason to believe something, then I can be criticized for using a premise that you reject. Your beliefs are no basis for criticism, however, if all I want is to show my own reasons for believing the conclusion. Thus, to evaluate an argument properly, we often need to determine not only whether the argument is being used to justify a belief but also which kind of justification is sought and who the audience is.

EXERCISE I

Write the best brief argument you can to justify each of the following claims to someone who does not believe them.

1. Nine is not a prime number.
2. Seven is a prime number.
3. A molecule of water has three atoms in it.
4. Water is not made up of carbon.
5. The U.S. president lives in Washington, D.C.
6. The Earth is not flat.
7. Humans have walked on the moon.
8. Most bicycles have two wheels.

DISCUSSION QUESTION

When, if ever, is it legitimate to try to convince someone else to believe something on the basis of a premise that you yourself reject? Consider a variety of cases.

EXPLANATIONS

A different but equally important use of arguments is to provide explanations. Explanations answer questions about how or why something happened. We explain how a mongoose got out of his cage by pointing to a hole he dug under the fence. We explain why Smith was acquitted by saying that he got off on a technicality. The purpose of explanations is not to prove that something happened, but to make sense of things.

An example will bring out the difference between justification and explanation. One person claims that a school's flagpole is thirty-five feet tall, and someone else asks her to justify this claim. In response, she might produce a receipt from the Allegiance Flagpole Company acknowledging payment for a flagpole thirty-five feet in height. Alternatively, she may put a stick straight up into the ground, measure the stick's length and its shadow's length, then measure the length of the flagpole's shadow, and calculate the length of the flagpole. Neither of these justifications, however, will answer a different question: *Why* is the flagpole thirty-five feet tall? This new question could be answered in all sorts of ways, depending on context: The school could not afford a taller one. It struck the committee as about the right height for the location. That was the only size flagpole in stock. There is a state law limiting flagpoles to thirty-five feet. And so on. These answers help us understand why the flagpole is thirty-five feet tall. They explain its height.

Sometimes simply filling in the details of a story provides an explanation. For example, we can explain how a two-year-old girl foiled a bank robbery by saying that the robber tripped over her while fleeing from the bank. Here we have made sense out of an unusual event by putting it in the context of a plausible *narrative*. It is unusual for a two-year-old girl to foil a bank robbery, but there is nothing unusual about a person tripping over a child when running recklessly at full speed in a crowded area.

Although the narrative is probably the most common form of explanation in everyday life, we also often use arguments to give explanations. We can explain a certain event by deriving it from established principles and accepted facts. This argument then has the following form:

    (1) General principles or laws
    (2) A statement of initial conditions
∴(3) A statement of the phenomenon to be explained

The symbol "∴" is pronounced "therefore" and indicates that the premises above the line are supposed to give a reason for the conclusion below the line. By "initial conditions" we mean those facts in the context that, together with appropriate general principles and laws, allow us to derive the result that the event to be explained occurs.

This sounds quite abstract, but an example should clarify the basic idea. Suppose we put an ice cube into a glass and then fill the glass with water to the brim. The ice will stick out above the surface of the water. What will happen when the ice cube melts? Will the water overflow? Will it remain at the same level? Will it go down? Here we are asking for a *prediction*, and it will, of course, make sense to ask a person to *justify* whatever prediction he or she makes. Stumped by this question, we let the ice cube melt to see what happens. We observe that the water level remains unchanged. After a few experiments, we convince ourselves that this result always occurs. We now have a new question: *Why* does this occur? Now we want an explanation of this phenomenon. The explanation turns upon the law of buoyancy, which says that an object in water is buoyed up by a force equal to the weight of the water it displaces. This law implies that, if we put an object in water, it will continue to sink until it displaces a volume of water whose weight is equal to its own weight (or else the object hits the bottom of the container). With this in mind, go back to the original problem. An ice cube is itself simply water in a solid state. Thus, when it melts, it will exactly fill in the volume of water it displaced, so the water level will remain unchanged.

We can now see how this explanation conforms to the argumentative pattern mentioned above:

(1) General principles or laws (Primarily the law of buoyancy)
(2) Initial conditions (An ice cube in a glass of water filled to the brim)
∴(3) Phenomenon explained (The level of the water remaining unchanged after the ice cube melts)

This explanation is fairly good. People with only a slight understanding of science can follow it and see why the water level remains unchanged. We should also notice that it is not a *complete* explanation, because certain things are simply taken for granted—for example, that things do not change weight when they pass from a solid to a liquid state. To put the explanation into perfect argumentative form, this assumption and many others would have to be stated explicitly. This is never done in everyday life and is only rarely done in the most exact sciences.

Is this explanation any good? Explanations are satisfactory if they remove bewilderment or surprise by telling us *how* or *why* something happened in a way that is relevant to the concerns of a particular context. Our example does seem to accomplish that much. However, it might seem that even the best explanations are not very useful because they take so much for granted. In explaining why the water level remains the same when the ice cube melts, we cited the law of buoyancy. Now, why should that law be true? What explains *it*? To explain the law of buoyancy, we would have to derive it from other laws that are more general and, perhaps, more intelligible. In fact, this has been done. Archimedes simultaneously proved and explained the law of buoyancy by deriving it from the laws of the lever. How about the laws of the lever? Can they be proved and explained by deriving them from still higher and more comprehensive laws? Perhaps. Yet reasons give out, and sooner or later explanation (like justification) comes to an end. It is the task of science and all rational inquiry to move that boundary further and further back. But even when there is more to explain, that does not show that a partial explanation is totally useless. As we have seen, explanations can be useful even when they are incomplete, and even though they are not used to justify any disputed claim. Explanation is, thus, a separate use of arguments.

EXERCISE II

Houses in Indonesia sometimes have their electrical outlets in the middle of the wall rather than at floor level. Why? A beginning of an explanation is that flooding is a danger in the Netherlands. Citing this fact does not help much, however, unless one remembers that Indonesia was formerly a Dutch colony. We can understand why the Dutch might put their electrical outlets above floor level in the Netherlands. It is safer in a country where flooding is a danger. Is flooding, then, a similar danger in Indonesia? Apparently not; so why did the Dutch continue this practice in Indonesia? The answer is that colonial settlers tend to preserve their home customs, practices, and styles. The Dutch continued to build Dutch-style houses with the electrical outlets where (for them) they are normally placed—that is, in the middle of the wall rather than at floor level. Restate this explanation in the form of an argument (that is, specify its premises and conclusion).

EXERCISE III

Write a brief argument to explain each of the following. Indicate what facts and what general principles are employed in your explanations. (Do not forget those principles that may seem too obvious to mention.)

1. Why a lighter-than-air balloon rises.
2. Why there is an international date line.
3. Why average temperatures tend to be higher closer to the equator.
4. Why there are usually more college freshmen who plan to go to medical school than there are seniors who still plan to go to medical school.
5. Why almost no textbooks are more than eighteen inches high.
6. Why most cars have four tires (instead of more or fewer).
7. Why paintings by Van Gogh cost so much.
8. Why wages go up when unemployment goes down.

It is sometimes said that science tells us *how* things happen but does not tell us *why* they happen. In what ways is this contention right, and in what ways is it wrong?

COMBINATIONS: AN EXAMPLE

Although justification and explanation are distinct uses of arguments, we often want to know both *what* happened and also *why* it happened. Then we need to combine justifications and explanations. We can see how this works by considering a fictional crime.

Imagine that Madison was arrested for murdering her husband, Victor. Now she is on trial, and you are on the jury. Presumably, the police and the prosecuting attorneys would not have arrested and prosecuted her if they did not believe that Madison committed the murder, but are their beliefs justified? Should she be convicted and sent to prison? That's up to you and the other jurors to decide.

You do not want to convict her arbitrarily, of course, so you need arguments to justify you in believing that Madison is guilty. The goal of prosecuting attorneys is to provide such justification. Their means of reaching this goal is to present evidence and arguments during the trial. Although their ultimate conclusion is that you should find Madison guilty of murder, the prosecutors need to justify lots of little claims along the way.

It might seem too obvious to mention, but the prosecution first needs an argument to show that the victim died. After all, if nobody died, nobody was killed. This first argument can be pretty simple: This person was walking and talking before he was shot in the head; now his heart has stopped beating for a long time; so he must be dead. There can be complications, since some gunshot victims can be revived, but let's assume that an argument like this justifies the claim that the victim is dead.

We also want to know who the victim was. The body was identified by several of Victor's friends, we assume, so all the prosecution needs to argue is that identifications like this are usually correct, so it was Victor who died. This second argument also provides a justification, but it differs from the first argument in several ways. The first argument referred directly to the facts about Victor that show he died, whereas this second argument does not say which features of the victim show that it was Victor. Instead, this argument relies on trusting other people—Victor's friends—without knowing what it was about the victim's face that made them think it was Victor. Such appeals to authority will be discussed in more detail in Chapters 3 and 15.

The third issue is the cause of death. Here it is common to appeal to a medical authority. In our case, the coroner or medical examiner makes observations or runs scientific tests that provide premises for another argument that is supposed to justify the conclusion that Victor's death was caused by a bullet to the head. This argument is also an appeal to an authority, but here the authority is a scientific expert rather than a friend.

Yet another argument, possibly based on firing marks on the bullet, can then justify you in believing that the bullet came from a certain gun. More arguments, possibly based on eyewitnesses, then justify the claims that Madison was the person who fired that gun at Victor. And so on.

All of these arguments depend on background assumptions. When you see the marks on the bullet that killed Victor line up with the marks on another bullet that was fired from the alleged murder weapon, you assume that guns leave distinctive marks on bullets and that nobody switched the bullets. A good prosecutor will provide arguments for these assumptions, but nobody can prove everything. Arguments always start from assumptions. This problem will occupy us at several points later, including parts of Chapters 3 and 5. The point for now is just that the prosecution needs to produce several arguments of various kinds in order to justify the claim that Madison killed Victor.

It is also crucial that killing violates the law. If not, then Madison should not be found guilty for killing Victor. So, how can the prosecutor justify the assumption that such killing is illegal? Prosecutors usually just quote a statute or cite a common law principle and apply it to the case, but that argument assumes a lot of background information. In the case of a statute, there must be a duly elected legislature, it must have jurisdiction over the place and time where and when the killing occurred, it must follow required procedures, and the content of the law must be constitutionally permissible. Given such a context, if the legislature says that a certain kind of killing is illegal, then it is illegal. It is fascinating that merely announcing that something is illegal thereby makes it illegal. We will explore such performatives and speech acts in Chapter 2. For now we will simply assume that all of these arguments could be provided if needed.

Even so, Madison might have had some justification for killing Victor, such as self-defense. This justification for her act can be presented in an argument basically like this: I have a reason to protect my own life, and I need to kill Victor first in order to protect my own life, so I have a reason to kill Victor. This justification differs in several ways from the kind of justification that we have been discussing so far. For one thing, this argument provides a reason for a different person—a reason for Madison—whereas the preceding arguments provided a reason for you as a juror. This argument also provides a reason with a different kind of object, since it justifies an action (killing Victor) whereas the previous arguments justified a belief (the belief that Madison did kill Victor). It provides a practical reason instead of an intellectual reason. Despite these differences, however, if her attorneys want to show that Madison has this new kind of justification, they need to give an argument to show that she was justified in doing what she did.

Even if Madison had no justification, she still might have had an excuse. Whereas a justification is supposed to show that the act was the right thing to do, an excuse admits that the act was wrong but tries to show that the agent was not fully responsible for doing it. Madison might, for example, argue that she honestly believed that Victor was going to kill her if she did not kill him first. If she offers this only as an excuse, she can admit that her belief was mistaken, so she had no justification for killing Victor. Her claim is, instead, that she was not fully responsible for his death because she was only trying to defend herself.

Excuses like this are, in effect, explanations. By citing her mistake, Madison explains why she did what she did. If she had killed Victor because she hated him or because she wanted to take his money, then she would have no excuse. Her act is less blameworthy, however, if she was mistaken. Of course, you should be careful before you shoot someone, so Madison could still be guilty of carelessness or negligence. But that is not as bad as killing someone out of hatred or for money. Her mistake might even be reasonable. If Victor was aiming a gun at her, then, even if it turned out not to be loaded, any rational person in her position might have thought that Victor was on the attack. Such reasonable mistakes might reduce or even remove responsibility. Thus, by explaining her act as a mistake, Madison puts her act in a better light than it would appear without that explanation. In general, an excuse is just an explanation of an act that puts that act in a better light by reducing the agent's responsibility.

To offer an excuse, then, Madison's defense attorneys will need to give arguments whose purpose is not justification but explanation. This excuse will then determine what she is guilty of. Whether Madison is guilty of first-degree murder or some lesser charge, such as second-degree murder or manslaughter, or even no crime at all, depends on the explanation for her act of killing Victor.

Several of the earlier arguments also provided explanations. The medical examiner cited the head wound to explain why Victor stopped breathing. The victim's identity explained why his friends said he was Victor. The fact that the bullet came out of a particular gun explained why it had certain markings. The legislature's vote explained why the killing was illegal. And so on.

In this way, what appears at first to be a simple case actually depends on a complex chain of arguments that mixes justifications with explanations. All of these justifications and explanations can be understood by presenting them explicitly in the form of arguments.

One final point is crucial. Suppose that Madison has no justification or excuse for killing Victor. It is still not enough for the prosecutor to give any old argument that Madison killed Victor. The prosecution must prove guilt beyond a reasonable doubt. This burden of proof makes the strength of the argument crucial. You as a juror should not convict, even if you think Madison is guilty, unless the prosecution's argument meets this high standard. In this case, as in many others, it is not enough just to be able to identify the argument and to understand its purpose. You also need to determine how strong it is.

For such reasons, we all need to understand arguments and to be able to evaluate them. This need arises not only in law but also in life, such as when we decide which candidate to vote for, what course to take, whether to believe that your spouse is cheating on you, and so on. The goal of this book is to teach the skills needed for understanding and assessing arguments about important issues like these.

DISCUSSION QUESTION

In his famous testimony to the United Nations Security Council on February 5, 2003, which was forty-two days before U.S. troops entered Iraq, Secretary of State Colin Powell gave several arguments for his main conclusion that Saddam Hussein was at that time still trying to obtain fissile material for a nuclear weapons program. His arguments mix justification with explanation. For each of his arguments, determine whether it is a justification or an explanation. How does each argument work? How strong is it? How would you respond if you disagreed? How would you defend that part against criticisms? It will, of course, be difficult to answer these questions before studying the rest of this book. However, it is worthwhile to reflect on how much you already understand at the start. It is also useful to have some concrete examples to keep in mind as you study arguments in more depth.

Let me turn now to nuclear weapons. We have no indication that Saddam Hussein has ever abandoned his nuclear weapons program. On the contrary, we have more than a decade of proof that he remains determined to acquire nuclear weapons.

To fully appreciate the challenge that we face today, remember that in 1991 the inspectors searched Iraq's primary nuclear weapons facilities for the first time, and they found nothing to conclude that Iraq had a nuclear weapons program. But, based on defector information, in May of 1991, Saddam Hussein's lie was exposed. In truth, Saddam Hussein had a massive clandestine nuclear weapons program that covered several different techniques to enrich uranium, including electromagnetic isotope separation, gas centrifuge and gas diffusion.

We estimate that this illicit program cost the Iraqis several billion dollars. Nonetheless, Iraq continued to tell the IAEA that it had no nuclear weapons program. If Saddam had not been stopped, Iraq could have produced a nuclear bomb by 1993, years earlier than most worst case assessments that had been made before the war.

In 1995, as a result of another defector, we find out that, after his invasion of Kuwait, Saddam Hussein had initiated a crash program to build a crude

(continued)

nuclear weapon, in violation of Iraq's UN obligations. Saddam Hussein already possesses two out of the three key components needed to build a nuclear bomb. He has a cadre of nuclear scientists with the expertise, and he has a bomb design.

Since 1998, his efforts to reconstitute his nuclear program have been focused on acquiring the third and last component: sufficient fissile material to produce a nuclear explosion. To make the fissile material, he needs to develop an ability to enrich uranium. Saddam Hussein is determined to get his hands on a nuclear bomb.

He is so determined that he has made repeated covert attempts to acquire high-specification aluminum tubes from eleven different countries, even after inspections resumed. These tubes are controlled by the Nuclear Suppliers Group precisely because they can be used as centrifuges for enriching uranium.

By now, just about everyone has heard of these tubes and we all know that there are differences of opinion. There is controversy about what these tubes are for. Most U.S. experts think they are intended to serve as rotors in centrifuges used to enrich uranium. Other experts, and the Iraqis themselves, argue that they are really to produce the rocket bodies for a conventional weapon, a multiple rocket launcher.

Let me tell you what is not controversial about these tubes. First, all the experts who have analyzed the tubes in our possession agree that they can be adapted for centrifuge use.

Second, Iraq had no business buying them for any purpose. They are banned for Iraq.

I am no expert on centrifuge tubes, but this is an old army trooper. I can tell you a couple things.

First, it strikes me as quite odd that these tubes are manufactured to a tolerance that far exceeds U.S. requirements for comparable rockets. Maybe Iraqis just manufacture their conventional weapons to a higher standard than we do, but I don't think so.

Second, we actually have examined tubes from several different batches that were seized clandestinely before they reached Baghdad. What we notice in these different batches is a progression to higher and higher levels of specification, including in the latest batch an anodized coating on extremely smooth inner and outer surfaces.

Why would they continue refining the specifications? Why would they go to all that trouble for something that, if it was a rocket, would soon be blown into shrapnel when it went off?

The high-tolerance aluminum tubes are only part of the story. We also have intelligence from multiple sources that Iraq is attempting to acquire magnets and high-speed balancing machines. Both items can be used in a gas centrifuge program to enrich uranium.

In 1999 and 2000, Iraqi officials negotiated with firms in Romania, India, Russia and Slovenia for the purchase of a magnet production plant. Iraq wanted the plant to produce magnets weighing twenty to thirty grams. That's the same weight as the magnets used in Iraq's gas centrifuge program before the Gulf War.

This incident, linked with the tubes, is another indicator of Iraq's attempt to reconstitute its nuclear weapons program.

Intercepted communications from mid-2000 through last summer showed that Iraqi front companies sought to buy machines that can be used to balance gas centrifuge rotors. One of these companies also had been involved in a failed effort in 2001 to smuggle aluminum tubes into Iraq.

People will continue to debate this issue, but there is no doubt in my mind. These illicit procurement efforts show that Saddam Hussein is very much focused on putting in place the key missing piece from his nuclear weapons program, the ability to produce fissile material.

2

THE WEB OF LANGUAGE

Arguments are made up of language, so we cannot understand arguments without first understanding language. This chapter will examine some of the basic features of language, stressing three main ideas. First, language is conventional. *Words acquire meaning within a rich system of linguistic conventions and rules. Second, the uses of language are* diverse. *We use language to communicate information, but we also use it to ask questions, issue orders, write poetry, keep score, formulate arguments, and perform an almost endless number of other tasks. Third, meaning is often conveyed* indirectly. *To understand the significance of many utterances, we must go beyond what is literally said to examine what is conversationally implied by saying it.*

LANGUAGE AND CONVENTION

The preceding chapter stressed that arguing is a *practical* activity. More specifically, it is a *linguistic* activity. Arguing is one of the many things that we can do with words. In fact, unlike things that we can accomplish both with words and without words (like making people happy, angry, and so forth), arguing is something we can *only* do with words or other meaningful symbols. That is why nonhuman animals never give arguments. To understand how arguments work, then, it is crucial to understand how language works.

Unfortunately, our understanding of human language is far from complete, and linguistics is a young science in which disagreement exists on many important issues. Still, certain facts about language are beyond dispute, and recognizing them will provide a background for understanding how arguments work.

As anyone who has bothered to think about it knows, language is conventional. There is no reason why we, as English speakers, use the word "dog" to refer to a dog rather than to a cat, a tree, or the number of planets in our solar system. It seems that any word might have been used to stand for anything. Beyond this, there seems to be no reason why we put words together the way we do. In English, we put adjectives before the nouns they modify. We thus speak of a "green salad." In French, adjectives usually follow the noun, and so, instead of saying "verte salade," the French say "salade verte."

The conventions of our own language are so much with us that it strikes us as odd when we discover that other languages have different conventions. A French diplomat once praised his own language because, as he said, it followed the natural order of thought. This strikes English speakers as silly, but in seeing why it is silly, we see that the word order in our own language is conventional as well.

Although it is important to realize that language is conventional, it is also important not to misunderstand this fact. From the idea that language is conventional, it is easy to conclude that language is totally arbitrary. If language is totally arbitrary, then it might seem that it really does not matter which words we use or how we put them together. It takes only a little thought to see that this view, however daring it might seem, misrepresents the role of conventions in language. If we wish to communicate with others, we must follow the system of conventions that others use. Grapefruits are more like big lemons than like grapes, so you might want to call them "mega-lemons." Still, if you order a glass of mega-lemon juice in a restaurant, you will get stares and smirks but no grapefruit juice. The same point lies behind this famous passage in *Through the Looking Glass,* by Lewis Carroll:

> "There's glory for you!"
> "I don't know what you mean by 'glory'," Alice said.
> Humpty Dumpty smiled contemptuously.
> "Of course you don't—till I tell you. I meant 'there's a nice knock-down argument for you!'"
> "But 'glory' doesn't mean 'a nice knock-down argument'," Alice objected.
> "When I use a word," Humpty Dumpty said, in a rather scornful tone, "it means just what I choose it to mean—neither more nor less."
> "The question is," said Alice, "whether you can make words mean so many different things."

The point, of course, is that Humpty Dumpty cannot make a word mean whatever he wants it to mean, and he cannot communicate if he uses words in his own peculiar way without regard to what those words themselves mean. Communication can take place only within a shared system of conventions. Conventions do not destroy meaning by making it arbitrary; conventions bring meaning into existence.

A misunderstanding of the conventional nature of language can lead to pointless disputes. Sometimes, in the middle of a discussion, someone will declare that "the whole thing is just a matter of definition" or "what you say is true by your definition, false by mine." There are times when definitions are important and the truth of what is said turns on them, but usually this is not the case. Suppose someone has fallen off a cliff and is heading toward certain death on the rocks below. Of course, it is a matter of convention that we use the word "death" to describe the result of the sudden, sharp stop at the end of the fall. We might have used some other word—perhaps "birth"—instead. But it certainly will not help a person who is falling to his certain death to shout out, "By 'birth' I mean death." It will not help even if *everyone* agrees to use these words in this new way. If we all decided to adopt this new convention, we would then say, "He is falling from the cliff to his certain birth" instead of "He is falling from the cliff to his certain death." But speaking in this way will not change the facts. It will not save him from perishing. It will not make those who care for him feel better.

The upshot of this simple example is that the *truth* of what we say is rarely just a matter of definition. Whether what we have said is true or not will depend, for the most part, on how things stand in the world. Abraham Lincoln, during his days as a trial lawyer, is reported to have cross-examined a witness like this:

"How many legs does a horse have?"
"Four," said the witness.
"Now, if we call a tail a leg, how many legs does a horse have?"
"Five," answered the witness.
"Nope," said Abe, "calling a tail a leg don't make it a leg."

In general, then, though the *meaning of* what we say is dependent on convention, the *truth* of what we say is not.

In the preceding sentence we used the qualifying phrase, "in general." To say that a claim holds *in general* indicates that there may be exceptions. This qualification is needed because sometimes the truth of what we say *is* simply a matter of definition. Take a simple example: The claim that a triangle has three sides is true by definition, because a triangle is defined as "a closed figure having three sides." Again, if someone says that sin is wrong, he or she has said something that is true by definition, for a sin is defined as, among other things, "something that is wrong." In unusual cases like these, things are true merely as a matter of convention. Still, in general, the truth of what we say is settled not by appealing to definitions but, instead, by looking at the facts. In this way, language is not arbitrary, even though it is conventional.

LINGUISTIC ACTS

In the previous section we saw that a language is a system of shared conventions that allows us to communicate with one another. If we examine language, we will see that it contains many different kinds of conventions. These conventions govern what we will call linguistic acts, speech acts, and conversational acts. We will discuss linguistic acts first.

We have seen that words have meanings conventionally attached to them. The word "dog" is used conventionally to talk about dogs. Given what our words mean, it would be incorrect to call dogs "airplanes." Proper names are also conventionally assigned, for Harry Jones could have been named

Wilbur Jones. Still, given that his name is not Wilbur, it would be improper to call him Wilbur. Rules like these, which govern meaning and reference, can be called *semantic* rules.

Other conventions concern the ways words can be put together to form sentences. These are often called *syntactic* or *grammatical* rules. Using the three words "John," "hit," and "Harry," we can formulate sentences with very different meanings, such as "John hit Harry" and "Harry hit John." We recognize that these sentences have different meanings, because we understand the grammar of our language. This grammatical understanding also allows us to see that the sentence "Hit John Harry" has no determinate meaning, even though the individual words do. (Notice that "Hit John, Harry!" *does* mean something: It is a way of telling Harry to hit John.) Grammatical rules are important, for they play a part in giving a meaning to combinations of words, such as sentences.

Some of our grammatical rules play only a small role in this important task of giving meaning to combinations of words. It is bad grammar to say, "If I was you, I wouldn't do that," but it is still clear what information the person is trying to convey. What might be called stylistic rules of grammar are of relatively little importance for logic, but grammatical rules that affect the meaning or content of what is said are essential to logical analysis. Grammatical rules of this kind can determine whether we have said one thing rather than another, or perhaps failed to say anything at all and have merely spoken nonsense.

It is sometimes hard to tell what is nonsense. Consider "The horse raced past the barn fell." This sentence usually strikes people as nonsense when they hear it for the first time. To show them that it actually makes sense, all we need to do is insert two words: "The horse that was raced past the barn fell." Since English allows us to drop "that was," the original sentence means the same as the slightly expanded version. Sentences like these are called "garden path sentences," because the first few words "lead you down the garden path" by suggesting that some word plays a grammatical role that it really does not play. In this example, "The horse raced . . ." suggests at first that the main verb is "raced." That makes it hard to see that the main verb really is "fell."

Another famous example is "Buffalo buffalo buffalo." Again, this seems like nonsense at first, but then someone points out that "buffalo" can be a verb meaning "to confuse." The sentence "Buffalo buffalo buffalo" then means "North American bison confuse North American bison." Indeed, we can even make sense out of "Buffalo buffalo Buffalo buffalo buffalo buffalo Buffalo buffalo Buffalo buffalo buffalo." This means "North American bison from Buffalo, New York, that North American bison from Buffalo, New York, confuse also confuse North American bison from Buffalo, New York, that North American bison from Buffalo, New York, confuse."

Examples like these show that sentences can have linguistic meaning when they seem meaningless. To be meaningful, sentences need to follow both *semantic* conventions that govern meanings of individual words and also *syntactic* or *grammatical* conventions that lay down rules for combining words into meaningful wholes. When a sentence satisfies essential semantic and syntactic conventions, we will say that the person who uttered that sentence performed a *linguistic act:* The speaker said something meaningful in a language.[1] The ability to perform linguistic acts shows a command of a language. What the speaker says may be false, irrelevant, boring, and so on; but, if in saying it linguistic rules are not seriously violated, then that person can be credited with performing a linguistic act.

Later, in Chapters 13 and 14, we will look more closely at semantic and syntactic conventions, for they are common sources of fallacies and other confusions. In particular, we shall see how these conventions can generate fallacies of ambiguity and fallacies of vagueness. Before examining the defects of our language, however, we should first appreciate that language is a powerful and subtle tool that allows us to perform a wide variety of jobs important for living in the world.

EXERCISE I

Read each of the following sentences aloud. Did you perform a linguistic act? If so, explain what the sentence means and why it might not seem meaningful.

1. The old man the ship.
2. Colorless green ideas sleep furiously.
3. Time flies like an arrow. Fruit flies like bananas.
4. The cotton clothing is made of grows in Mississippi.
5. The square root of pine is tree.
6. The man who whistles tunes pianos.
7. " 'Twas brillig, and the slithy toves did gyre and gimble in the wabe." (From Lewis Carroll)

And now some weird examples from Dan Wegner's Hidden Brain Damage Scale. If these make sense to you, it might be a sign of hidden brain damage. If they don't make sense, explain why:

8. People tell me one thing one day and out the other.
9. I feel as much like I did yesterday as I do today.
10. My throat is closer than it seems.
11. I've lost all sensation in my shirt.
12. There's only one thing for me.

DISCUSSION QUESTIONS

1. When someone hums (but does not sing) the "Star-Spangled Banner," does she perform a linguistic act? Why or why not?
2. Can a speaker mispronounce a word in a sentence without performing any linguistic act? Why or why not?

SPEECH ACTS

When asked about the function of language, it is natural to reply that we use language to describe objects and communicate ideas. These are, however, only some of the purposes for which we use language. Other purposes become obvious as soon as we look at the ways in which our language actually works. Adding up a column of figures is a linguistic activity—though it is rarely looked at in this way—but it does not describe any objects (since numbers are not objects) or communicate any ideas to others. When I add the figures, I am not even communicating anything to myself; I am just trying to figure something out. A look at our everyday conversations produces a host of other examples of language being used for different purposes. Grammarians, for example, have divided sentences into various moods, among which are:

Indicative: Barry Bonds hit a home run.

Imperative: Get in there and hit a home run, Barry!

Interrogative: Did Barry Bonds hit a home run?

Expressive: Hurray for Barry Bonds!

The first sentence states a fact. We can use it to communicate information about something that Barry Bonds did. If we use it in this way, then what we say will be either true or false. Notice that none of the other sentences can be called either true or false even though they are all meaningful.

PERFORMATIVES

The different types of sentences recognized by traditional grammarians show that we use language to do more than convey information, but they still give only a small sample of the wide variety of things that we can accomplish using language. Sometimes, for example, we use language to perform an action. In one familiar setting, if one person says, "I do," and another person says, "I do," and finally a third person says, "I now pronounce you husband and wife," the relationship between the first two people changes in a fundamental way: They thereby become married. With luck, they begin a life of wedded bliss, but they also alter their legal relationship. For example, they may now file joint income tax returns and may not legally marry other people without first getting divorced. The philosopher J. L. Austin labeled such utterances *performatives* in order to contrast performing an action with simply stating or describing something.[2]

Performatives come in a wide variety of forms. They are often in the first person (like "I do"), but not always. For example, "You're all invited to my house after the game" is in the second person, but uttering it performs the act of inviting. Even silence can amount to a performative act in special situations. When the chairperson of a meeting asks if there are any objections to a ruling and none is voiced, then the voters, through their silence, have accepted the ruling.

Because of this diversity of forms, it is not easy to formulate a definition that covers all performatives, so we will not even try to define performatives here. Instead, we will concentrate on one particularly clear subclass of performatives, which J. L. Austin called *explicit performatives*. All explicit performatives are utterances in the first-person singular indicative noncontinuous[3] present. But not all utterances of that form are explicit performatives. There is one more requirement:

> An utterance of that form is an explicit performative if and only if it yields a true statement when plugged into the following pattern:
> In saying "I _____" in appropriate circumstances, I thereby _____.

For example, "I congratulate you" expresses an explicit performative, because in saying "I congratulate you," I thereby congratulate you. Here a quoted expression occurs on the left side of the word "thereby" but not on the right side. This reflects the fact that the formula takes us from the words (which are quoted) to the world (the actual act that is performed). The *saying*, which is referred to on the left side of the pattern, amounts to the *doing* referred to on the right side of the word "thereby." We will call this the *thereby test* for explicit performatives.

The thereby test includes an important qualification: *The context of the utterance must be appropriate.* You have not congratulated anyone if you say, "I congratulate you," when no one is around, unless you are congratulating yourself. Congratulations said by an actor in a play are not real congratulations, and so on.

Assuming an appropriate context, all of the following sentences meet the thereby test:

> I promise to meet you tomorrow.
>
> I bid sixty-six dollars. (Said at an auction)
>
> I bid one club. (Said in a bridge game)
>
> I resign from this club.
>
> I apologize for being late.

Notice that it doesn't make sense to *deny* any of these performatives. If someone says, "I bid sixty-six dollars," it is not appropriate for someone to reply "No, you don't" or "That's false." It could, however, be appropriate for someone to reply, "You can't bid sixty-six dollars, because the bidding is already up to seventy dollars." In this case, the person tried to make a bid, but failed to do so.

Several explicit performatives play important roles in constructing arguments. These include sentences of the following kind:

> I *conclude* that this bill should be voted down.
>
> I *base* my conclusion on the assumption that we do not want to hurt the poor.
>
> I *stipulate* that anyone who earns less than $10,000 is poor.
>
> I *assure* you that this bill will hurt the poor.
>
> I *concede* that I am not absolutely certain.
>
> I *admit* that there is much to be said on both sides of this issue.
>
> I *give my support* to the alternative measure.
>
> I *deny* that this alternative will hurt the economy.
>
> I *grant* for the sake of argument that some poor people are lazy.
>
> I *reply* that most poor people contribute to the economy.
>
> I *reserve comment* on other issues raised by this bill.

We will call this kind of performative an *argumentative performative.* Studying such argumentative performatives can help us to understand what is going on in arguments, which is one main reason why we are studying performatives here.

In contrast to the above utterances, which pass the thereby test, none of the following utterances does:

> I agree with you. (This describes one's thoughts or beliefs, so, unlike a performative, it can be false.)

I am sorry for being late. (This describes one's feelings and could be false.)

Yesterday I bid sixty dollars. (This is a statement about a past act and might be false.)

I'll meet you tomorrow. (This utterance may only be a prediction that can turn out to be false.)

Questions, imperatives, and exclamations are also not explicit performatives, because they cannot sensibly be plugged into the thereby test at all. They do not have the right form, since they are not in the first-person singular indicative noncontinuous present.

EXERCISE II

Using the thereby test as described above, indicate which of the following sentences express explicit performatives (EP) and which do not express explicit performatives (N) in appropriate circumstances:

1. I pledge allegiance to the flag.
2. We pledge allegiance to the flag.
3. I pledged allegiance to the flag.
4. I always pledge allegiance at the start of a game.
5. You pledge allegiance to the flag.
6. He pledges allegiance to the flag.
7. He doesn't pledge allegiance to the flag.
8. Pledge allegiance to the flag!
9. Why don't you pledge allegiance to the flag?
10. Pierre is the capital of South Dakota.
11. I state that Pierre is the capital of South Dakota.
12. I order you to leave.
13. Get out of here!
14. I didn't take it.
15. I swear that I didn't take it.
16. I won't talk to you.
17. I refuse to talk to you.
18. I'm out of gas.
19. I feel devastated.
20. Bummer!
21. I claim this land for England.
22. I bring you greetings from home.

KINDS OF SPEECH ACTS

Recognizing explicit performatives introduces us to a kind of act distinct from linguistic acts. We will call them *speech acts.*[4] They include such acts as stating, promising, swearing, and refusing. A speech act is the conventional move that a remark makes in a language exchange. It is what is done *in* saying something.

Speech acts are distinct from linguistic acts, because the same linguistic act can play different roles in different contexts. This is shown by the following brief conversations.

    A: Is there any pizza left?

    B: Yes.

    A: Do you promise to pay me back by Friday?

    B: Yes.

    A: Do you swear to tell the truth?

    B: Yes.

    A: Do you refuse to leave?

    B: Yes.

Here the same linguistic act, uttering the word "yes," is used to do four different things: to state something, to make a promise, to take an oath, and to refuse to do something.

We can make this idea of a speech act clearer by using the notion of an explicit performative. The basic idea is that different speech acts are named by the different verbs that occur in explicit performatives. We can thus use the thereby test to search for different kinds of speech acts. For example:

If I say, "I promise," I thereby promise. So "I promise" is a performative, and *promising* is a kind of speech act.

If I say, "I resign," I thereby resign. So "I resign" is a performative, and *resigning* is a kind of speech act.

If I say, "I apologize," I thereby apologize. So "I apologize" is a performative, and *apologizing* is a kind of speech act.

If I say, "I question his honesty," I thereby question his honesty. So "I question his honesty" is a performative, and *questioning* is a kind of speech act.

If I say, "I conclude that she is guilty," I thereby conclude that she is guilty. So "I conclude that she is guilty" is a performative, and *concluding* is a kind of speech act.

The main verbs that appear in such explicit performatives can be called *performative verbs.* Performative verbs name kinds of speech acts.

Still, the same speech act can also be accomplished without any performative verb. I can deny my opponent's claim by saying either "I deny that" or simply "No way!" Both utterances perform the speech act of denying, even though only the former is a performative. The latter is not a performative and does not contain any performative verb, but it still performs a speech act.

Nonetheless, speech acts depend on context in much the same way as performatives. If a baseball umpire during a game shouts, "You're out!" to a batter then the batter is out. By way of contrast, if someone in the stands shouts, "You're out!" or "He's out!" the batter is not *thereby* out, although the person who shouts this may be encouraging the umpire to call the batter out or complaining because he didn't. And even an umpire cannot call a player out if the player is not at bat, but is pitching or in the dugout. The identity of the speaker and the audience as well as the circumstances thus determines whether the speech act is accomplished. Similarly, in a less formal setting, I cannot invite someone to your party (unless you gave me permission to do so), and I cannot congratulate you for losing your job (at least not sincerely). This example shows that a speech act will *fail to come off* or will be *void* unless certain rules or conventions are satisfied. These rules or conventions that must be satisfied for a speech act to come off and not be void can be called *speech act rules*.

EXERCISE III

Which of the following verbs names a speech act?

1. *capture* the suspect
2. *assert* that the suspect is guilty
3. *stare* accusingly at the suspect
4. *find* the defendant guilty
5. *punish* the defendant
6. *take* the defendant away
7. *revoke* the defendant's driver's license
8. *welcome* the prisoner to prison
9. *order* the prisoner to be silent
10. *lock* the cell door

EXERCISE IV

Using a dictionary, find ten verbs that can be used to construct explicit performatives that have not yet been mentioned in this chapter.

DISCUSSION QUESTIONS

1. *Do* the speech acts in which people get married presuppose that the people who are getting married are of different sexes? *Should* these speech acts presuppose this fact? Why or why not?

2. The importance of deciding what kind of speech act has been performed is illustrated by a classic case from the law of contracts, *Hawkins v. McGee.*[5] McGee performed an operation on Hawkins that proved unsuccessful, and Hawkins sued for damages. He did not sue on the basis of malpractice, however, but on the basis of breach of contract. His attorney argued that the doctor initiated a contractual relationship in that he tried to persuade Hawkins to have the operation by saying things such as "I will guarantee to make the hand a hundred percent perfect hand." He made statements of this kind a number of times, and Hawkins finally agreed to undergo the operation on the basis of these remarks. Hawkins's attorney maintained that these exchanges, which took place in the doctor's office on a number of occasions, constituted an offer of a contract that Hawkins explicitly accepted. The attorney for the surgeon replied that these words, even if uttered, would not constitute an offer of a contract, but merely expressed a *strong belief*, and that reasonable people should know that doctors cannot guarantee results.

   It is important to remember that contracts do not have to be written and signed to be binding. A proper verbal offer and acceptance are usually sufficient to constitute a contract. The case, then, turned on two questions: (1) Did McGee utter the words attributed to him? In other words, did McGee perform the *linguistic act* attributed to him? The jury decided that he did. (2) The second, more interesting question was whether these words, when uttered in this particular context, amounted to an offer of a contract, as Hawkins's attorney maintained, or merely were an expression of strong belief, as McGee's attorney held. In other words, the fundamental question in this case was what kind of *speech act* McGee performed when trying to convince Hawkins to have the operation.

   Explain how you would settle this case. (The court actually ruled in favor of Hawkins, but you are free to disagree.)

CONVERSATIONAL ACTS

In examining linguistic acts (saying something meaningful in a language) and then speech acts (doing something in using words), we have largely ignored a central feature of language: It is normally a *practical* activity with certain goals. We use language in order to inform people of things, get them to do things, amuse them, calm them down, and so on. We can capture this practical aspect of language by introducing the notion of a *conversational exchange*, that is, a situation where various speakers use speech acts in order to bring about some effects in each other. We will call this act of using a speech act to cause a standard effect in another a *conversational act.*

Suppose, for example, Amy says to Bobbi, "Someone is following us." In this case, Amy has performed a linguistic act; that is, she has uttered a meaningful sentence in the English language. Amy has also performed a speech act—specifically, she has *stated* that they are being followed. The point of performing this speech act is to produce in Bobbi a particular belief—namely, that they are being followed. (Amy's utterance might also have other purposes, such as to alert Bobbi to some danger, but it accomplishes those other purposes by means of getting Bobbi to believe they are being followed.) If Amy is successful in this, then Amy has successfully performed the conversational act of producing this belief in Bobbi. Amy, of course, might fail in her attempt to do this. Amy's linguistic act could be successful and her speech act successful as well, yet, for whatever reason, Bobbi might not accept as true what Amy is telling her. Perhaps Bobbi thinks that Amy is paranoid or just trying to frighten her as some kind of joke. In that case, Amy failed to perform her intended conversational act, even though she did perform her intended linguistic and speech acts.

Here are some other examples of the difference between performing a speech act and performing a conversational act:

We can *warn* people about something in order to *put them on guard* concerning it.
Here warning is the speech act; putting them on guard is the intended conversational act.

We can *urge* people to do things in order to *persuade* them to do these things.
Here urging is the speech act; persuading is the intended conversational act.

We can *assure* people concerning something in order to *instill confidence in them.*
Here assuring is the speech act; instilling confidence is the intended conversational act.

We can *apologize* to people in order to *make them feel better about us.*
Here apologizing is the speech act; making them feel better about us is the intended conversational act.

In each of these cases, our speech act may not succeed in having its intended conversational effect. Our urging, warning, and assuring may, respectively, fail to persuade, put on guard, or instill confidence. Indeed, speech acts may bring about the opposite of what was intended. People who brag (a speech act) in order to impress others (the intended conversational act) often actually make others think less of them (the actual effect). In many ways like these, we can perform a speech act without performing the intended conversational act.

The relationship between conversational acts and speech acts is confusing, because both of them can be performed at once by the same utterance. Suppose Carl says, "You are invited to my party." By means of this single utterance, he performs a linguistic act of uttering this meaningful sentence, a speech act of inviting you, and perhaps also a conversational act of getting you to come to his party. Indeed, he would not be able to perform this conversational act without also performing such a speech act, assuming that you would not come to his party if you were not invited. He would also not be able to perform this speech act without performing this linguistic act or something like it, since he cannot invite you by means of an inarticulate grunt or by asking, "Are you invited to my party?"

As a result, we cannot sensibly ask whether Carl's utterance of "You are invited to my party" is a linguistic act, a speech act, or a conversational act. That single utterance performs all three acts at once. Nonetheless, we can distinguish those kinds of acts that Carl performs in terms of the verbs that describe the acts. Some verbs describe speech acts; other verbs describe conversational acts. We can tell which verbs describe which kinds of acts by asking whether the verb passes the thereby test (in which case the verb describes a speech act) or whether, instead, it describes a standard effect of the utterance (in which case the verb describes a conversational act).

EXERCISE V

Indicate whether the verbs in the following sentences name a speech act, a conversational act, or neither. Assume a standard context. Explain your answers.

1. She *thought* that he did it.
2. She *asserted* that he did it.
3. She *convinced* them that he did it.
4. She *condemned* him in front of everyone.
5. She *challenged* his integrity.
6. She *embarrassed* him in front of them.
7. He *denied* doing it.
8. They *believed* her.
9. They *encouraged* him to admit it.
10. She *told* him to get lost.
11. He *praised* her lavishly.
12. His praise *made* her happy.
13. He *threatened* to reveal her secret.
14. He *submitted* his resignation.
15. Her news *frightened* him half to death.
16. He *advised* her to go into another line of work.
17. She *blamed* him for her troubles.
18. His lecture *enlightened* her.
19. His jokes *amused* her.
20. His book *confused* her.

CONVERSATIONAL RULES

Just as there are rules that govern linguistic acts and other rules that govern speech acts, so too there are rules that govern conversational acts. This should not be surprising, because conversations can be complicated interpersonal activities in need of rules to make them effective in attaining their goals. These underlying rules are implicitly understood by users of the language, but the philosopher Paul Grice was the first person to examine them in careful detail.[6]

We can start by examining standard or normal conversational exchanges where conversation is a cooperative venture—that is, where the people involved in the conversation have some common goal they are trying to achieve in talking with one another. (A prisoner being interrogated and a shop owner being robbed are *not* in such cooperative situations.) According to Grice, such exchanges are governed by what he calls the *Cooperative Principle.* This principle states that the parties involved should use language in a way that contributes toward achieving their common goal. It tells them to cooperate.

This general principle gains more content when we consider other forms of cooperation. Carpenters who want to build a house need enough nails and wood, but not too much. They need the right kinds of nails and wood. They also need to put the nails and wood together in the relevant way—that is, according to their plans. And, of course, they also want to perform their tasks quickly and in the right order. Rational people who want to achieve common goals must follow similar general restrictions in other practical activities. Because cooperative conversations are one such practical activity, speakers who want to cooperate with one another must follow rules analogous to those for carpenters.

Grice spells out four such rules. The first he calls the rule of *Quantity.* It tells us to give the right amount of information. More specifically:

1. Make your contribution as informative as is required (for the current purposes of the exchange);

and possibly:

2. Do not make your contribution more informative than is required.

Here is an application of this rule: A person rushes up to you and asks, "Where is a fire extinguisher?" You know that there is a fire extinguisher five floors away in the basement, and you also know that there is a fire extinguisher just down the hall. Suppose you say that there is a fire extinguisher in the basement. Here you have said something true, but you have violated the first part of the rule of Quantity. You have failed to reveal an important piece of information that, under the rule of Quantity, you should have produced. A violation of the second version of the rule would look like this: As smoke billows down the hall, you say where a fire extinguisher is located on each floor, starting with the basement. Eventually you will get around to saying that there is a fire extinguisher just down the hall, but you bury the point in a mass of unnecessary information.

Grice's second rule is called the rule of *Quality*. In general: Try to make your contribution one that is true. More specifically:

1. Do not say what you believe to be false.
2. Do not say that for which you lack adequate evidence.

In a cooperative activity, you are not supposed to tell lies. Beyond this, you are expected not to talk off the top of your head either. When we make a statement, we can be challenged by someone asking, "Do you really believe that?" or "Why do you believe that?" That a person has the right to ask such questions shows that statement making is governed by the rule of Quality.

In a court of law, witnesses promise to tell the whole truth and nothing but the truth. The demand for *nothing but the truth* reflects the rule of Quality. The demand for *the whole truth* roughly reflects the rule of Quantity. Obviously, nobody really tells every truth he or she knows. Here the *whole* truth concerns all the known truths that are relevant in the context.

This brings us to our next rule, the rule of *Relevance.* Simply stated, the rule of Relevance says:

Be relevant!

Though easy to state, the rule is not easy to explain, because relevance itself is a difficult notion. It is, however, easy to illustrate. If someone asks me where he can find a doctor, I might reply that there is a hospital on the next block. Though not a direct answer to the question, it does not violate the rule of Relevance because it provides a piece of useful information. If, however, in response I tell the person that I like his haircut, then I have violated the rule of Relevance. Clear-cut violations of this principle often involve *changing the subject.*

Another rule concerns the manner of our conversation. We are expected to be clear in what we say. Under the general rule of *Manner* come various special rules:

1. Avoid obscurity of expression.
2. Avoid ambiguity.
3. Be brief.
4. Be orderly.

As an example of the fourth part of this rule, when describing a series of events, it is usually important to state them in the order in which they occurred. It would certainly be misleading to say that two people had a child and got married when, in fact, they had a child after they were married.

Many other rules govern our conversations. "Be polite!" is one of them. "Be charitable!" is another. That is, we should put the best interpretation on what others say, and our replies should reflect this. We should avoid quibbling and being picky. For the most part, however, we will not worry about these other rules.

EXERCISE VI

Indicate which, if any, of Grice's conversational rules are violated by the italicized sentence of each of the following conversations. Assume a standard context. More than one rule might be violated.

1. "Did you like her singing?" *"Her costume was beautiful."*
2. *"The governor has the brains of a three-year-old."*
3. *"The Lone Ranger rode into the sunset and jumped on his horse."*
4. *"Without her help, we'd be up a creek without a paddle."*
5. "Where is Palo Alto?" *"On the surface of the Earth."*
6. *"It will rain tomorrow."* "How do you know?" "I just guessed."
7. *"Does the dog need to go out for a W-A-L-K [spelled out]?"*
8. "Why did the chicken cross the road?" *"To get to the other side."*

"What are you implying?"

CONVERSATIONAL IMPLICATION

In a normal setting where people are cooperating toward reaching a shared goal, they often conform quite closely to Grice's conversational rules. If, on the whole, people did not do this, we could not have the linguistic practices we do. If we thought, for example, that people very often lied (even about the most trivial matters), the business of exchanging information would be badly damaged.

Still, people do not always follow these conversational rules. They withhold information, they elaborate needlessly, they assert what they know to be false, they say the first thing that pops into their heads, they wander off the subject, and they talk vaguely and obscurely. When we observe actual conversations, it is sometimes hard to tell how any information gets communicated at all.

The explanation lies in the same conversational rules. Not only do we usually follow these conventions, we also (1) implicitly realize that we are following them, and (2) expect others to assume that we are following them. This mutual understanding of the commitments involved in a conversational act has the following important consequence: People are able to convey a great deal of information without actually saying it.

A simple example will illustrate this point. Again suppose that a person, with smoke billowing behind him, comes running up to you and asks, "Where's a fire extinguisher?" You reply, "There's one in the lobby." Through a combination of conversational rules, notably relevance, quantity, and manner, this commits you to the claim that this is the closest, or at least the most accessible, fire extinguisher. Furthermore, the person you are speaking to assumes that you are committed to this. Of course, you have not actually *said* that it is the closest fire extinguisher; but you have, we might say, *implied* this. When we do not actually say something but imply it by virtue of a mutually understood conversational rule, the implication is called a *conversational implication*.

It is important to realize that conversational implication is a pervasive feature of human communication. It is not something we employ only occasionally for special effect. In fact, virtually every conversation relies on these implications, and most conversations would fall apart if people refused to go beyond literal meanings to take into account the implications of saying things. In the following conversation, B is literal-minded in just this way:

A: Do you know what time it is?

B: Not without looking at my watch.

B has answered A's question, but it is hard to imagine that A has received the information she was looking for. Presumably, she wanted to know what time it was, not merely whether B, at that very moment, knew the time. Finding B rather obtuse, A tries again:

A: Can you tell me what time it is?

B: Oh, yes, all I have to do is look at my watch.

Undaunted, A gives it another try:

A: Will you tell me what time it is?

B: I suppose I will as soon as you ask me.

Finally:

A: What time is it?

B: Two o'clock. Why didn't you ask me that in the first place?

Notice that in each of these exchanges *B* gives a direct and accurate answer to *A*'s question; yet, in all but the last answer, *B* does not provide *A* with what *A* wants. Like a computer in a science-fiction movie, *B* is taking *A*'s questions too literally. More precisely, *B* does nothing *more* than take *A*'s remarks literally. In a conversational exchange, we expect others to take our remarks in the light of the obvious purpose we have in making them. We expect them to share our commonsense understanding of why people ask questions. At the very least, we expect people to respond to us in ways that are *relevant* to our purposes. Except at the end, *B* seems totally oblivious to the point of *A*'s questions. That is what makes *B* unhelpful and annoying.

Though all the conversational rules we have examined can be the basis of conversational implication, the rule of Relevance is particularly powerful in this respect. Normal conversations are dense with conversational implications that depend on the rule of Relevance. Someone says, "Dinner's ready," and that is immediately taken to be a way of asking people to come to the table. Why? Because dinner's being ready is a transparent *reason* to come to the table to eat. This is an ordinary context that most people are familiar with. Change the context, however, and the conversational implications can be entirely different. Suppose the same words, "Dinner's ready," are uttered when guests have failed to arrive on time. In this context, the conversational implication, which will probably be reflected in an annoyed tone of voice, will be quite different.

EXERCISE VII

Assuming a natural conversational setting, what might a person intend to conversationally imply by making the following remarks? Briefly explain why each of these conversational implications holds; that is, explain the relationship between what the speaker *literally* says and what the speaker intends to convey through conversational implication. Finally, for each example, find a context where the standard conversational implication would fail and another arise in its place.

1. It's getting a little chilly in here. (Said by a visitor in your home)
2. Do you mind if I borrow your pen? (Said to a friend while studying)
3. We are out of soda. (Said by a child to her parents)
4. I got here before he did. (Said in a ticket line)
5. Don't blame me if you get in trouble. (Said by someone who advised you not to do what you did)
6. Has this seat been taken? (Said in a theater before a show)
7. Don't ask me. (Said in response to a question)
8. I will be out of town that day. (Said in response to a party invitation)

GARFIELD © 1999 Paws, Inc. Reprinted with permission of UNIVERSAL UCLICK All rights reserved.

RHETORICAL DEVICES

Many rhetorical devices work by openly violating conversational rules in order to generate conversational implications. Consider exaggeration. When someone claims to be hungry enough to eat a horse, it does not dawn on us to treat this as a literal claim about how much she can eat. To do so would be to attribute to the speaker a blatant violation of Grice's first rule of Quality—namely, do not say what you believe to be false. Consequently, her audience will naturally interpret her remark figuratively, rather than literally. They will assume that she is exaggerating the amount she can eat in order to conversationally imply that she is very hungry. This rhetorical device is called *overstatement* or *hyperbole*. It is commonly employed, often in heavy-handed ways.

Sometimes, then, we do not intend to have others take our words at face value. Even beyond this, we sometimes expect our listeners to interpret us as claiming just the *opposite* of what we assert. This occurs, for example, with *irony* and *sarcasm*. Suppose at a crucial point in a game, the second baseman fires the ball ten feet over the first baseman's head, and someone shouts, "Great throw." Literally, it was not a great throw; it was the opposite of a great throw, and this is just what the person who says "Great throw" is indicating. How do the listeners know they are supposed to interpret it in this way? Sometimes this is indicated by tone of voice. A sarcastic tone of voice usually indicates that the person means the opposite of what he or she is saying. Even without the tone of sarcasm, the remark "Great throw" is not likely to be taken literally. The person who shouts this knows that it was not a great throw, as do the people who hear it. Rather than attributing an obviously false belief to the shouter, we assume that the person is blatantly violating the rule of Quality to draw our attention to just how bad the throw really was.

Metaphors and similes are perhaps the most common forms of figurative language. A *simile* is, roughly, an explicit figurative comparison. A word such as "like" or "as" makes the comparison explicit, and the comparison is figurative because it would be inappropriate if taken literally. To say that the home team fought like tigers does not mean that they clawed the opposing team and took large bites out of them. To call someone as dumb as a post is not to claim that they have no brain at all.

With a *metaphor*, we also compare certain items, but without words such as "like" or "as." Metaphorical comparisons are still figurative because the vocabulary, at a literal level, is not appropriate to the subject matter. George Washington was not literally the father of his country. Taken literally, it hardly makes sense to speak of someone fathering a country. But the metaphor is so natural (or so familiar) that it does not cross our minds to treat the remark literally, asking, perhaps, who the mother was.

Taken literally, metaphors are usually obviously false, and then they violate Grice's rule of Quality. Again, as with irony, when someone says something obviously false, we have to decide what to make of that person's utterance. Perhaps the person is very stupid or a very bad liar, but often neither suggestion is plausible. In such a situation, sometimes the best supposition is that the person is speaking metaphorically rather than literally.

EXERCISE VIII

Identify each of the following sentences as irony, metaphor, or simile. For each sentence, write another expressing its literal meaning.

1. He missed the ball by a mile.
2. He acted like a bull in a china shop.
3. The exam blew me away.
4. He had to eat his words.
5. It was a real team effort. (Said by a coach after his team loses by forty points)
6. They are throwing the baby out with the bathwater.
7. This is a case of the tail wagging the dog.
8. "Religion is the opiate of the masses." (Marx)

EXERCISE IX

Unpack the following political metaphors by giving their literal content:

1. We can't afford a president who needs on-the-job training.
2. It's time for people on the welfare wagon to get off and help pull.
3. If you can't stand the heat, get out of the kitchen.
4. We need to restore a level playing field.
5. The special interests have him in their pockets.
6. He's a lame duck.

DISCUSSION QUESTION

At the start of the U.S. war with Iraq in 2003, some described Iraq as another Vietnam, while others described Saddam Hussein (Iraq's president) as another Hitler. Which metaphor was used by supporters of the war? Which was used by opponents? How can you tell? How do these metaphors work?

SUMMARY

In this chapter we have developed a rather complex picture of the way our language functions. In the process, we have distinguished three kinds or levels of acts that are performed when we employ language. We have also examined the rules associated with each kind or level of act. The following table summarizes this discussion:

THREE LEVELS OF LANGUAGE

Kinds of Acts	Governing Rules
A LINGUISTIC ACT is an act of saying something meaningful in a language. It is the basic act that is needed to make anything part of language.	Semantic rules (such as definitions) and syntactic rules (as in grammar).
A SPEECH ACT concerns the move a person makes in saying something. Different kinds of speech acts are indicated by the various verbs found in explicit performatives.	Speech act rules about special agents and circumstances appropriate to different kinds of speech acts.
A CONVERSATIONAL ACT is a speaker's act of causing a standard kind of effect in the listener; it is what I do by saying something—for example, I persuade someone to do something.	Conversational rules (the Cooperative Principle; Quantity, Quality, Relevance, and Manner).

EXERCISE X

1. It is late, and *A* is very hungry. *A* asks *B*, "When will dinner be ready?" Describe the linguistic act, the speech act, and some of the conversational acts this person may be performing in this context.

2. Someone is trying to solve the following puzzle: One of thirteen balls is heavier than the others, which are of equal weight. In no more than three weighings on a balance scale, determine which ball is the heavier one. The person is stumped, so someone says to her: "Begin by putting four balls in each pan of the scale." Describe the linguistic act, the speech act, and the conversational act of the person who makes this suggestion.

NOTES

[1] J. L. Austin used the phrase "locutionary act" to refer to a level of language closely related to what we refer to as a "linguistic act." See J. L. Austin, *How to Do Things with Words*, 2nd ed. (Cambridge, MA: Harvard University Press, 1975), 94–109.

[2] See, for example, J. L. Austin's *How to Do Things with Words*.

[3] An example of the continuous present is "I bet ten dollars every week in the lottery." Since this sentence is not used to make a bet, this sentence and others with the continuous present do not pass the thereby test or express explicit performatives.

[4] Austin calls speech acts "illocutionary acts." See *How to Do Things with Words*, 98–132.

[5] Supreme Court of New Hampshire, 1929, 84 N.H. 114, A. 641.

[6] This discussion of conversational rules and implications is based on Paul Grice's important essay, "Logic and Conversation," which appears as the second chapter of his *Studies in the Way of Words* (Cambridge, MA: Harvard University Press, 1989). To avoid British references that some readers might find perplexing, we have sometimes altered Grice's wording.

3

THE LANGUAGE OF ARGUMENT

Using the techniques developed in Chapter 2, this chapter will examine the use of language to formulate arguments and will provide methods to analyze genuine arguments in their richness and complexity. The first stage in analyzing an argument is the discovery of its basic structure. *To do this, we will examine the words, phrases, and special constructions that indicate the premises and conclusions of an argument. The second stage is the study of techniques used to* protect *an argument. These include* guarding *premises so that they are less subject to criticism,* offering assurances *concerning debatable claims, and* discounting *possible criticisms in advance.*

ARGUMENT MARKERS

In Chapter 2, we saw that language is used for a great many different purposes. One important thing that we do with language is construct arguments. Arguments are constructed out of statements, but arguments are not just lists of statements. Here is a simple list of statements:

Socrates is a man.

All men are mortal.

Socrates is mortal.

This list is not an argument, because none of these statements is presented as a reason for any other statement. It is, however, simple to turn this list into an argument. All we have to do is to add the single word "therefore":

Socrates is a man.

All men are mortal.

Therefore, Socrates is mortal.

Now we have an argument. The word "therefore" converts these sentences into an argument by signaling that the statement following it is a *conclusion,* and the statement or statements that come before it are offered as *reasons* on behalf of this conclusion. The argument we have produced in this way is a good one, because the conclusion follows from the reasons stated on its behalf.

There are other ways of linking these sentences to form an argument. Here is one:

Since Socrates is a man,

and all men are mortal,

Socrates is mortal.

Notice that the word "since" works in roughly the opposite way that "therefore" does. The word "therefore" is a *conclusion marker*, because it indicates that the statement that follows it is a conclusion. In contrast, the word "since" is a *reason marker*, because it indicates that the following statement or statements are reasons. In our example, the conclusion comes at the end, but there is a variation on this. Sometimes the conclusion is given at the start:

Socrates is mortal, since all men are mortal and Socrates is a man.

"Since" flags reasons; the remaining connected statement is then taken to be the conclusion, whether it appears at the beginning or at the end of the sentence.

Many other terms are used to introduce an argumentative structure into language by marking either reasons or conclusions. Here is a partial list:

REASON MARKERS	CONCLUSION MARKERS
since	therefore
because	hence
for	thus
as	then

We shall call such terms "argument markers," because each presents one or more statements as part of an argument or backing for some other statement.

It is important to realize that these words are not always used as argument markers. The words "since" and "then" are often used as indicators of time, as in, "He's been an American citizen since 1973" and "He ate a hot dog, then a hamburger." The word "for" is often used as a preposition, as in "John works for IBM." Because some of these terms have a variety of meanings, it is not possible to identify argument markers in a mechanical way just by looking at words. It is necessary to examine the function of words in the context in which they occur. One test of whether a word is functioning as an argument marker in a particular sentence is whether you can substitute another argument marker without changing the meaning of the sentence. In the last example, it makes no sense to say, "John works since IBM."

Many *phrases* are also available to signal that an argument is being given. Here is just a small sample:

from which it follows that . . .

from which we may conclude that . . .

from which we see that . . .

which goes to show that . . .

which establishes that . . .

We can also indicate conclusions and reasons by using *argumentative performatives*, which we examined briefly in Chapter 2. If someone says, "I conclude that . . . ," the words that follow are given the status of a conclusion. More pretentiously, if someone says, "Here I base my argument on the claim that . . . ," what comes next has the status of a reason.

Examination of actual arguments will show that we have a great many ways of introducing an argumentative structure into our language by using the two forms of argument markers: reason markers and conclusion markers. The first, and in many ways the most important, step in analyzing an argument is to identify the conclusion and the reasons given on its behalf. We do this by paying close attention to these argument markers.

IF . . . , THEN . . .

If-then sentences, which are also called *conditionals*, often occur in arguments, but they do not present arguments by themselves. To see this, consider the following conditional:

If the Dodgers improve their hitting, then they will win the Western Division.

The sentence between the "if" and the "then" is called the *antecedent* of the conditional. The sentence after the "then" is called its *consequent*. In uttering such a conditional, we are not asserting the truth of its antecedent, and we are not asserting the truth of its consequent either. Thus, the person who makes the above remark is not claiming that the Dodgers will win the Western Division. All she is saying is that *if* they improve their hitting, *then* they will win. Furthermore, she is not saying that they will improve their hitting. Because the speaker is not committing herself to either of these claims, she is not presenting an argument. This becomes clear when we contrast this conditional with a statement that does formulate an argument:

CONDITIONAL: *If* the Dodgers improve their hitting, *then* they will win the Western Division.

ARGUMENT: *Since* the Dodgers will improve their hitting, they will win the Western Division.

The sentence that follows the word "since" is asserted. That is why "since" is an argument marker, whereas the connective "if . . . then . . ." is not an argument marker.

Even though conditionals by themselves do not mark arguments, there is a close relationship between conditionals and arguments: Indicative conditionals provide *patterns* that can be converted into an argument whenever the antecedent is said to be true. (We also get an argument when the consequent is said to be false, but we will focus here on the simpler case of asserting the antecedent.) Thus, we often hear people argue in the following way:

> If inflation continues to grow, there will be an economic crisis. But inflation will certainly continue to grow, so an economic crisis is on the way.

The first sentence is an indicative conditional. It makes no claims one way or the other about whether inflation will grow or whether an economic crisis will occur. The next sentence asserts the antecedent of this conditional and then draws a conclusion signaled by the argument marker "so." We might say that when the antecedent of an indicative conditional is found to be true, the conditional can be *cashed in* for an argument.

Often the antecedent of a conditional is not asserted explicitly but is conversationally implied. When asked which player should be recruited for a team, the coach might just say, "If Deon is as good as our scouts say he is, then we ought to go for Deon." This conditional does not actually assert that Deon is as good as the scouts report. Nonetheless, it would be irrelevant and pointless for the coach to utter this conditional alone if he thought that the scouts were way off the mark. The coach might immediately add that he disagrees with the scouting reports. But unless the coach cancels the conversational implication in some way, it is natural to interpret him as giving an argument that we ought to pick Deon. In such circumstances, then, an indicative conditional can conversationally imply an argument, even though it does not state the argument explicitly.

This makes it easy to see why indicative conditionals are a useful feature of our language. By providing patterns for arguments, they prepare us to draw conclusions when the circumstances are right. Much of our knowledge of the world around us is contained in such conditionals. Here is an example: If your computer does not start, the plug might be loose. This is a useful piece of practical information, for when your computer does not start, you can immediately infer that the plug might be loose, so you know to check it out.

Other words function in similar ways. When your computer fails to start, a friend might say, "Either the plug is loose or you are in deep trouble." Now, if you also assert, "The plug is not loose," you can conclude that you are in deep trouble. "Either . . . or . . ." sentences thus provide patterns for arguments, just as conditionals do. However, neither if-then sentences nor either-or sentences by themselves explicitly assert enough to present a complete argument, so "if . . ., then . . ." and "either . . . or . . ." should not be labeled as argument markers.

Indicate which of the following italicized words or phrases is a reason marker, a conclusion marker, or neither.

1. He apologized, *so* you should forgive him.
2. He apologized. *Accordingly,* you should forgive him.
3. *Since* he apologized, you should forgive him.
4. *Provided that* he apologized, you should forgive him.
5. *In view of the fact that* he apologized, you should forgive him.
6. He apologized. *Ergo,* you should forgive him.
7. *Given that* he apologized, you should forgive him.
8. He apologized, and *because of that* you should forgive him.
9. *After* he apologizes, you should forgive him.
10. He apologized. *As a result,* you should forgive him.
11. *Seeing as* he apologized, you should forgive him.
12. He apologized. *For that reason alone,* you should forgive him.

Indicate whether each of the following sentences is an argument.

1. Charles went bald, and most men go bald.
2. Charles went bald because most men go bald.
3. My roommate likes to ski, so I do, too.
4. My roommate likes to ski, and so do I.
5. I have been busy since Tuesday.
6. I am busy, since my teacher assigned lots of homework.

ARGUMENTS IN STANDARD FORM

Because arguments come in all shapes and forms, it will help to have a standard way of presenting arguments. For centuries, logicians have used a format of the following kind:

(1) All men are mortal.
(2) Socrates is a man.
∴ (3) Socrates is mortal. (from 1–2)

The reasons (or premises) are listed and numbered. Then a line is drawn below the premises. Next, the conclusion is numbered and written below the line. The symbol "∴"—which is read "therefore"—is then added to the left of the conclusion in order to indicate the relation between the premises and the conclusion. Finally, the premises from which the conclusion is supposed to be derived are indicated in parentheses. Arguments presented in this way are said to be in *standard form*.

The notion of a standard form is useful because it helps us see that the same argument can be expressed in different ways. For example, the following three sentences formulate the argument that was given in standard form above.

Socrates is mortal, since all men are mortal, and Socrates is a man.

All men are mortal, so Socrates is mortal, because he is a man.

All men are mortal, and Socrates is a man, which goes to show that
    Socrates is mortal.

More important, by putting arguments into standard form, we perform the most obvious, and in some ways most important, step in the analysis of an argument: the identification of its premises and conclusion.

EXERCISE III

Identify which of the following sentences expresses an argument. For each that does, (1) circle the argument marker (or markers), (2) indicate whether it is a reason marker or a conclusion marker, and (3) restate the argument in standard form.

1. Since Chicago is north of Boston, and Boston is north of Charleston, Chicago is north of Charleston.
2. Toward evening, clouds formed and the sky grew darker; then the storm broke.
3. Texas has a greater area than Topeka, and Topeka has a greater area than the Bronx Zoo, so Texas has a greater area than the Bronx Zoo.
4. Both houses of Congress may pass a bill, but the president may still veto it.
5. Other airlines will carry more passengers, because United Airlines is on strike.
6. Since Jesse James left town, taking his gang with him, things have been a lot quieter.
7. Things are a lot quieter, because Jesse James left town, taking his gang with him.
8. Witches float because witches are made of wood, and wood floats.
9. The hour is up, so you must hand in your exams.
10. Joe quit, because his boss was giving him so much grief.

A PROBLEM AND SOME SOLUTIONS

After identifying an argument and putting it in standard form, the natural question to ask is this: Is the argument any good? If the argument is used for justification, then we can reformulate the question like this: Do the argument's premises provide a good reason to believe its conclusion?

This question will occupy us in several later chapters, but some simple examples should already be clear. Imagine that you want to buy a house, and your real estate agent shows you a particular one that looks pretty good. Then the agent tells you that this house will double in value over the next ten years. You ask, "How do you know?" The agent argues, "All of the house values in this neighborhood will double over the next ten years, so this one will double, too." Notice that this argument *does* give you a reason to believe that the conclusion is true *if* you have a reason to believe that its premise is true. However, if you have no reason to believe the premise, then the argument gives you no reason at all to believe its conclusion. In short, the argument is no good without a reason to believe its premise.

How can the real estate agent solve this problem? He needs to provide an argument for the premise, so next he argues, "All of the house values in this *city* will double over the next ten years, so all of the house values in this *neighborhood* will double over the next ten years." And if you question this new premise, he can go on to give an argument for it: "All of the house values in this *state* will double over the next ten years, so all of the house values in this *city* will double over the next ten years." And so on.

Now the problem should be obvious: An argument that aims at justification is no good unless its premises are justified. However, to justify a premise, the arguer needs to give a second argument with that premise as its conclusion. But then that second argument depends on its own premises. The second argument is no good at justifying the premise in the first argument unless the second argument's premises are justified themselves. But to justify these new premises requires a third argument, and that argument will depend on its premises being justified, which will require yet another argument, and so on. The whole process of justification seems to go on forever, requiring argument after argument without end. It now looks as if every argument, to be successful, will have to be infinitely long.

This potential regress causes deep problems in theoretical philosophy, leading some philosophers to adopt total skepticism. In everyday life, however, we try to avoid these problems by relying on shared beliefs—beliefs that will not be challenged. Beyond this, we expect people to believe us when we cite information that only we possess. But there are limits to this expectation, for we all know that people sometimes believe things that are false and sometimes lie about what they know to be true. This presents a practical problem: How can we present our reasons in a way that does not produce

just another demand for an argument—a demand for more reasons? Here
we tend to use three main strategies:

1. *Assuring*: Indicating that there are backup reasons even though we are
   not giving them fully right now.
2. *Guarding*: Weakening our claims so that they are less subject to attack.
3. *Discounting*: Anticipating criticisms and dismissing them.

In these three ways we build a defensive perimeter around our premises.
Each of these defenses is useful, but each can also be abused.

ASSURING

When will we want to give assurances about some statement we have
made? If we state something that we know everyone believes, assurances
are not necessary. For that matter, if everyone believes something, we may
not even state it at all; we let others fill in this step in the argument. We
offer assurances when we think that someone might doubt or challenge
what we say.

There are many ways to give assurances. Sometimes we cite authorities:

Doctors agree . . .

Recent studies have shown . . .

An unimpeachable source close to the White House says . . .

It has been established that . . .

Here we indicate that authorities have these reasons without specifying
what their reasons are. We merely indicate that good reasons exist, even if
we ourselves cannot—or choose not to—spell them out. When the authority cited can be trusted, this is often sufficient, but authorities often can
and should be questioned. This topic will be discussed at greater length in
Chapter 15.

Another way to give assurances is to comment on the strength of our own
belief:

I'm certain that . . .

I'm sure that . . .

I can assure you that . . .

I'm not kidding. . . .

Over the years, I have become more and more convinced that . . .

Again, when we use these expressions, we do not explicitly present reasons,
but we conversationally imply that there are reasons that back our assertions.

A third kind of assurance abuses the audience:

Everyone with any sense agrees that . . .

Of course, no one will deny that . . .

It is just common sense that . . .

There is no question that . . .

Nobody but a fool would deny that . . .

These assurances not only do not give any reason; they also suggest that there is something wrong with you if you ask for a reason. We call this the *trick of abusive assurances.*

Just as we can give assurances that something is true, we can also give assurances that something is false. For example,

It is no longer held that . . .

It is wholly implausible to suppose that . . .

No intelligent person seriously maintains that . . .

You would have to be pretty dumb to think that . . .

The last three examples clearly involve abusive assurances.

Although many assurances are legitimate, we as critics should always view assurances with some suspicion. People tend to give assurances only when they have good reasons to do so. Yet assuring remarks often mark the weakest parts of the argument, not the strongest. If someone says "I hardly need argue that . . . ," it is often useful to ask why she has gone to the trouble of saying this. When we distrust an argument—as we sometimes do— this is precisely the place to look for weakness. If assurances are used, they are used for some reason. Sometimes the reason is a good one. Sometimes, however, it is a bad one. In honest argumentation, assurances save time and simplify discussion. In a dishonest argument, they are used to paper over cracks.

GUARDING

Guarding represents a different strategy for protecting premises from attack. We reduce our claim to something less strong. Thus, instead of saying "all," we say "many." Instead of saying something straight out, we use a qualifying phrase, such as "it is likely that . . ." or "it is very possible that. . . ." Law school professors like the phrase "it is arguable that. . . ." This is wonderfully noncommittal, for it does not indicate how strong the argument is, yet it does get the statement into the discussion.

Broadly speaking, there are three main ways of guarding what we say:

1. Weakening the *extent* of what has been said: retreating from "all" to "most" to "a few" to "some," and so on.

2. Introducing *probability* phrases such as "It is virtually certain that . . . ," "It is likely that . . . ," "It might happen that . . . ," and so on.

3. Reducing our *level of commitment*: moving from "I know that . . ." to "I

believe that . . ." to "I suspect that . . . ," and so on.

Such terms guard premises when they are used in place of stronger alternatives. "Madison probably quit the volleyball team" is weaker than "She definitely quit" but stronger than "She could have quit." Thus, if the context makes one expect a strong claim, such as "I know she quit," then it is guarding to say, "She probably quit." In contrast, if the context is one of speculating about who might have quit the team, then it is not guarding to say, "She probably quit." That is a relatively strong claim when others are just guessing. Thus, you need to pay careful attention to the context in order to determine whether a term has the function of guarding. When a term is used for guarding, you should be able to specify a stronger claim that the guarding term replaces and why that stronger term would be expected in the context.

Guarding terms and phrases are often legitimate and useful. If you want to argue that a friend needs fire insurance for her house, you do not need to claim that her house *will* burn down. All you need to claim is that there is a significant *chance* that her house will burn down. Your argument is better if you start with this weaker premise, because it is easier to defend and it is enough to support your conclusion.

If we weaken a claim sufficiently, we can make it completely immune to criticism. What can be said against a remark of the following kind: "There is some small chance that perhaps a few politicians are honest on at least some occasions"? You would have to have a *very* low opinion of politicians to deny this statement. On the other hand, if we weaken a premise too much, we pay a price. The premise no longer gives strong support to the conclusion.

The goal in using guarding terms is to find a middle way: We should weaken our premises sufficiently to avoid criticism, but not weaken them so much that they no longer provide strong enough evidence for the conclusion. Balancing these factors is one of the most important strategies in making and criticizing arguments.

Just as it was useful to zero in on assuring terms, so it is also useful to keep track of guarding terms. One reason is that, like assuring terms, guarding terms are easily corrupted. A common trick is to use guarding terms to *insinuate* things that cannot be stated explicitly in a conversation. Consider the effect of the following remark: "Perhaps the secretary of state has not been candid with the Congress." This does not actually say that the secretary of state has been less than candid with the Congress, but, by the rule of Relevance, clearly suggests it. Furthermore, it suggests it in a way that is hard to combat.

A more subtle device for corrupting guarding terms is to introduce a statement in a guarded form and then go on to speak as if it were not guarded at all.

Perhaps the secretary of state has not been candid with the Congress. Of course, he has a right to his own views, but this is a democracy where officials are accountable to Congress. It is time for him to level with us.

The force of the guarding term "perhaps" that begins this passage disappears at the end, where it is taken for granted that the secretary of state has not been candid. This can be called *the trick of the disappearing guard*.

What is commonly called *hedging* is a sly device that operates in the opposite direction from our last example. With hedging, one shifts ground from a strong commitment to something weaker. Things, as they say, get "watered down" or "taken back." Strong statements made at one stage of an argument are later weakened without any acknowledgment that the position has thereby been changed in a significant way. A promise to *pass* a piece of legislation is later whittled down to a promise to *bring it to a vote*.

DISCOUNTING

The general pattern of discounting is to cite a possible criticism in order to reject it or counter it. Notice how different the following statements sound:

The ring is beautiful, but expensive.

The ring is expensive, but beautiful.

Both statements assert the same facts—that the ring is beautiful and that the ring is expensive. Both statements also suggest that there is some opposition between these facts. Yet these statements operate in different ways. We might use the first as a reason for *not* buying the ring; we can use the second as a reason *for* buying it. The first sentence acknowledges that the ring is beautiful, but overrides this by pointing out that it is expensive. In reverse fashion, the second statement acknowledges that the ring is expensive, but overrides this by pointing out that it is beautiful. Such assertions of the form "*A* but *B*" thus have four components:

1. The assertion of *A*
2. The assertion of *B*
3. The suggestion of some opposition between *A* and *B*
4. The indication that the truth of *B* is more important than the truth of *A*

The word "but" thus discounts the statement that comes before it in favor of the statement that follows it.

"Although" is also a discounting connective, but it operates in reverse fashion from the word "but." We can see this, using the same example:

Although the ring is beautiful, it is expensive.

Although the ring is expensive, it is beautiful.

Here the statement following the word "although" is discounted in favor of the connected statement.

A partial list of terms that typically function as discounting connectives includes the following conjunctions:

although	even if	but	nevertheless
though	while	however	nonetheless
even though	whereas	yet	still

These terms are not always used to discount. The word "still," for example, is used for discounting in (a) "He is sick; still, he is happy" but not in (b) "He is still happy" (or "Sit still"). We can tell whether a term is being used for discounting by asking whether the sentence makes sense when we substitute another discounting term: It makes sense to say, "He is sick, but he is happy." It makes no sense to say, "He is but happy." It is also illuminating to try to specify the objection that is being discounted. If you cannot say which objection is discounted, then the term is probably not being used for discounting.

The clearest cases of discounting occur when we are dealing with facts that point in different directions. We discount the facts that go against the position we wish to take. But discounting is often more subtle than this. We sometimes use discounting to block certain conversational implications of what we have said. This comes out in examples of the following kind:

Jones is an aggressive player, but he is not dirty.

The situation is difficult, but not hopeless.

The Republicans have the upper hand in Congress, but only for the time being.

A truce has been declared, but who knows for how long?

Take the first example. There is no opposition between Jones being aggressive and his not being dirty. Both would be reasons to pick Jones for our team. However, the assertion that Jones is aggressive might *suggest* that he is dirty. The "but" clause discounts this suggestion without, of course, denying that Jones is aggressive.

The nuances of discounting terms can be subtle, and a correct analysis is not always easy. All the same, the role of discounting terms is often important. It can be effective in an argument to beat your opponents to the punch by anticipating and discounting criticisms before your opponents can raise them. The proper use of discounting can also help you avoid side issues and tangents.

Still, discounting terms, like the other argumentative terms we have examined, can be abused. People often spend time discounting *weak* objections to their views in order to avoid other objections that they know are harder to counter. Another common trick is to discount objections no one would raise. This is called *attacking straw men*. Consider the following remark: "A new building would be great, but it won't be free." This does not actually say that the speaker's opponents think we can build a new building for free, but it does conversationally imply that they think this, because otherwise it would be irrelevant to discount that objection. The speaker is thus trying to make the opponents look bad by putting words in their mouths that they would never say themselves. To counter tricks like this, we need to ask whether a discounted criticism is one that really would be raised, and whether there are stronger criticisms that should be raised.

EXERCISE IV

For each of the numbered words or expressions in the following sentences, indicate whether it is an argument marker, an assuring term, a guarding term, a discounting term, or none of these. For each argument marker, specify what the conclusion and the reasons are, and for each discounting term, specify what criticism is being discounted and what the response to this criticism is.

1. *Although* [1] no mechanism has been discovered, *most* [2] *researchers in the field agree* [3] that smoking *greatly increases the chances* [4] of heart disease.
2. *Since* [5] *historically* [6] public debt leads to inflation, *I maintain* [7] that, *despite* [8] recent trends, inflation will return.
3. *Take it from me* [9], there hasn't been a decent center fielder *since* [10] Joe DiMaggio.
4. *Whatever anyone tells you* [11], there is *little* [12] to the rumor that Queen Elizabeth II will step down *for* [13] her son, Prince Charles.
5. The early deaths of Janis Joplin and Jimi Hendrix *show* [14] that drugs are *really* [15] dangerous.
6. I *think* [16] he is out back somewhere.
7. I *think* [17], *therefore* [18] I am.
8. I *concede* [19] that the evidence is *hopelessly* [20] weak, *but* [21] I still think he is guilty.
9. I *deny* [22] that I had *anything* [23] to do with it.
10. The wind has shifted to the northeast, *which means* [24] that snow is *likely* [25].

EXERCISE V

1. Construct three new and interesting examples of statements containing assuring terms, and indicate which kind of assuring it is.
2. Do the same for guarding terms, and indicate which stronger claim is being reduced in strength.
3. Do the same for discounting terms, and indicate which statement is being discounted in favor of the other.
4. Do the same for argument markers, and indicate what is presented as a reason for what.

EVALUATIVE LANGUAGE

Arguments are often filled with evaluations, so it is important to figure out what evaluative language means. We will begin with the clearest cases of evaluative language, which occur when we say simply that something is *good* or *bad,* that some course of action is *right* or *wrong*, or that something *should* or *should not* (or *ought to* or *ought not to*) be done.

Such evaluative terms often come into play when one is faced with a choice or decision. If you are deciding which shirt to buy, and a friend tells you, "That one's good," your friend would normally be taken to be suggesting that you get it. A passenger who says, "That's the wrong turn," is telling the driver not to turn that way. Evaluative language is, in these ways, used to perform speech acts of *prescribing action*.

Evaluative language is also often used to *express emotion*. When a fan says, "That band is great," this usually expresses admiration for their music and perhaps a desire to hear more. After a meal, someone who announces, "That was horrible," is often expressing aversion or even disgust at the food. To say, "That's too bad," is often to express disappointment or sadness.

Evaluative language is also typically used to bring about certain effects. When a mother tells her son that that he ought to keep his promises, she not only prescribes that her son not lie and expresses disapproval of lying; she also standardly intends to have an effect on his behavior—she tries to get him to keep his promises. And when war protesters call a war immoral, they are normally trying to get anyone listening to join their protest or at least share their disapproval. Thus, evaluative language is used to perform conversational acts of *changing people's behavior and feelings*.

There is still more to the meaning of evaluative language. In most cases, we call something "good" or "right" because we believe that it meets or satisfies some relevant standard, and we call something "bad" or "wrong" because we believe that it violates some relevant standard. This is, roughly, the content of evaluative claims.

On this account, calling something good or bad by itself can be fairly empty, because to say that something satisfies or violates *some* standard does not explicitly specify *which* standard is satisfied or violated. Such remarks gain content—sometimes a very rich content—by virtue of the particular standards they invoke. This explains why the word "good" can be applied to so many different kinds of things. When we say that Hondas are good cars, we are probably applying standards that involve reliability, efficiency, comfort, and so on. We call someone a good firefighter because we think the person is skilled at the tasks of a firefighter, is motivated to do those tasks, works well with other firefighters, and so on. Our standards for calling someone an ethically good person concern honesty, generosity, fairness, and so on. The standards we have for calling something a good car, a good firefighter, and an (ethically) good person have little in common. Even so, the word "good" functions in the same way in all three cases: It invokes standards that are relevant in a given context and indicates that something adequately satisfies these standards.

Because evaluative statements invoke standards, they stand in contrast to utterances that *merely* express personal feelings. If I say that I like a particular singer, then I am expressing a personal taste. It would normally be very odd for someone to reply, "No, you don't like that singer." On the other hand, if I call someone a good singer (or the best singer in years), then I am going beyond expressing my personal tastes. I am saying something that others may accept or reject. Of course, the standards for judging singers may be imprecise, and they may shift from culture to culture. Still, to call someone a good singer is to evaluate that person as a singer, which goes beyond merely expressing feelings, because it invokes standards and indicates that the person in question meets them.

The words "good" and "bad" are general evaluative terms. Other evaluative terms are more restrictive in their range of application. The word "delicious" is usually used for evaluating the taste of foods; it means "good-tasting." A *sin* is a kind of wrong action, but, more specifically, it is an action that is wrong according to religious standards. A *bargain* has a good price. An *illegal* action is one that is legally wrong. Our language contains a great many specific terms of evaluation like these. Here are a few more examples:

beautiful	dangerous	wasteful	sneaky	cute
murder	prudent	nosy	sloppy	smart

Each of these words expresses either a positive or a negative evaluation of a quite specific kind.

Positive and negative evaluations can be subtle. Consider a word like "clever." It presents a positive evaluation in terms of quick mental ability. In contrast, "cunning" often presents a negative evaluation of someone for misusing mental abilities. It thus makes a difference which one of these words we choose. It also makes a difference where we apply them. When something is supposed to be profound and serious, it is insulting to call it merely clever. Prayers, for example, should not be clever.

Sometimes seemingly innocuous words can shift evaluative force. The word "too" is the perfect example of this. This word introduces a negative evaluation, sometimes turning a positive quality into a negative one. Compare the following sentences:

John is smart.	John is too smart.
John is honest.	John is too honest.
John is ambitious.	John is too ambitious.
John is nice.	John is too nice.
John is friendly.	John is too friendly.

The word "too" indicates an excess, and thereby contains a criticism.

The difference between an evaluative term and a descriptive term is not always obvious. To see this, consider the terms "homicide" and "murder." The words are closely related but do not mean the same thing. "Homicide" is a descriptive term meaning "the killing of a human being." "Murder" is an evaluative term meaning, in part at least, "the *wrongful* killing of a human being." It takes more to show that something is a murder than it does to show that something is a homicide.

Just as it is easy to miss evaluative terms because we fail to recognize the evaluative component built into their meanings, it is also possible to interpret neutral words as evaluative because of positive or negative associations with the words. The word "nuclear," for example, has bad connotations for some people because of its association with bombs and wars, but the word itself is purely descriptive. To call people nuclear scientists is not to say that they are bad in any way.

The test for an evaluative term then is this: Does the word explicitly say that something is good or bad (right or wrong) in a particular way? A word is not evaluative when it merely suggests evaluation in some special contexts. It counts as evaluative only if its semantic content or meaning cannot be fully explained without using clearly evaluative words.

EXERCISE VI

Indicate whether the following italicized terms are positively evaluative (E+), negatively evaluative (E–), or simply descriptive (D). Remember, the evaluations need not be moral evaluations.

1. Janet is an *excellent* golfer.
2. The group was playing very *loudly*.
3. The group was playing *too* loudly.
4. William was *rude* to his parents.
5. William *shouted* at his parents.
6. They mistakenly turned *right* at the intersection.
7. *Fascists* ruled Italy for almost twenty years.
8. That's a *no-no*.
9. *Bummer*.
10. Debbie *lied*.
11. Debbie *said something false*.
12. Joe *copped out*.
13. Jake is a *bully*.
14. Mary Lou was a *gold medalist*.
15. She is *sick*.
16. He suffers from a hormonal *imbalance*.

EXERCISE VII

For each of the following sentences, construct two others—one that reverses the evaluative force, and one that is as neutral as possible. The symbol "0" stands for neutral, "+" for positive evaluative force, and "−" for negative evaluative force. Try to make as little change as possible in the descriptive content of the sentence.

Example: − Professor Conrad is rude.

+ Professor Conrad is uncompromisingly honest in his criticisms.

0 Professor Conrad often upsets people with his criticisms.

1. − Larry is a lazy lout.

2. + Brenda is brave.

3. − Sally is a snob.

4. + Bartlett is a blast.

5. − George is a goody-goody

6. − Walter is a weenie.

7. + Carol is caring.

8. − Bill is bossy.

9. − Oprah is opinionated

10. − This is a Mickey Mouse exercise.

DEEP ANALYSIS

Arguments in everyday life rarely occur in isolation. They usually come in the middle of much verbiage that is not essential to the argument itself. Everyday arguments are also rarely complete. Essential premises are often omitted. Many such omissions are tolerable because we are able to convey a great deal of information indirectly by conversational implication. Nevertheless, to understand and evaluate an argument, it is necessary to isolate the argument from extraneous surroundings, to make explicit unstated parts of the argument, and to arrange them in a systematic order. This reconstruction puts us in a better position to decide how good the argument really is. This chapter will develop methods for reconstructing arguments so that they may be analyzed and assessed in a fair and systematic fashion. These methods will then be illustrated by applying them to an important disagreement that depends on fundamental principles.

GETTING DOWN TO BASICS

To understand an argument, it is useful to put it into standard form. As we saw in Chapter 3, this is done simply by writing down the numbered premises, drawing a line, adding "∴" followed by the conclusion, and indicating which premises are supposed to be reasons for the conclusion. That is all we write down in standard form, but there is often a lot more in the passage that includes the argument. It is not uncommon for the stated argument to stretch over several pages, whereas the basic argument has only a few premises and a single conclusion.

One reason for this is that people often go off on *tangents*. They start to argue for one claim, but that reminds them of something else, so they talk about that for a while; then they finally return to their original topic. One example occurred during the Republican presidential candidates' debate on October 9, 2007, when Governor Mitt Romney said,

> We're also going to have to get serious about treating Ahmadinejad [the President of Iran] like the rogue and buffoon that he is. And it was outrageous for the United Nations to invite him to come to this country. It was outrageous for Columbia to invite him to speak at their university. This is a person who denied

the Holocaust, a person who has spoken about genocide, is seeking the means to carry it out. And it is unacceptable to this country to allow that individual to have control of launching a nuclear weapon. And so we will take the action necessary to keep that from happening.[1]

Romney's criticisms of the United Nations and Columbia are not really part of his argument, because they do not support his conclusion that the United States needs to keep nuclear weapons out of the hands of Ahmadinejad.

Such tangents can be completely irrelevant or unnecessary, and they often make it hard to follow the argument. Some people even go off on tangents on purpose to confuse their opponents and hide gaping holes in their arguments. The irrelevant diversion is sometimes called a *red herring* (reportedly after a man who, when pursued by hounds, threw them off his scent by dragging a red herring across his trail). More generally, this maneuver might be called the *trick of excess verbiage*. It violates the conversational rules of Quantity, Relevance, or Manner, which were discussed in Chapter 2.

To focus on the argument itself, we need to look carefully at each particular sentence to determine whether it affects the validity or strength of the argument or the truth of its premises. If we decide that a sentence is not necessary for the argument, then we should not add it when we list the premises and conclusion in standard form. Of course, we have to be careful not to omit anything that would improve the argument, but we also do not want to include too much, because irrelevant material simply makes it more difficult to analyze and evaluate the argument.

Another source of extra material is repetition. Consider Senator John Edwards's response to a question about the Defense of Marriage Act in the Democratic presidential candidates' debate on January 22, 2004:

> These are issues that should be left [to the states]. Massachusetts, for example, has just made a decision—the Supreme Court at least has made a decision—that embraces the notion of gay marriage. I think these are decisions the states should have the power to make. And the Defense of Marriage Act, as I understand it— you're right, I wasn't there when it was passed—but as I understand it, would have taken away that power. And I think that's wrong—that power should not be taken away from the states.[2]

Now compare:

> These are issues that should be left to the states.

> These are decisions that states should have the power to make.

> That power should not be taken away from the states.

All three of these sentences say pretty much the same thing, so we do not need them all.

Why do people repeat themselves like this? Sometimes they just forget that they already made the point before, but often repetition accomplishes a goal. Good speakers regularly repeat their main points to remind their audience of what was said earlier. Repetition is subtler when it is used to explain something.

A point can often be clarified by restating it in a new way. Repetition can also function as a kind of assurance, as an expression of confidence, or as an indication of how important a point is. Some writers seem to think that if they say something often enough, people will come to believe it. Whether or not this trick works, if two sentences say equivalent things, there is no need to list both sentences when the argument is put into standard form. Listing the same premise twice will not make the argument any better from a logical point of view.

Sometimes *guarding* terms can also be dropped. If I say, "I think Miranda is at home, so we can probably meet her there," this argument might be represented in standard form thus:

(1) I think Miranda is at home.

∴ (2) We can probably meet her there. (from 1)

This is misleading. My *thoughts* are not what make us able to meet Miranda at home. My thoughts do not even increase the probability that she is at home or that we can meet her there. It is the *fact* that Miranda is at home that provides a reason for the conclusion. Thus, it is clearer to drop the guarding phrase ("I think") when putting the argument into standard form. But you have to be careful, for not all guarding phrases can be dropped. When I say "We can *probably* meet her there," I might not want to say simply, "We *can* meet her there." After all, even if she is there now, we might not be able to get there before she leaves. Then to drop "probably" from my conclusion would distort what I meant to say and would make my argument more questionable, so you should not drop that guarding term if you want to understand my argument charitably and accurately.

Here's another example: If a friend says that you ought to buckle your seat belt because you could have an accident, it would distort her argument to drop the guarding term ("could"), because she is not claiming that you definitely will have an accident, or even that you probably will have one. The *chance* of an accident is significant enough to show that you ought to buckle your seat belt, so this guarding term should be kept when the argument is put into standard form.

It is also possible to drop *assuring* terms in some cases. Suppose someone says, "You obviously cannot play golf in Alaska in January, so there's no point in bringing your clubs." There is no need to keep the assuring term ("obviously") in the premise. It might even be misleading, because the issue is whether the premise is true, not whether it is obvious. The argument cannot be refuted by showing that, even though you in fact cannot play golf in Alaska in January, this is not obvious, since there might be indoor golf courses. In contrast, assuring terms *cannot* be dropped in some other cases. For example, if someone argues, "We know that poverty causes crime, because many studies have shown that it does," then the assuring terms ("We know that . . ." and "studies have shown that . . .") cannot be dropped without turning the argument into an empty shell: "Poverty causes crime, because it does." The point of this argument is to cite the sources of our knowledge ("studies") and to show that we have knowledge instead of just a hunch. That point is lost if we drop the assuring terms.

Unfortunately, there is no mechanical method for determining when guarding or assuring terms and phrases can be dropped, or whether certain sentences are unnecessary tangents or repetition. We simply have to look closely at what is being said and think hard about what is needed to support the conclusion. It takes great skill, care, and insight to pare an argument down to its essential core without omitting anything that would make it better. And that is the goal: If you want to understand someone's argument, you should try to make that argument as good as it can be. You should interpret it charitably. Distorting and oversimplifying other people's arguments might be fun at times and can win points in debates, but it cannot help us understand or learn from other people's arguments.

EXERCISE I

Put the following arguments into standard form and omit anything that does not affect the validity of the argument or the truth of its premises:

1. Philadelphia is rich in history, but it is not now the capital of the United States, so the U.S. Congress must meet somewhere else.

2. Not everybody whom you invited is going to come to your party. Some of them won't come. So this room should be big enough.

3. I know that my wife is at home, since I just called her there and spoke to her. We talked about our dinner plans.

4. I'm not sure, but Joseph is probably Jewish. Hence, he is a rabbi if he is a member of the clergy.

5. Some students could not concentrate on the lecture, because they did not eat lunch before class, although I did.

6. The most surprising news of all is that Johnson dropped out of the race because he thought his opponent was better qualified than he was for the office.

7. The liberal candidate is likely to win, since experts agree that more women support him.

8. It seems to me that married people are happier, so marriage must be a good thing, or at least I think so.

DISCUSSION QUESTION

In the quotation above (p. 80), is it fair to drop "I think" from the start of Edwards's sentences "I think these are decisions the states should have the power to make" and "I think that's wrong—that power should not be taken away from the states"? Why or why not? Is this phrase "I think" used for guarding or assuring or some other purpose in this context? Explain why Edwards adds these words.

CLARIFYING CRUCIAL TERMS

After the essential premises and conclusion are isolated, we often need to clarify these claims before we can begin our logical analysis. The goal here is not perfect clarity, for there probably is no such thing. It is, however, often necessary to eliminate ambiguity and reduce vagueness before we can give an argument a fair assessment. In particular, it is usually helpful to specify the referents of pronouns, because such references can depend on a context that is changed when the argument is put into standard form. "You are wrong" or "That's wrong" can be perfectly clear when said in response to a particular claim, but they lose their clarity when they are moved into the conclusion of an argument in standard form. We also often need to specify whether a claim is about all, most, many, or just some of its subject matter. When people say, "Blues music is sad," do they mean all, most, some, or typical blues music?

Another common problem arises when someone argues like this:

You should just say "No" to drugs, because drugs are dangerous.

What counts as a drug? What about penicillin or aspirin? The speaker might seem to mean "drugs like cocaine," but "like" them in which respects? Maybe what is meant is "addictive drugs," but what about alcohol and nicotine (which are often addictive)? You might think that the speaker means "dangerous drugs," but then the premise becomes empty: "Dangerous drugs are dangerous." Or maybe the idea is "illegal drugs," but that seems to assume that the law is correct about what is dangerous. In any case, we cannot begin to evaluate this argument if we do not know the extent of what it claims.

Of course, we should not try to clarify every term in the argument. Even if this were possible, it would make the argument extremely long and boring. Instead, our goal is to clarify anything that seems likely to produce confusion later if it is not cleared up now. As our analysis continues, we can always return and clarify more if the need arises, but it is better to get the most obvious problems out of the way at the start.

Some problems, however, just won't go away. Don't get frustrated if you cannot figure out how to clarify a crucial term in someone else's argument. The fault might lie with the person who gave the argument. Often an argument leaves a crucial term vague or ambiguous, because serious defects in the argument would become apparent if its terms were made more precise. We will discuss such tricks in detail in Chapters 13 and 14. For now, we just need to try our best to understand and clarify the essential terms in the argument.

DISSECTING THE ARGUMENT

A single sentence often includes several clauses that make separate claims. When this happens, it is usually useful to dissect the sentence into its smallest parts, so that we can investigate each part separately. Because simpler steps are easier to follow than complex ones, we can understand the argument better when it is broken down. Dissection makes us more likely to notice any flaws in the argument. It also enables us to pinpoint exactly where the argument fails, if it does.

The process of dissecting an argument is a skill that can be learned only by practice. Let's start with a simple example:

> Joe won his bet, because all he had to do was eat five pounds of oysters, and he ate nine dozen oysters, which weigh more than five pounds.

The simplest unpacking of this argument yields the following restatement in standard form:

> (1) All Joe had to do was eat five pounds of oysters, and he ate nine
>   dozen oysters, which weigh more than five pounds.
> ∴(2) Joe won his bet. (from 1)

If we think about the premise of this argument, we see that it actually contains three claims. The argument will be clearer if we separate these claims into independent premises and add a few words for the sake of clarity. The following, then, is a better representation of this argument:

> (1) All Joe had to do (to win his bet) was eat five pounds of oysters.
>
> (2) Joe ate nine dozen oysters.
>
> (3) Nine dozen oysters weigh more than five pounds.
> ∴(4) Joe won his bet. (from 1–3)

With the premise split up in this way, it becomes obvious that there are three separate ways in which the argument could fail. One possibility is that the first premise is false because Joe had to do more than just eat five pounds of oysters to win his bet: Maybe what he bet was that he could eat five pounds in five minutes. Another possibility is that the second premise is false because Joe did not really eat nine dozen oysters: Maybe he really ate one dozen oysters cut into nine dozen pieces. A final way in which the argument could fail is if the third premise is false because nine dozen oysters do not weigh more than five pounds: Maybe the oysters that Joe ate were very small, or maybe nine dozen oysters weigh more than five pounds only when they are still in their shells, but Joe did not eat the shells. In any case, breaking down complex premises into simpler ones makes it easier to see exactly where the argument goes wrong, if it does. Consequently, we can be more confident that an argument does not go wrong if we do not see any problem in it even after we have broken it down completely.

Although it is a good idea to break down the premises of an argument when this is possible, we have to be careful not to do this in a way that changes the logical structure of the argument. Suppose someone argues like this:

Socialism is doomed to failure because it does not provide the incentives that are needed for a prosperous economy.

The simplest representation of this argument yields the following standard form:

(1) Socialism does not provide the incentives that are needed for a prosperous economy.

∴(2) Socialism is doomed to failure. (from 1)

It is tempting to break up the first premise into two parts:

(1) Socialism does not provide incentives.

(2) Incentives are needed for a prosperous economy.

∴(3) Socialism is doomed to failure. (from 1–2)

In this form, the argument is open to a fatal objection: Socialism *does* provide *some* incentives. Workers often get public recognition and special privileges when they produce a great deal in socialist economies. But this does not refute the original argument. The point of the original argument was not that socialism does not provide any incentives at all, but only that socialism does not provide *enough* incentives or the right *kind* of incentives to create a prosperous economy. This point is lost if we break up the premise in the way suggested. A better attempt is this:

(1) Socialism does not provide adequate incentives.

(2) Adequate incentives are needed for a prosperous economy.

∴(3) Socialism is doomed to failure. (from 1–2)

The problem now is to specify when incentives are *adequate*. What kinds of incentives are needed? How much of these incentives? The answer seems to be "enough for a prosperous economy." But then premise 2 reduces to "Enough incentives for a prosperous economy are needed for a prosperous economy." This is too empty to be useful. Thus, we are led back to something like the original premise:

(1) Socialism does not provide enough incentives for a prosperous economy.

∴(2) Socialism is doomed to failure. (from 1)

In this case, we cannot break the premise into parts without distorting the point.

ARRANGING SUBARGUMENTS

When the premises of an argument are dissected, it often becomes clear that some of these premises are intended as reasons for others. The premises then form a chain of simpler arguments that culminate in the ultimate conclusion, but only after some intermediate steps. Consider this argument:

> There's no way I can finish my paper before the 9 o'clock show, since I have to do the reading first, so I won't even start writing until at least 9 o'clock.

It might seem tempting to put this argument into standard form as:

> (1) I have to do the reading first.
> (2) I won't even start writing until at least 9 o'clock.
> ∴(3) I can't finish my paper before the 9 o'clock show. (from 1–2)

This reformulation does include all three parts of the original argument, but it fails to indicate the correct role for each part. The two argument markers in the original argument indicate that there are really *two* conclusions. The word "since" indicates that what precedes it is a conclusion, and the word "so" indicates that what follows it is also a conclusion. We cannot represent this as a single argument in standard form, because each argument in standard form can have only one conclusion. Thus, the original sentence must have included two arguments. The relationship between these arguments should be clear: The conclusion of the first argument functions as a premise or reason in the second argument. To represent this, we let the two arguments form a chain. This is the first argument:

> (1) I have to do the reading first.
> ∴(2) I won't even start writing until at least 9 o'clock. (from 1)

This is the second argument:

> (2) I won't even start writing until at least 9 o'clock.
> ∴(3) I can't finish my paper before the 9 o'clock show. (from 2)

If we want to, we can then write these two arguments in a chain like this:

> (1) I have to do the reading first.
> ∴(2) I won't even start writing until at least 9 o'clock. (from 1)
> ∴(3) I can't finish my paper before the 9 o'clock show. (from 2)

This chain of reasoning can also be diagrammed like this:

(1)

(2)

(3)

The arrows indicate which claims are supposed to provide reasons for which other claims. Because these premises and arrows all fall on a single line, it is natural to call this structure *linear*.

Although it is often illuminating to break an argument into stages and arrange them in a linear series, this can be misleading if done incorrectly. For example, the first sentences of Kyl's speech cited in Chapter 4 read as follows:

> Mr. Speaker, I oppose this measure. I oppose it first because it is expensive. I further oppose it because it is untimely.

If we try to force this into a simple line, we might get this:

(1) This measure is expensive.

∴(2) This measure is untimely. (from 1)

∴(3) I oppose this measure. (from 2)

This reconstruction suggests that the measure's being expensive is what makes it untimely. That might be true (say, during a temporary budget crisis), but it is not what Kyl actually says. Instead, Kyl is giving two separate reasons for the same conclusion. First,

(1) This measure is expensive.

∴(2) I oppose this measure. (from 1)

Second,

(1*) This measure is untimely.

∴(2) I oppose this measure. (from 1*)

The structure of this argument can now be diagrammed as a branching tree:

The two arrows indicate that there are two separate reasons for the conclusion. Because this structure resembles the way branches split off from the trunk of a tree, we can describe this structure as *branching*. We have to be careful not to confuse branching arguments like this with linear chains of arguments that do not branch.

We also need to distinguish this branching structure from cases where several premises work together to support a single conclusion. Consider this argument:

> My keys must be either at home or at the office. They can't be at the office, because I looked for them there. So they must be at home.

With some clarifications, we can put this argument in standard form:

(1) My keys are either at my home or at my office.

(2) My keys are not at my office.

∴(3) My keys are at my home. (from 1–2)

Although this argument has two premises, it does not give two separate reasons for its conclusion. Neither premise by itself, without the other, is enough to give us any reason to believe the conclusion: "My keys are either at my home or at my office" alone is not enough to support "My keys are at my home," and "My keys are not at my office" alone is also not enough to support "My keys are at my home." The premises work only when they work together. Thus, it would be misleading to diagram this argument in the same way as Kyl's argument.

Instead, we need to indicate that the premises work together. Here's a simple way:

The symbol "+" with a single arrow indicates that the two premises work together to provide a single reason for the conclusion. The line under the premises that are joined together makes it clear that those are the premises that lead to the conclusion at the end of the arrow. If three or more premises provided a single reason, then we could simply add to the list—(1) + (2) + (3), and so on—then draw a line under the premises to show which ones work together. Because these premises work jointly rather than separately, we can call this structure *joint*.

The argument that we are diagramming included one part that we have not incorporated yet:

They can't be at the office, because I looked for them there.

The standard form is this:

(2*) I looked for my keys at my office.

∴ (2) My keys can't be at my office. (from 2*)

By itself, this argument has this diagram:

Since the conclusion of this background argument is a premise in the other part of the argument, we can put the diagrams together like this:

The fact that the arrow goes from (2*) to (2) but not to (1) indicates that this background argument supports premise (2), but not the other premise. In cases like this, you need to be careful where you draw your arrows.

Argument structures can get very complex, but we can diagram most arguments by connecting the simple forms that we illustrated. Begin by identifying the premises and conclusions. Give each different claim a different number. When two premises work together to support a single conclusion, put a "+" between the premises and a line under them connected to a single arrow that points to the conclusion. When two or more premises (or sets of premises) provide separate reasons for a conclusion, draw separate arrows from each reason to the conclusion. When a conclusion of one argument is a premise in another, put it in the middle of a chain. The complete diagram together will then show how the parts of the argument fit together and form a complex whole.

EXERCISE II

Put the following arguments into standard form. Break up the premises and form chains of arguments wherever this can be done without distorting the argument. Then diagram the argument.

1. I know that Pat can't be a father, because she is not a male. So she can't be a grandfather either.

2. Either Jack is a fool or Mary is a crook, because she ended up with all of his money.

3. Our team can't win this Saturday, both because they are not going to play, and because they are no good, so they wouldn't win even if they did play.

4. Mercury is known to be the only metal that is liquid at room temperature, so a pound of mercury would be liquid in this room, which is at room temperature, and it would also conduct electricity, since all metals do. Therefore, some liquids do conduct electricity.

5. Since he won the lottery, he's rich and lucky, so he'll probably do well in the stock market, too, unless his luck runs out.

6. Joe is not a freshman, since he lives in a fraternity, and freshmen are not allowed to live in fraternities. He also can't be a senior, since he has not declared a major, and every senior has declared a major. And he can't be a junior, because I never met him before today, and I would have met him before now if he were a junior. So Joe must be a sophomore.

7. Since many newly emerging nations do not have the capital resources necessary for sustained growth, they will continue to need help from industrial nations to avoid mass starvation.

EXERCISE III

In "A Piece of 'God's Handiwork'" (Exercise II in Chapter 4), Robert Redford argues that the Bureau of Land Management (BLM) should not allow Conoco to drill for oil in Utah's Grand Staircase-Escalante National Monument. The following passage is a crucial part where Redford answers an objection. Arrange its subarguments in standard form so as to reveal the structure of his argument. Then diagram the overall argument.

(continued)

The BLM says its hands are tied. Why? Because these lands were set aside subject to "valid existing rights," and Conoco has a lease that gives it the right to drill. Sure Conoco has a lease—more than one, in fact—but those leases were originally issued without sufficient environmental study or public input. As a result, none of them conveyed a valid right to drill. What's more, in deciding to issue a permit to drill now, the BLM did not conduct a full analysis of the environmental impacts of drilling in these incomparable lands, but instead determined there would be no significant environmental harm on the basis of an abbreviated review that didn't even look at drilling on the other federal leases. Sounds like Washington double-speak to me.[3]

EXERCISE IV

During the Republican candidates' debate on October 9, 2007, Chris Matthews asked Senator John McCain, ". . . Do you believe that Congress has to authorize a strategic attack, not an attack on—during hot pursuit, but a strategic attack on weaponry in Iran—do you need congressional approval as commander and chief?" Read McCain's response, then arrange its subarguments in standard form so as to reveal the structure of his argument. Then diagram the overall argument.

McCain: We're dealing, of course, with hypotheticals. If the situation is that it requires immediate action to ensure the security of the United States of America, that's what you take your oath to do, when you're inaugurated as president of the United States. If it's a long series of build-ups, where the threat becomes greater and greater, of course you want to go to Congress; of course you want to get approval, if this is an imminent threat to the security of the United States of America. So it obviously depends on the scenario. But I would, at minimum, consult with the leaders of Congress because there may come a time when you need the approval of Congress. And I believe that this is a possibility that is, maybe, closer to reality than we are discussing tonight.[4]

SOME STANDARDS FOR EVALUATING ARGUMENTS

After identifying the explicit premises and conclusion and then placing them all into a unified structure, the next step is to look for missing parts. Arguments in everyday life are rarely completely explicit. They usually depend on unstated assumptions that are taken for granted by those in the conversation. We need to bring out those implicit elements in order to complete the argument and assess it fully.

This step raises a crucial question: When is it legitimate to add premises that the arguer did not state openly? It would be unfair to criticize an argument for assuming something that it does not really need to assume. Nonetheless, if an argument does need to meet certain standards in order to support its conclusion, then it is legitimate to add premises that really are necessary for the argument to meet those standards. Thus, in order to determine which assumptions we can fairly ascribe to an argument, we first need to determine precisely which standards that argument needs to meet in order to succeed or be good.

Evaluating arguments is a complex business. In fact, this entire book is aimed primarily at developing procedures for doing so. We will find that different standards apply to different arguments. There are, however, certain basic terms used in evaluating many arguments that we can introduce briefly now. They are validity, truth, and soundness. Here they will be introduced informally. Later (in Chapters 6 and 7) they will be examined with more rigor.

VALIDITY

In some good arguments, the conclusion is said to follow from the premises. However, this commonsense notion of *following from* is hard to pin down precisely. The conclusion follows from the premises only when the content of the conclusion is related appropriately to the content of the premises, but which relations count as appropriate?

To avoid this difficult question, most logicians instead discuss whether an argument is *valid*. Calling something "valid" can mean a variety of things, but in this context validity is a technical notion. Here "valid" does not mean "good," and "invalid" does not mean "bad." This will be our definition of validity:

> An argument is *valid* if and only if it is not possible that all of its premises are true and its conclusion false.

Alternatively, one could say that its conclusion *must* be true if its premises are all true (or, again, that at least one of its premises *must* be false if its conclusion is false). The point is that a certain combination—true premises and a false conclusion—is ruled out as impossible.

The following argument passes this test for validity:

(1) All senators are paid.

(2) Sam is a senator.

∴(3) Sam is paid. (from 1–2)

Clearly, if the two premises are both true, there is no way for the conclusion to fail to be true. To see this, just try to tell a coherent story in which every single senator is paid and Sam is a senator, but Sam is not paid. You can't do it.

Contrast this example with a different argument:

(1) All senators are paid.
(2) Sam is paid.
∴(3) Sam is a senator. (from 1–2)

Here the premises and the conclusion are all in fact true, let's assume, but that is still not enough to make the argument valid, because validity concerns what is possible or impossible, not what happens to be true. This conclusion *could* be false even when the premises are true, for Sam *could* leave the Senate but still be paid for some other job, such as lobbyist. That possibility shows that this argument is invalid.

Another very common form of argument is called *modus ponens:*

(1) If it is snowing, then the roads are slippery.

(2) It is snowing.
∴(3) The roads are slippery. (from 1–2)

This argument is valid, because it is not possible for its premises to be true when its conclusion is false. We can show that by assuming that the conclusion is false and then reasoning backwards. Imagine that the roads are not slippery. Then there are two possibilities. Either it is snowing or it is not snowing. If it is not snowing, then the second premise is false. If it is snowing, then the first premise must be false, since we are supposing that it is snowing and that the roads are not slippery. Thus, at least one premise has to be false when the conclusion is false. Hence, this argument is valid.

This argument might seem similar to another:

(1) If it is snowing, then the roads are slippery.
(2) It is not snowing.
∴(3) The roads are not slippery. (from 1–2)

This argument is clearly invalid, because there are several ways for its premises to be true when its conclusion is false. It might have just stopped snowing or ice might make the roads slippery. Then the roads are slippery, so the conclusion is false, even if both premises are true.

Yet another form of argument is often called *process of elimination:*

(1) Either Joe or Jack or Jim or Jerry committed the murder.
(2) Joe didn't do it.
(3) Jack didn't do it.
(4) Jim didn't do it.
∴(5) Jerry committed the murder. (from 1–4)

The first premise asserts that at least one of these four suspects is guilty. That couldn't be true if all of the other premises were true and the conclusion were false, because that combination would exclude all four of these suspects. So this argument is valid.

Now compare this argument:

(1) Either Joe or Jack or Jim or Jerry committed the murder.
(2) Joe did it.

∴(3) Jerry did not commit the murder. (from 1–2)

To show that this argument is invalid, all we have to do is explain how the premises could be true and the conclusion false. Here's how: Joe and Jerry did it together. In that case, Jerry did it, so the conclusion is false; Joe also did it, so the second premise is true; and the first premise is true, because it says that at least one of these four suspects did it, and that is true when more than one of the suspects did it. That possibility of complicity, thus, makes this argument invalid.

We will explore many more forms of argument in Chapters 6 and 7. The goal for now is just to get a feel for how to determine validity. In all of these examples, an argument is said to be *valid* if and only if there is no possible situation in which its premises are true and its conclusion is false. You need to figure out whether there could be any situation like this in order to determine whether an argument is valid. If so, the argument is invalid. If not, it is valid.

This definition shows why validity is a valuable feature for an argument to possess: There can be no valid argument that leads one from true premises to a false conclusion. This should square with your commonsense ideas about reasoning. If you reason well, you should not be led from truth into error.

What are known as *deductive* arguments are put forward as meeting this standard of validity, so validity is one criterion for a good deductive argument. Other arguments—so-called *inductive* arguments—are not presented as meeting this standard. Roughly, an inductive argument is presented as providing strong support for its conclusion. The standards for evaluating inductive arguments will be examined in Chapters 8-10. For now, we will concentrate on deductive arguments.

TRUTH

Although a deductive argument must be valid in order to be a good argument, validity is not enough. One reason is that an argument can be valid even when some (or all) of the statements it contains are false. For example:

(1) No fathers are female.
(2) Sam is a father.

∴(3) Sam is not female. (from 1–2)

Suppose that Sam has no children or that Sam is female, so premise 2 is false. That would be a serious defect in this argument. Nonetheless, this argument satisfies our definition of validity: If the premises were true, then the conclusion could not be false. There is no way that Sam could be female if Sam is a father and no fathers are female. This example makes it obvious that validity is not the same as truth. It also makes it obvious that another requirement of a good argument is that *all of its premises must be true.*

SOUNDNESS

We thus make at least two demands of a deductive argument:

1. The argument must be valid.
2. The premises must be true.

When an argument meets both of these standards, it is said to be *sound*. If it fails to meet either one or the other, then it is *unsound*. Thus, an argument is unsound if it is invalid, and it is also unsound if at least one of its premises is false.

	ALL PREMISES TRUE	AT LEAST ONE FALSE PREMISE
Valid	Sound	Unsound
Invalid	Unsound	Unsound

Soundness has one great benefit: A sound argument must have a true conclusion. We know this because its premises are true and, since it is valid, it is not possible that its premises are true and its conclusion is false. This is why people who seek truth want sound arguments, not merely valid arguments.

EXERCISE V

Indicate whether each of the following arguments is valid and whether it is sound. Explain your answers where necessary.

1. Most professors agree that they are paid too little, so they are.
2. David Letterman is over four feet tall, so he is over two feet tall.
3. Lee can't run a company right, because he can't do anything right.
4. Barack Obama is smart and good-looking, so he is smart.
5. Barack Obama is either a Democrat or a Republican, so he is a Democrat.
6. Since Jimmy Carter was president, he must have won an election.
7. Since Gerald Ford was president, he must have won an election.
8. Pat is either a mother or a father. If Pat is a mother, then she is a parent. If Pat is a father, he is a parent. So, either way, Pat is a parent. (Assume that this conclusion is true.)
9. People who live in the Carolinas live in either North Carolina or South Carolina. Hillary Clinton does not live in North Carolina or South Carolina. Hence, she does not live in the Carolinas.
10. If all of Illinois were in Canada, then Chicago would be in Canada. But Chicago is not in Canada. Therefore, not all of Illinois is in Canada.

11. If George lives in Crawford, then George lives in Texas. If George lives in Texas, then George lives in the United States. Hence, if George lives in Crawford, he lives in the United States.

12. There can't be a largest six-digit number, because six-digit numbers are numbers, and there is no largest number.

EXERCISE VI

Assume that the following sentences are either true (T) or false (F) as indicated.

All my children are teenagers. (T)

All teenagers are students. (T)

All teenagers are my children. (F)

All my children are students. (T)

Using these assigned values, label each of the following arguments as (a) either valid or invalid, and (b) either sound or unsound.

1. All my children are teenagers.
   All teenagers are students.
   ∴ All my children are students.

2. All my children are students.
   All teenagers are students.
   ∴ All my children are teenagers.

3. All teenagers are my children.
   All my children are students.
   ∴ All teenagers are students.

4. All teenagers are students.
   All my children are students.
   ∴ All my children are students.

EXERCISE VII

Indicate whether each of the following sentences is true. For those that are true, explain why they are true. For those that are false, show why they are false by giving a counterexample.

1. Every argument with a false conclusion is invalid.

2. Every argument with a false premise is invalid.

3. Every argument with a false premise and a false conclusion is invalid.

4. Every argument with a false premise and a true conclusion is invalid.

(continued)

5. Every argument with true premises and a false conclusion is invalid.

6. Every argument with a true conclusion is sound.

7. Every argument with a false conclusion is unsound.

SUPPRESSED PREMISES

Now that we understand validity and soundness, we can use those standards to determine which assumptions can fairly be added to deductive arguments in order to complete them. If some extra premise is needed in order for a deductive argument to be valid or sound, then that argument needs that assumption in order to succeed as a deductive argument. That makes it legitimate to add that extra premise to the argument even though the person who gave that argument omitted that premise. The arguer did not openly state the extra premise, but he did assume it.

For example, if we are told that Chester Arthur was a president of the United States, we have a right to conclude a great many things about him— for example, that at the time he was president, he was a live human being. Appeals to facts of this kind lie behind the following argument:

Benjamin Franklin could not have been our second president, because he died before the second election was held.

This argument obviously turns on a question of fact: Did Franklin die before the second presidential election was held? (He did.) The argument would not be sound if this explicit premise were not true. But the argument also depends on a more general principle that ties the premise and conclusion together:

The dead cannot be president.

This new premise is needed to make the argument valid in the technical sense.

This new premise is also needed to explain *why* the premise supports the conclusion. You could have made the original argument valid simply by adding this:

If Franklin died before the second election was held, then he could not have been our second president.

Indeed, you can always make an argument valid simply by adding a conditional whose antecedent is the premises and whose consequent is the conclusion. However, this trick is often not illuminating; it does not reveal how the argument works. In our example, there is nothing special about Franklin, so it is misleading to add a conditional that mentions Franklin in particular. In contrast, when we add the general principle, "The dead cannot be president," this new premise not only makes the argument valid but also helps us understand how the conclusion is supposed to follow from the premise.

Traditionally, logicians have called premises that are not stated but are needed (to make the argument valid and explain how it works) *suppressed premises*. An argument depending on suppressed premises is called an *enthymeme* and is said to be *enthymematic*. If we look at arguments that occur in daily life, we discover that they are, almost without exception, enthymematic. Therefore, to trace the pathway between premises and conclusion, it is usually necessary to fill in these suppressed premises that serve as links between the stated premises and the conclusion.

CONTINGENT FACTS

Suppressed premises come in several varieties. They often concern facts or conventions that might have been otherwise—that are contingent rather than necessary. Our example assumed that the dead are not eligible for the presidency, but we can imagine a society in which the deceased are elected to public office as an honor (something like posthumous induction into the Baseball Hall of Fame). Our national government is not like that, however, and this is something that most Americans know. This makes it odd to come right out and say that the deceased cannot hold public office. In most settings, this would involve a violation of the conversational rule of Quantity, because it says more than needs to be said.

Even though it would be odd to state it, this fact plays a central role in the argument. To assert the conclusion without believing the suppressed premise would involve a violation of the conversational rule of Quality, because the speaker would not have adequate reasons for the conclusion. Furthermore, if this suppressed premise were not believed to be true, then to give the explicit premise as a reason for the conclusion would violate the conversational rule of Relevance (just as it would be irrelevant to point out that Babe Ruth is dead when someone asks whether he is in the Baseball Hall of Fame). For these reasons, anyone who gives the original argument conversationally implies a commitment to the suppressed premise.

Suppressed premises are not always so obvious. A somewhat more complicated example is this:

> Arnold Schwarzenegger cannot become president of the United States, because he was born in Austria.

Why should being from Austria disqualify someone from being president? It seems odd that the Founding Fathers should have something against that particular part of the world. The answer is that the argument depends on a more general suppressed premise:

> Only a natural-born U.S. citizen may become president of the United States.

It is this provision of the U.S. Constitution that lies at the heart of the argument. Knowing this provision is, of course, a more specialized piece of knowledge than knowing that you have to be alive to be president. For this reason, more people will see the force of the first argument (about Franklin) than the second (about Schwarzenegger). The second argument assumes an audience with more specialized knowledge.

The argument still has to draw a connection between being born in Austria and being a natural-born U.S. citizen. So it turns out that the argument has three stages:

> (1) Schwarzenegger was born in Austria.
> (2) Austria has never been part of the United States.
> ∴ (3) Schwarzenegger was born outside of the United States. (from 1–2)
> (4) Anyone who was born outside of the United States is not a natural-born U.S. citizen.
> ∴ (5) Schwarzenegger is not a natural-born U.S. citizen. (from 3–4)
> (6) Only a natural-born U.S. citizen may become president of the United States.
> ∴ (7) Schwarzenegger cannot become president of the United States. (from 5–6)

With the addition of suppressed premises (2), (4), and (6), the argument is technically valid, for, if (1)–(2) are true, (3) must be true; if (3)–(4) are true, (5) must also be true; and if (5)–(6) are true, then (7) must be true.

The argument is still not sound, however, because some of the suppressed premises that were added are not true. In particular, there is an exception to the suppressed premise about who is a natural-born U.S. citizen. This exception is well known to U.S. citizens who live overseas. People who were born in Austria are U.S. citizens if their parents were U.S. citizens. They also seem to count as natural-born citizens, since they are not naturalized. This is not completely settled, but it does not matter here, as Arnold Schwarzenegger's parents were not U.S. citizens when he was born. Thus, the second stage of the above argument can be reformulated as follows:

> (3) Schwarzenegger was born outside of the United States.
> (4*) Schwarzenegger's parents were not U.S. citizens when he was born.
> (4**) Anyone who was born outside of the United States and whose parents were not U.S. citizens at the time is not a natural-born U.S. citizen.
> ∴ (5) Schwarzenegger is not a natural-born U.S. citizen. (from 3, 4*, and 4**)

This much of the argument is now sound.

An argument with a single premise has grown to include three stages with at least four suppressed premises. Some of the added premises are obvious, but others are less well known, so we cannot assume that the person who gave the original argument had the more complete argument in mind. Many people would be convinced by the original argument even without all these added complexities. Nonetheless, the many suppressed premises are necessary to make the argument sound. Seeing this brings out the assumptions that must be true for the conclusion to follow from the premises. This process of making everything explicit enables us to assess these background assumptions directly.

EXERCISE VIII

There is one obscure exception to the premise that only a natural-born citizen may become president of the United States. The Constitution does allow a person who is not a natural-born citizen to become president if he or she was "a citizen of the United States at the time of the adoption of this Constitution." This exception is said to have been added to allow Alexander Hamilton to run for president, but it obviously does not apply to Schwarzenegger or to anyone else alive today. Nonetheless, this exception keeps the argument from being sound in its present form. Reformulate the final stage of the argument to make it sound.

LINGUISTIC PRINCIPLES

Often an argument is valid, but it is still not clear *why* it is valid. It is not clear *how* the conclusion follows from the premises. Arguments are like pathways between premises and conclusions, and some of these pathways are more complicated than others. Yet even the simplest arguments reveal hidden complexities when examined closely. For example, there is no question that the following argument is valid:

(1) Harriet is in New York with her son.

∴ (2) Harriet's son is in New York.

It is not possible for the premise to be true and the conclusion false. If asked why this conclusion follows from the premise, it would be natural to reply that:

You cannot be someplace with somebody unless that person is there, too.

This is not something we usually spell out, but it is the principle that takes us from the premise to the conclusion.

One thing to notice about this principle is that it is quite general—that is, it does not depend on any special features of the people or places involved. It is also true that if Benjamin is in St. Louis with his daughter, then Benjamin's daughter is in St. Louis. Although the references have changed, the general pattern that lies behind this inference will seem obvious to anyone who understands the words used to formulate it. For this reason, principles of this kind are basically *linguistic* in character.

If we look at arguments as they occur in everyday life, we will discover that almost all of them turn on unstated linguistic principles. To cite just one more example: Alice is taller than her husband, so there is at least one woman who is taller than at least one man. This inference relies on the principles that husbands are men and wives are women. We do not usually state these linguistic principles, for to do so will often violate the rule of Quantity. (Try to imagine a context in which you would come right out and say, "Husbands, you know, are men." Unless you were speaking to someone just learning the language, this would be a peculiar remark.) Nonetheless, even if it would usually be peculiar to come right out and state such linguistic principles, our arguments still typically presuppose them. This observation reveals yet another way in which our daily use of language moves within a rich, though largely unnoticed, framework of linguistic rules, as we emphasized in Chapter 2.

EVALUATIVE SUPPRESSED PREMISES

We have examined two kinds of suppressed premises, factual and linguistic. Many arguments also contain unstated evaluative premises. As we saw in Chapter 3, evaluation comes in many kinds. The following argument involves moral evaluation:

> It is immoral to buy pornography, because pornography leads to violence toward women.

This argument clearly relies on the moral principle that it is immoral to buy anything that leads to violence toward women. A different example contains religious premises:

> You shouldn't take the name of the Lord in vain, for this shows disrespect.

The suppressed premise here is that you should not do anything that shows disrespect (to the Lord). One more example is about economics:

> It is unwise to invest all of your money in one stock, since this increases the risk that you will lose everything.

The suppressed premise here is that it is unwise to increase the risk that you will lose everything. More examples could be given, but the point should be clear. Most arguments depend on unstated assumptions, and many of these assumptions are evaluative in one way or another.

USES AND ABUSES OF SUPPRESSED PREMISES

Talk about *suppressed* premises may bring to mind suppressing a rebellion or an ugly thought, and using *hidden* premises may sound somewhat sneaky. However, the way we are using them, these expressions do not carry such negative connotations. A suppressed or hidden premise is simply an *unstated* premise. It is often legitimate to leave premises unstated. It is legitimate if (1) those who are given the argument can easily supply these unstated premises for themselves, and (2) the unstated premises are not themselves controversial. If done properly, the suppression of premises can add greatly to the efficiency of language. Indeed, without the judicious suppression of obvious premises, many arguments would become too cumbersome to be effective.

On the other hand, suppressed premises can also be used improperly. People sometimes suppress questionable assumptions so that their opponents will not notice where an argument goes astray. For example, when election debates turn to the topic of crime, we often hear arguments like this:

My opponent is opposed to the death penalty, so he must be soft on crime.

The response sometimes sounds like this:

Since my opponent continues to support the death penalty, he must not have read the most recent studies, which show that the death penalty does not deter crime.

The first argument assumes that anyone who is opposed to the death penalty is soft on crime, and the second argument assumes that anyone who read the studies in question would be convinced by them and would turn against the death penalty. Both of these assumptions are questionable, and the questions they raise are central to the debate. If we want to understand these issues and address them directly, we have to bring out these suppressed premises openly.

EXERCISE IX

The following arguments depend for their validity on suppressed premises of various kinds. For each of them, list enough suppressed premises to make the argument valid and also to show why it is valid. This might require several suppressed premises of various kinds.

EXAMPLE: Carol has no sisters, because all her siblings are brothers.

SUPPRESSED PREMISES: A sister would be a sibling.
A brother is not a sister.

1. Britney Spears is under age thirty-five. Therefore, she cannot run for president of the United States.
2. Nixon couldn't have been president in 1950 because he was still in the Senate.
3. 81 is not a prime number, because 81 is divisible by 3.
4. There's no patient named Rupert here; we have only female patients.
5. Columbus did not discover the New World because the Vikings explored Newfoundland centuries earlier.
6. There must not be any survivors, since they would have been found by now.
7. Lincoln could not have met Washington, because Washington was dead before Lincoln was born.
8. Philadelphia cannot play Los Angeles in the World Series, since they are both in the National League.

9. Mildred must be over forty-three, since she has a daughter who is thirty-six years old.

10. He cannot be a grandfather because he never had children.

11. That's not modern poetry; you can understand it.

12. Harold can't play in the Super Bowl, because he broke his leg.

13. Shaquille must be a basketball player, since he is so tall.

14. Dan is either stupid or very cunning, so he must be stupid.

15. Susan refuses to work on Sundays, which shows that she is lazy and inflexible.

16. Jim told me that Mary is a professor, so she can't be a student, since professors must already have degrees.

17. This burglar alarm won't work unless we are lucky or the burglar uses the front door, so we can't count on it.

18. His natural talents were not enough; he still lost the match because he had not practiced sufficiently.

THE METHOD OF RECONSTRUCTION

We can summarize the discussion so far by listing the steps to be taken in reconstructing an argument. The first two steps were discussed in Chapters 4 and 3, respectively.

1. Do a *close analysis* of the passage containing the argument.

2. List all explicit premises and the conclusion in *standard form*.

3. *Clarify* the premises and the conclusion where necessary.

4. *Break up* the premises and the conclusion into smaller parts where this is possible.

5. *Arrange* the parts of the argument into a chain or tree of subarguments where this is possible.

6. Assess each argument and subargument for *validity*.[5]

7. If any argument or subargument is not valid, or if it is not clear why it is valid, add *suppressed premises* that will show how to get from the premises to the conclusion.

8. Assess the *truth* of the premises.

Remember that the goal of reconstruction is not just technical validity but is, instead, to understand why and how the conclusion is supposed to follow from the premises.

After reconstructing the argument, it is often helpful to add some indication of its structure. This can be done by numbering the premises and then, after each conclusion, listing the premises from which that conclusion follows. (We did this in our examples.) The argument's structure can also be shown by a diagram like those discussed above. Either way, we need to make it clear exactly how the separate parts of the argument are supposed to fit together.

This method is not intended to be mechanical. Each step requires care and intelligence. As a result, a given argument can be reconstructed in various ways with varying degrees of illumination and insight. The goal of this method is to reveal as much of the structure of an argument as possible and to learn from it as much as you can. Different reconstructions approach this goal more or less closely.

The whole process is more complex than our discussion thus far has suggested. This is especially clear in the last three steps of reconstruction, which must be carried out simultaneously. In deciding whether an argument is acceptable, we try to find a set of true suppressed premises that, if added to the stated premises, yields a sound argument for the conclusion. Two problems typically arise when we make this effort:

1. We find a set of premises strong enough to support the conclusion, but at least one of these premises is false.

2. We modify the premises to avoid falsehood, but the conclusion no longer follows from them.

The reconstruction of an argument typically involves shifting back and forth between the demand for a valid argument and the demand for true premises. Eventually, either we show the argument to be sound or we abandon the effort. In the latter case, we conclude that the argument in question has no sound reconstruction. It is still possible that *we* were at fault in not finding a reconstruction that showed the argument to be sound. Perhaps we did not show enough ingenuity in searching for a suppressed premise that would do the trick. There is, in fact, no purely formal or mechanical way of dealing with this problem. A person presenting an argument may reasonably leave out steps, provided that they can easily be filled in by those to whom the argument is addressed. So, in analyzing an argument, we should be charitable, but our charity has limits. After a reasonable search for those suppressed premises that would show the argument to be sound, we should not blame ourselves if we fail to find them. Rather, the blame shifts to the person who formulated the argument for not doing so clearly.

EXERCISE X

Reconstruct and diagram the main arguments in:

1. The passages at the end of Chapters 1 and 4.

2. An editorial from your local paper.

3. Your last term paper or a friend's last term paper.

Not all arguments are serious or good. The following silly argument comes from a famous scene in *Monty Python and the Holy Grail*. Reconstruct the argument that is supposed to show that the woman is a witch.

CROWD: We have found a witch. May we burn her? . . .

WOMAN: I'm not a witch! I'm not a witch! . . .

LEADER: What makes you think she is a witch?

MAN #1: She turned me into a newt!

LEADER: A newt?

MAN #1: I got better.

CROWD: Burn her anyway!

LEADER: Quiet! Quiet! There are ways of telling whether she is a witch.

CROWD: Are there? What are they? Tell us. Do they hurt?

LEADER: Tell me, what do you do with witches?

CROWD: Burn them!

LEADER: And what do you burn apart from witches?

MAN #2: More witches!

MAN #3: Wood.

LEADER: So, why do witches burn?

MAN #1: 'Cause they're made of wood.

LEADER: Good! . . . So, how do we tell whether she is made of wood?

CROWD: Build a bridge out of her.

LEADER: Ah, but can you not also make bridges out of stone?

CROWD: Oh yeah.

LEADER: Does wood sink in water?

CROWD: No, it floats. Throw her into the pond!

LEADER: What also floats in water?

CROWD: Bread. Apples. Very small rocks. Cider! Great gravy. Cherries. Mud. Churches. Lead.

ARTHUR: A duck!

LEADER: Exactly. So, logically, —

MAN #3: If she weighs the same as a duck, she's made of wood.

LEADER: And therefore?

CROWD: A witch! . . . A duck. A duck. Here's a duck!

LEADER: We shall use my largest scales.

CROWD: Burn the witch! (Woman is placed on scales opposite a duck.)

LEADER: Remove the supports. (Woman balances duck.)

CROWD: A witch!

WOMAN: It's a fair cop.

AN EXAMPLE OF RECONSTRUCTION: CAPITAL PUNISHMENT

We can illustrate the methods of reconstruction by examining the difficult question of the constitutionality of capital punishment. It has been argued that the U.S. Supreme Court should declare the death penalty unconstitutional because it is a cruel and unusual punishment. The explicitly stated argument has the following basic form:

(1) The death penalty is a cruel and unusual punishment.

∴(2) The death penalty should be declared unconstitutional. (from 1)

This argument plainly depends on two suppressed premises:

SP1: The Constitution prohibits cruel and unusual punishments.

SP2: Anything that the Constitution prohibits should be declared unconstitutional.

These premises and this entire argument refer to the relevant jurisdiction, which is the United States. So the argument, more fully spelled out, looks like this:

(1) The death penalty is a cruel and unusual punishment.
(2) SP: The Constitution prohibits cruel and unusual punishments.

∴(3) The Constitution prohibits the death penalty. (from 1–2)
(4) SP: Anything that the Constitution prohibits should be declared unconstitutional.

∴(5) The death penalty should be declared unconstitutional. (from 3–4)

This reconstruction seems to be a fair representation of the intent of the original argument.

We can now turn to an assessment of this argument. First, the argument is valid: Given the premises, the conclusion does follow. All that remains is to determine the truth of the premises one by one.

Premise 4 seems uncontroversial. This premise is so much an accepted part of our system that no one would challenge it in a courtroom proceeding today.

Premise 2 is clearly true, for the U.S. Constitution does, in fact, prohibit cruel and unusual punishments. Its Eighth Amendment reads, "Excessive bail shall not be required, nor excessive fines imposed, nor cruel and unusual punishments inflicted." It is not clear, however, just what this prohibition amounts to. In particular, does the punishment have to be *both* cruel *and* unusual to be prohibited, or is it prohibited whenever it is *either* cruel *or* unusual? This would make a big difference if cruel punishments were usual, or if some unusual punishments were not cruel. For the moment, let us interpret the language as meaning "both cruel and unusual."

The first premise—"The death penalty is a cruel and unusual punish-ment"—obviously forms the heart of the argument. What we would expect, then, is a good supporting argument to be put forward on its behalf. The following argument by Supreme Court Justice Potter Stewart (in *Furman v. Georgia*, 408 U.S. 239 at 309–310 [1972]) was intended to support this claim in particular cases in which the death penalty was imposed for rape and murder:

> In the first place, it is clear that these sentences are "cruel" in the sense that they excessively go beyond, not in degree but in kind, the punishments that the state legislatures have determined to be necessary. . . . In the second place, it is equally clear that these sentences are "unusual" in the sense that the penalty of death is infrequently imposed for murder, and that its imposition for rape is extraordinarily rare. But I do not rest my conclusion upon these two propositions alone. These death sentences are cruel and unusual in the same way that being struck by lightning is cruel and unusual. For, of all the people convicted of rapes and murders in 1967 and 1968, many just as reprehensible as these, the petitioners are among a capriciously selected random handful upon whom the sentence of death has in fact been imposed. My concurring brothers [the Justices who agree with Stewart] have demonstrated that, if any basis can be discerned for the selection of these few to be sentenced to die, it is the constitutionally impermissible basis of race.[6]

The first sentence argues that the death penalty is *cruel*. The basic idea is that punishments are cruel if they inflict harms that are much worse than what is necessary for any legitimate and worthwhile purpose. Stewart then seems to accept the state legislatures' view that the death penalty does go far beyond what is necessary. This makes it cruel.

Now let us concentrate on the part of this argument intended to show that the death penalty is an *unusual* punishment. Of course, in civilized nations, the death penalty is reserved for a small range of crimes, but this is hardly the point at issue. The point of the argument is that the death penalty is unusual even for those crimes that are punishable by death, including first-degree murder. Moreover, Stewart claims that, among those convicted of crimes punishable by death, who actually receives a death sentence is determined either capriciously or on the basis of race. The point seems to be that whether a person who is convicted of a capital crime will be given the death penalty depends on the kind of legal aid he or she receives, the prosecutor's willingness to offer a plea bargain, the judge's personality, the beliefs and attitudes of the jury, and many other considerations. At many points in the process, choices that affect the out-come could be based on mere whim or caprice, or even on the race of the defendant or the victim. Why are these factors mentioned? Because, as Stewart says, it is unconstitutional for sentencing to be based on caprice or race.

We can then restate this supporting argument more carefully:

(1) Very few criminals who were found guilty of crimes that are punishable by death are actually sentenced to death.
(2) Among those found guilty of crimes punishable by death, who is sentenced to death depends on caprice or race.
(3) It is unconstitutional for sentencing to depend on caprice or race.
(4) A punishment is unusual if it is imposed infrequently and on an unconstitutional basis.
∴(5) The death penalty is an unusual punishment. (from 1–4)

This conclusion is part of the first premise in our original argument. Now we can spread the entire argument out before us:

(1) An act is cruel if it inflicts harms that are much worse than what is necessary for any legitimate and worthwhile purpose.
(2) The death penalty inflicts harms that are much worse than what is necessary for any legitimate and worthwhile purpose.
∴(3) The death penalty is cruel. (from 1–2)
(4) Very few criminals who were found guilty of crimes that are punishable by death are sentenced to death.
(5) Among those found guilty of crimes punishable by death, who is sentenced to death depends on caprice or race.
(6) It is unconstitutional for sentencing to depend on caprice or race.
(7) A punishment is unusual if it is imposed infrequently and on an unconstitutional basis.
∴(8) The death penalty is an unusual punishment. (from 4–7)
∴(9) The death penalty is both cruel and unusual. (from 3 and 8)
(10) The Constitution prohibits cruel and unusual punishments.
∴(11) The Constitution prohibits the death penalty. (from 9–10)
(12) Anything that the Constitution prohibits should be declared unconstitutional.
∴(13) The death penalty should be declared unconstitutional. (from 11–12)

These propositions provide at least the skeleton of an argument with some force. The conclusion does seem to follow from the premises, and the premises themselves seem plausible. We have produced a charitable reconstruction of the argument.

This reconstruction enables us to see precisely how opponents can respond to the argument. Some opponents might deny Premise 2 and claim to the contrary that the death penalty does serve a legitimate purpose, such as retribution, deterrence, or incapacitation. Other opponents might deny Premise 5 and claim that courts do have good reasons for the death sentences that they approve. A more subtle objection denies Premise 7, because it is not the death penalty itself that is unusual or unfair in the relevant sense when the conditions in premise 7 are met. Instead, the problem is with the present administration of the death penalty. If so, maybe what we need is procedural reform instead of abolishing the death penalty itself. Of course, there are other objections as well as replies to every objection, so the debate goes on.

The point here is only that reconstructing the argument step by step using the method outlined in this chapter makes us able to understand the argument better and to determine more precisely whether and where it is vulnerable or not. This method can thereby help opponents understand each other and deal with their basic disagreements in an intelligent, humane, and civilized way.

EXERCISE XII

What is the best argument that Justice Stewart could give in support of the premise that the death penalty "excessively go[es] beyond" what is necessary for any legitimate and worthwhile purpose? Is this argument adequate to justify this premise? (For one such argument, see Justice Brennan's opinion in *Furman v. Georgia*.)

EXERCISE XIII

To solve a mystery, you need to determine which facts are crucial and then argue from those facts to a solution. Solve the following mysteries and reconstruct your own argument for your solution. These stories come from *Five-Minute Whodunits*, by Stan Smith (New York: Sterling, 1997). The first passage introduces our hero:

Even those acquainted with Thomas P. Stanwick are often struck by his appearance. A lean and lanky young man, he stands six feet two inches tall. His long, thin face is complemented by a full head of brown hair and a droopy mustache. Though not husky in build, he is surprisingly strong and enjoys ruggedly good health. His origins and early life are obscure. He is undeniably well educated, however, for he graduated with high honors from Dartmouth College as a philosophy major.[7]

MYSTERY 1: A MERE MATTER OF DEDUCTION

■

Thomas P. Stanwick, the amateur logician, removed a pile of papers from the extra chair and sat down. His friend Inspector Matthew Walker had just returned to his office from the interrogation room, and Stanwick thought he looked unusually weary.

Source: Stanley Smith, "A Mere Matter of Deduction," from Five-Minute Whodunits. Copyright © 1997 by Stanley Smith. Reprinted with permission of Sterling Publishing Co., Inc., NY, NY.

"I'm glad you dropped by, Tom," said Walker. "We have a difficult case on hand. Several thousand dollars' worth of jewelry was stolen from Hoffman's Jewel Palace yesterday morning. From some clues at the scene and a few handy tips, we have it narrowed down to three suspects: Addington, Burke, and Chatham. We know that at least one of them was involved, and possibly more than one."

"Burke has been suspected in several other cases, hasn't he?" asked Stanwick as he filled his pipe.

"Yes, he has," Walker replied, "but we haven't been able to nail him yet. The other two are small potatoes, so what we really want to know is whether Burke was involved in this one."

"What have you learned about the three of them?"

"Not too much. Addington and Burke were definitely here in the city yesterday. Chatham may not have been. Addington never works alone, and carries a snub-nosed revolver. Chatham always uses an accomplice, and he was seen lurking in the area last week. He also refuses to work with Addington, who he says once set him up."

"Quite a ragamuffin crew!" Stanwick laughed. "Based on what you've said, it's not too hard to deduce whether Burke was involved."

Was Burke involved or not?

MYSTERY 2: TRIVIA AND SIGNIFICA

"For April, this is starting out to be a pretty quiet month," remarked Inspector Walker as he rummaged in his desk drawer for a cigar.

Thomas P. Stanwick, the amateur logician, finished lighting his pipe and leaned back in his chair, stretching his long legs forward.

"That is indeed unusual," he said. "Spring usually makes some young fancies turn to crime. The change is welcome."

"Not that we police have nothing to do." Walker lit his cigar. "A couple of the youth gangs, the Hawks and the Owls, have been screeching at each other lately. In fact, we heard a rumor that they were planning to fight each other this Wednesday or Thursday, and we're scrambling around trying to find out whether it's true."

"The Hawks all go to Royston North High, don't they?" asked Stanwick.

"That's right. The Owls are the street-smart dropouts who hang out at Joe's Lunch Cafe on Lindhurst. You know that only those who eat at Joe's collect green matchbooks?"

Stanwick blinked and smiled. "I beg your pardon?"

"That's right." Walker picked up a few papers from his desk. "That's the sort of trivia I'm being fed in my reports. Not only that, but everyone at Royston North High wears monogrammed jackets. What else have I got here? Only kids who hang out on Laraby Street fight on weekdays. Laraby is three blocks from Lindhurst. The Hawks go out for pizza three times a week."

(continued)

Source: Stanley Smith, "A Mere Matter of Deduction," from Five-Minute Whodunits. Copyright © 1997 by Stanley Smith. Reprinted with permission of Sterling Publishing Co., Inc., NY, NY.

"Keep going," chuckled Stanwick. "It's wonderful."

"A hog for useless facts, eh? No one who eats at Joe's wears a monogrammed jacket. The Owls elect a new leader every six months, the Hawks every year. Elections! Furthermore, everyone who hangs out on Laraby Street collects green matchbooks. Finally, the older (but not wiser) Owls buy beer at Johnny's Package Store."

Stanwick laughed heartily. "Lewis Carroll," he said, "the author of *Symbolic Logic* and the 'Alice in Wonderland' books, taught logic at Oxford, and he used to construct soriteses, or polysyllogisms [that is, chains of categorical syllogisms], out of material like that. In fact, his were longer and much wilder and more intricate, but of course they were fiction.

"As it is, the information you've cited should ease your worries. Those gangs won't get together to fight until at least Saturday."

How does he know?

NOTES

[1] *CQ Transcripts Wire,* Tuesday, October 9, 2007, washingtonpost.com.

[2] LexisNexis™ Academic, Copyright 2004 Federal News Service, Inc.

[3] Robert Redford, "A Piece of 'God's Handiwork'," *The Washington Post,* November 25, 1997, A19.

[4] *CQ Transcripts Wire,* Tuesday, October 9, 2007, washingtonpost.com.

[5] We assess inductive arguments for *strength* instead of validity, but here we focus on deductive arguments. Inductive arguments will be examined in Part III, Chapters 8–12.

[6] Supreme Court Justice Potter Stewart, Concurring Opinion, *Furman v. Georgia,* 408 U.S. 239 at 309–310 [1972].

[7] Stan Smith, *Five-Minute Whodunits* (New York: Sterling, 1997).

PROPOSITIONAL LOGIC

This chapter begins our investigation of evaluating arguments by means of formal deductive logic. The first part of the chapter will show how the crucial standard of validity, which was introduced in Chapter 5, can be developed rigorously in one area—what is called propositional logic. This branch of logic deals with connectives such as "and" and "or," which allow us to build up compound propositions from simpler ones. Throughout most of the chapter, the focus will be theoretical rather than immediately practical. It is intended to provide insight into the concept of validity by examining it in an ideal setting. The chapter will close with a discussion of the relationship between the ideal language of symbolic logic and the language we ordinarily speak.

THE FORMAL ANALYSIS OF ARGUMENTS

When we carry out an informal analysis of an argument, we pay close attention to the key words used to present the argument and then ask ourselves whether these key terms have been used properly. So far, we have no exact techniques for answering the question of whether a word is used correctly. We rely, instead, on linguistic instincts that, on the whole, are fairly good.

In a great many cases, people can tell whether an argument marker, such as "therefore," is used correctly in indicating that one claim follows from another. However, if we go on to ask the average intelligent person *why* one claim follows from the other, he or she will probably have little to say except, perhaps, that it is just obvious. In short, it is often easy to see *that* one claim follows from another, but to explain *why* can be difficult. The purpose of this chapter is to provide such an explanation for some arguments.

This quality of "following from" is elusive, but it is related to the technical notion of validity, which was introduced in Chapter 5. The focus of our attention will be largely on the *concept* of validity. We are not, for the time being at least, interested in whether this or that argument is valid; we want to understand validity itself. To this end, the arguments we will examine are so simple that you will not be able to imagine anyone not understanding them at a glance. Who needs logic to deal with arguments of this kind?

There is, however, good reason for dealing with simple—trivially simple—arguments at the start. The analytic approach to a complex issue is first to break it down into subissues, repeating the process until we reach problems simple enough to be solved. After these simpler problems are solved, we can reverse the process and construct solutions to larger and more complex problems. When done correctly, the *result* of such an analytic process may seem dull and obvious—and it often is. The *discovery* of such a process, in contrast, often demands the insight of genius.

The methods of analysis to be discussed here are *formal* in a specific way. In Chapter 5, we gave the following argument as an example of a valid argument: "All Senators are paid, and Sam is a Senator, so Sam is paid." The point could have been made just as well with many similar examples: (a) "All Senators are paid, and Sally is a Senator, so Sally is paid." (b) "All plumbers are paid, and Sally is a plumber, so Sally is paid." (c) "All plumbers are dirty, and Sally is a plumber, so Sally is dirty." These arguments are all valid (though not all are sound). Thus, we can change the person we are talking about, the group that we say the person is in, and the property that we ascribe to the person and to the group, all without affecting the validity of the argument at all. That flexibility shows that the validity of this argument does not depend on the particular content of its premises and conclusion. Instead, the validity of this argument results solely from its form. Formal validity of this kind is what formal logics try to capture.

BASIC PROPOSITIONAL CONNECTIVES

CONJUNCTION

The first system of formal logic that we will examine concerns propositional (or sentential) connectives. *Propositional connectives* are terms that allow us to build new propositions from old ones, usually combining two or more propositions into a single proposition. For example, given the propositions "John is tall" and "Harry is short," we can use the term "and" to *conjoin* them, forming a single compound proposition: "John is tall and Harry is short."

Let us look carefully at the simple word "and" and ask how it functions. "And" is a curious word, for it does not seem to stand for anything, at least in the way in which a proper name ("Churchill") and a common noun ("dog") seem to stand for things. Instead of asking what this word stands for, we can ask a different question: What *truth conditions* govern this connective? That is, under what conditions are propositions containing this connective true? To answer this question, we imagine every possible way in which the component propositions can be true or false. Then, for each combination, we decide what truth value to assign to the entire proposition. This may sound complicated, but an example will make it clear:

John is tall.	Harry is short.	John is tall and Harry is short.
T	T	T
T	F	F
F	T	F
F	F	F

Here the first two columns cover every possibility for the component propositions to be either true or false. The third column states the truth value of the whole proposition for each combination. Clearly, the conjunction of two propositions is true if both of the component propositions are true; otherwise, it is false.

Our reflections have not depended on the particular propositions in our example. We could have been talking about dinosaurs instead of people, and we still would have come to the conclusion that the conjunction of two propositions is true if both propositions are true, but false otherwise. This neglect of the particular content of propositions is what makes our account *formal*.

To reflect the generality of our concerns, we can drop the reference to particular sentences altogether and use variables instead. Just as the lowercase letters "x," "y," and "z" can be replaced by any numbers in mathematics, so we can use the lowercase letters "p," "q," "r," "s," and so on as variables that can be replaced by any propositions in logic. We will also use the symbol "&" (called an *ampersand*) for "and."

Consider the expression "$p \& q$." Is it true or false? There is obviously no answer to this question. This is not because we do not know what "p" and "q" stand for, for in fact "p" and "q" do not stand for any proposition at all. Just as "$x + y$" is not any particular number in mathematics, so "$p \& q$" is not a proposition. Instead, "$p \& q$" is a pattern for a whole series of propositions. To reflect this, we will say that "$p \& q$" is a *propositional form*. It is a pattern, or form, for a whole series of propositions, including "John is tall and Harry is short" as well as many other propositions.

To specify precisely which propositions have the form "$p \& q$," we need a little technical terminology. The central idea is that we can pass from a proposition to a propositional form by replacing propositions with propositional variables.

Proposition	*Propositional Form*
John is tall and Harry is short.	$p \& q$

When we proceed in the opposite direction by uniformly substituting propositions for propositional variables, we get what we will call a *substitution instance* of that propositional form.

Propositional Form	*Substitution Instance*
$p \& q$	Roses are red and violets are blue.

Thus, "John is tall and Harry is short" and "Roses are red and violets are blue" are both substitution instances of the propositional form "$p \& q$."

To get clear about these ideas, it is important to notice that "p" is also a propositional form, with *every* proposition, including "Roses are red and violets are blue," among its substitution instances. There is no rule against substituting compound propositions for propositional variables. Perhaps a bit more surprisingly, our definitions allow "Roses are red and roses are red" to be a substitution instance of "$p \& q$." This example makes sense if you compare it to variables in mathematics. Using only positive integers, how many solutions are there to the equation "$x + y = 4$"? There are three: $3 + 1$, $1 + 3$, and $2 + 2$. The fact that "$2 + 2$" is a solution to "$x + y = 4$" shows that "2" can be substituted for both "x" and "y" in the same solution. That's just like allowing "Roses are red" to be substituted for both "p" and "q," so that "Roses are red and roses are red" is a substitution instance of "$p \& q$" in propositional logic.

In general, then, we get a substitution instance of a propositional form by uniformly replacing the same variable with the same proposition throughout, but different variables do not have to be replaced with different propositions. The rule is this:

Different variables may be replaced with the same proposition, but different propositions may not be replaced with the same variable.

According to this rule:

"Roses are red and violets are blue" is a substitution instance of "$p \& q$."

"Roses are red and violets are blue" is also a substitution instance of "p."

"Roses are red and roses are red" is a substitution instance of "$p \& q$."

"Roses are red and roses are red" is a substitution instance of "$p \& p$."

"Roses are red and violets are blue" is *not* a substitution instance of "$p \& p$."

"Roses are red" is *not* a substitution instance of "$p \& p$."

We are now in a position to give a perfectly general definition of conjunction with the following truth table, using propositional variables where previously we used specific propositions:

p	q	$p \& q$
T	T	T
T	F	F
F	T	F
F	F	F

There is no limit to the number of propositions we can conjoin to form a new proposition. "Roses are red and violets are blue; sugar is sweet and so are you" is a substitution instance of "$p \& q \& r \& s$." We can also use parentheses to group propositions. This last example could be treated as a substitution instance of "$(p \& q) \& (r \& s)$"—that is, as a conjunction of two conjunctions. Later we will see that, just as in mathematics, parentheses can make an important difference to the meaning of a total proposition.

One cautionary note: The word "and" is not always used to connect two distinct sentences. Sometimes a sentence has to be rewritten for us to see that it is equivalent to a sentence of this form. For example,

Serena and Venus are tennis players.

is simply a short way of saying

Serena is a tennis player, and Venus is a tennis player.

At other times, the word "and" is *not* used to produce a conjunction of propositions. For example,

Serena and Venus are playing each other.

does *not* mean that

Serena is playing each other, and Venus is playing each other.

That does not even make sense, so the original sentence cannot express a conjunction of two propositions. Instead, it expresses a single proposition about two people taken as a group. Consequently, it should not be symbolized as "$p \& q$." Often, unfortunately, it is unclear whether a sentence expresses a conjunction of propositions or a single proposition about a group. The sentence

Serena and Venus are playing tennis.

could be taken either way. Maybe Serena and Venus are playing each other. If that is what it means, then the sentence expresses a single proposition about a group, so it should not be symbolized as "$p \& q$." But maybe Serena is playing one match, while Venus is playing another. If that would make it true, then the sentence expresses a conjunction of propositions, so it may be symbolized as "$p \& q$."

When a sentence containing the word "and" expresses the conjunction of two propositions, we will say that it expresses a *propositional conjunction.* When a sentence containing "and" does not express the conjunction of two propositions, we will say that it expresses a *nonpropositional conjunction.* In this chapter we are concerned only with sentences that express propositional conjunctions. A sentence should be translated into the symbolic form "$p \& q$" only if it expresses a propositional conjunction. There is no mechanical procedure that can be followed to determine whether a certain sentence expresses a conjunction of two propositions. You must think carefully about what the sentence means and about the context in which that sentence is used. This takes practice.

EXERCISE I

The proposition "The night is young, and you're so beautiful" is a substitution instance of which of the following propositional forms?

1. p 5. $p \& q \& r$
2. q 6. $p \& p$
3. $p \& q$ 7. p or q
4. $p \& r$

EXERCISE II

Which of the following propositions is a substitution instance of "$p \& q \& q$"?

1. The night is young, and you're so beautiful, and my flight leaves in thirty minutes.
2. The night is young, and you're so beautiful, and my flight leaves in thirty minutes, and my flight leaves in thirty minutes.
3. You're so beautiful, and you're so beautiful, and you're so beautiful.

EXERCISE III

For each of the following propositions, give three different propositional forms of which that proposition is a substitution instance.

1. The night is young, and you're so beautiful, and my flight leaves in thirty minutes.
2. The night is young, and you're so beautiful, and you're so beautiful.

EXERCISE IV

Indicate whether each of the following sentences expresses a propositional conjunction or a nonpropositional conjunction—that is, whether or not it expresses a conjunction of two propositions. If the sentence could be either, then specify a context in which it would naturally be used to express a propositional conjunction and a different context in which it would naturally be used to express a nonpropositional conjunction.

1. A Catholic priest married John and Mary.
2. Fred had pie and ice cream for dessert.
3. The winning presidential candidate rarely loses both New York and California.

4. Susan got married and had a child.
5. Jane speaks both French and English.
6. Someone who speaks both French and English is bilingual.
7. Ken and Naomi are two of my best friends.
8. Miranda and Nick cooked dinner.
9. I doubt that John is poor and happy.

Now we can look at an argument involving conjunction. Here is one that is ridiculously simple:

Harry is short and John is tall.
∴ Harry is short.

This argument is obviously valid. But why is it valid? Why does the conclusion follow from the premise? The answer in this case seems obvious, but we will spell it out in detail as a guide for more difficult cases. Suppose we replace these particular propositions with propositional forms, using a different variable for each distinct proposition throughout the argument. This yields what we will call an *argument form*. For example:

$p \& q$
∴ p

This is a pattern for endlessly many arguments, each of which is called a substitution instance of this argument form. Every argument that has this general form will also be valid. It really does not matter which propositions we put into this schema; the resulting argument will be valid—so long as we are careful to substitute the same proposition for the same variable throughout.

Let's pursue this matter further. If an argument has true premises and a false conclusion, then we know at once that it is invalid. But in saying that an argument is *valid*, we are not only saying that it does not have true premises and a false conclusion; we are also saying that the argument *cannot* have a false conclusion when the premises are true. Sometimes this is true because the argument has a structure or form that rules out the very possibility of true premises and a false conclusion. We can appeal to the notion of an argument form to make sense of this idea. A somewhat more complicated truth table will make this clear:

p	q	PREMISE $p \& q$	CONCLUSION p
T	T	T	T
T	F	F	T
F	T	F	F
F	F	F	F

The first two columns give all the combinations for the truth values of the propositions that we might substitute for "*p*" and "*q*." The third column gives the truth value of the premise for each of these combinations. (This column is the same as the definition for "&" given above.) Finally, the fourth column gives the truth value for the conclusion for each combination. (Here, of course, this merely involves repeating the first column. Later on, things will become more complicated and interesting.) If we look at this truth table, we see that no matter how we make substitutions for the variables, we never have a case in which the premise is true and the conclusion is false. In the first line, the premise is true and the conclusion is also true. In the remaining three lines, the premise is not true, so the possibility of the premise being true and the conclusion false does not arise.

Here it is important to remember that a valid argument can have false premises, for one proposition can follow from another proposition that is false. Of course, an argument that is sound cannot have a false premise, because a sound argument is defined as a valid argument with true premises. But our subject here is validity, not soundness.

Let's summarize this discussion. In the case we have examined, validity depends on the form of an argument and not on its particular content. A first principle, then, is this:

An *argument* is valid if it is an instance of a valid argument form.

Hence, the argument "Harry is short and John is tall; therefore, Harry is short" is valid because it is an instance of the valid argument form "*p* & *q*; ∴ *p*.*"

Next we must ask what makes an argument form valid. The answer to this is given in this principle:

An argument *form* is valid if and only if it has no substitution instances in which the premises are true and the conclusion is false.

We have just seen that the argument form "*p* & *q*; ∴ *p*" passes this test. The truth table analysis showed that. Incidentally, we can use the same truth table to show that the following argument is valid:

John is tall.	p
Harry is short.	q
∴ John is tall and Harry is short.	∴ p & q

The argument on the left is a substitution instance of the argument form on the right. A glance at the truth table will show that there can be no cases for which all the premises could be true and the conclusion false. This pretty well covers the logical properties of conjunction.

Notice that we have not said that *every* argument that is valid is so in virtue of its form. There may be arguments in which the conclusion follows from the premises but we cannot show how the argument's validity is a matter of logical form. There are, in fact, some obviously valid arguments that have yet to be shown to be valid in terms of their form. Explaining validity by means of logical form has long been an ideal of logical theory, but there are arguments—many of them quite common—where this ideal has yet to be adequately fulfilled. Many arguments in mathematics fall into this category. At present, however, we will only consider arguments in which the strategy we used for analyzing conjunction continues to work.

EXERCISE V

Are the following arguments valid by virtue of their propositional form? Why or why not?

1. Donald owns a tower in New York and a palace in Atlantic City. Therefore, Donald owns a palace in Atlantic City.
2. Tom owns a house. Therefore, Tom owns a house and a piece of land.
3. Ilsa is tall. Therefore, Ilsa is tall, and Ilsa is tall.
4. Bernie has a son and a daughter. Bernie has a father and a mother. Therefore, Bernie has a son and a mother.
5. Mary got married and had a child. Therefore, Mary had a child and got married.
6. Bess and Katie tied for MVP. Therefore, Bess tied for MVP.

EXERCISE VI

For each of the following claims, determine whether it is true or false. Defend your answers.

1. An argument that is a substitution instance of a valid argument form is always valid.
2. An argument that is a substitution instance of an invalid argument form is always invalid.
3. An invalid argument is always a substitution instance of an invalid argument form.

DISCUSSION QUESTION

Is a valid argument always a substitution instance of a valid argument form? Why or why not?

DISJUNCTION

Just as we can form a conjunction of two propositions by using the connective "and," we can form a *disjunction* of two propositions by using the connective "or," as in the following compound sentence:

John will win or Harry will win.

Again, it is easy to see that the truth of this whole compound proposition depends on the truth of the component propositions. If they are both false, then the compound proposition is false. If just one of them is true, then the compound proposition is true. But suppose they are both true. What shall we say then?

Sometimes when we say "either-or," we seem to rule out the possibility of both. When a waiter approaches your table and tells you, "Tonight's dinner will be chicken or steak," this suggests that you cannot have both. In other cases, however, it does not seem that the possibility of both is ruled out—for example, when we say to someone, "If you want to see tall mountains, go to California or Colorado."

One way to deal with this problem is to say that the English word "or" has two meanings: one *exclusive,* which rules out both, and one *inclusive,* which does not rule out both. Another solution is to claim that the English word "or" always has the inclusive sense, but utterances with "or" sometimes conversationally imply the exclusion of both because of special features of certain contexts. It is, for example, our familiarity with common restaurant practices that leads us to infer that we cannot have both when the waiter says, "Tonight's dinner will be chicken or steak." If we may have both, then the waiter's utterance would not be as informative as is required for the purpose of revealing our options, so it would violate Grice's conversational rule of Quantity (as discussed in Chapter 2). That explains why the waiter's utterance seems to exclude both.

Because such explanations are plausible, and because it is simpler as well as traditional to develop propositional logic with the inclusive sense of "or," we will adopt that inclusive sense. Where necessary, we will define the exclusive sense using the inclusive sense as a starting point. Logicians symbolize disjunctions using the connective "∨" (called a *wedge*). The truth table for this connective has the following form:

p	q	$p \vee q$
T	T	T
T	F	T
F	T	T
F	F	F

We will look at some arguments involving this connective in a moment.

NEGATION

With conjunction and disjunction, we begin with two propositions and construct a new proposition from them. There is another way in which we can construct a new proposition from just one proposition—by *negating* it. Given the proposition "John is clever," we can get a new proposition, "John is not clever," simply by inserting the word "not" in the correct place in the sentence.

What, exactly, does the word "not" mean? This can be a difficult question to answer. Does it mean "nothing" or, maybe, "nothingness"? Although some respectable philosophers have sometimes spoken in this way, it is important to see that the word "not" does not stand for anything at all. It has an altogether different function in the language. To see this, think about how conjunction and disjunction work. Given two propositions, the word "and" allows us to construct another proposition that is true only when both original propositions are true, and false otherwise. With disjunction, given two propositions, the word "or" allows us to construct another proposition that is false only when both of the original propositions are false, and true otherwise. (Our truth table definitions reflect these facts.) Using these definitions as models, how should we define negation? A parallel answer is that the negation of a proposition is true just in the cases in which the original proposition is false, and it is false just in the cases in which original proposition is true. Using the symbol "~" (called a *tilde*) to stand for negation, this gives us the following truth table definition:

p	$\sim p$
T	F
F	T

Negation might seem as simple as can be, but people quite often get confused by negations. If Diana says, "I could not breathe for a whole minute," she might mean that there was a minute when something made her unable to breathe (maybe she was choking) or she might mean that she was able to hold her breath for a whole minute (say, to win a bet). If "A" symbolizes "Diana could breathe sometime during this minute," then "$\sim A$" symbolizes the former claim (that Diana was unable to breathe for this minute). Consequently, the latter claim (that Diana could hold her breath for this minute) should not also be symbolized by "$\sim A$." Indeed, this interpretation of the original sentence is not a negation, even though the original sentence did include the word "not." Moreover, some sentences are negations even though they do not include the word "not." For example, "Nobody owns Mars" is the negation of "Somebody owns Mars." If the latter is symbolized as "A," the former can be symbolized as "$\sim A$," even though the former does not include the word "not."

The complexities of negation can be illustrated by noticing that the simple sentence "Everyone loves running" can include negation at four distinct places: "Not everyone loves running," "Everyone does not love running," "Everyone loves not running," and the colloquial "Everyone loves running—not!" Some of these sentences can be symbolized in propositional logic as negations of "Everyone loves running," but others cannot.

To determine whether a sentence can be symbolized as a negation in propositional logic, it is often useful to reformulate the sentence so that it starts with "It is not the case that. . . ." For example, "I did none of the homework" would be reformulated as "It is not the case that I did any of the homework." If the resulting sentence means the same as the original (as it does in this example), then the original sentence can be symbolized as a propositional negation. In contrast, "I promise not to leave you" means something very different from "It is not the case that I promise to leave you," so "I promise not to leave you" should not be symbolized as a propositional negation.

Unfortunately, this test will not always work. There is no completely mechanical procedure for determining whether an English sentence can be symbolized as a negation. All you can do is think carefully about the sentence's meaning and context. The best way to get good at this is to practice.

EXERCISE VII

Explain the differences in meaning among "Not everyone loves running," "Everyone does not love running," "Everyone loves not running," and "Everyone loves running—not!" For each, is it a negation of "Everyone loves running"? Why or why not?

EXERCISE VIII

Negative terms or prefixes can often be interpreted in more than one way. Explain two ways to interpret each of the following sentences. Describe a context in which it would be natural to interpret it in each way.

1. You may not go to the meeting.
2. I cannot recommend him too highly.
3. He never thought he'd go to the Himalayas.
4. Have you not done all of your homework?
5. All of his friends are not students.
6. I will not go to some football games next season.
7. No smoking section available.
8. The lock on his locker was unlockable.

EXERCISE IX

Put each of the following sentences in symbolic form. Be sure to specify exactly which sentence is represented by each capital letter, and pay special attention to the placement of the negation. If the sentence could be interpreted in more than one way, symbolize each interpretation and describe a context in which it would be natural to interpret it in each way.

1. It won't rain tomorrow.
2. It might not rain tomorrow.
3. There is no chance that it will rain tomorrow.
4. I believe that it won't rain tomorrow.
5. Joe is not too smart or else he's very clever.
6. Kristin is not smart or rich.
7. Sometimes you feel like a nut; sometimes you don't. (from an advertisement for Mounds and Almond Joy candies, which are made by the same company and are exactly alike except that only one of them has a nut)

PROCESS OF ELIMINATION

Using only negation and disjunction, we can analyze the form of one common pattern of reasoning, which is called *process of elimination* or, more technically, *disjunctive syllogism*. As an example, consider this argument:

She is sitting alone and talking, so she must be either talking on a phone I don't see or talking to herself. She is clearly not talking to herself, since she's not crazy. So she must be talking on her phone.

After trimming off assurances and subarguments that support the premises, the core of this argument can be put in standard form:

(1) She is either talking to herself or talking on a phone.
(2) She is not talking to herself.
∴(3) She is talking on a phone. (from 1–2)

This core argument is then an instance of this argument form:

1. $p \vee q$
   $\sim p$
   ∴ q

It does not matter if we change the order of the disjuncts so that the first premise is "She must be either talking on a phone or talking to herself." Then the argument takes this form:

2. $p \vee q$
   $\sim q$
   ∴ p

Both of these argument forms are valid, so the core of the original argument is also valid.

EXERCISE X

Explain why argument forms 1–2 are valid. Use common language that would be understandable to someone who has not read this chapter.

Process of elimination is sometimes confused with a similar but crucially different pattern of reasoning, which can be called *affirming a disjunct*. This pattern includes both of these forms:

3. $p \vee q$ 4. $p \vee q$
    p q
∴ $\sim q$ ∴ $\sim p$

These forms of argument are invalid. This can be shown by the following single instance:

She is either talking to herself or talking on a phone.
She is talking to herself.
∴ She is not talking on a phone.

This argument might seem valid if one assumes that she cannot talk on the phone while talking to herself. The premises, however, do not specify that she cannot do both at once. If she mumbles a few quick words to herself in the midst of talking on the phone, then the premises are both true and the conclusion is false.

EXERCISE XI

Give other instances of argument forms 3–4 that are not valid. Explain why these instances are invalid and why they show that the general argument form is invalid.

HOW TRUTH-FUNCTIONAL CONNECTIVES WORK

We have now defined conjunction, disjunction, and negation. That, all by itself, is sufficient to complete the branch of modern logic called propositional logic. The definitions themselves may seem peculiar. They do not look like the definitions we find in a dictionary. But the form of these definitions is important, for it tells us something interesting about the character of such words as "and," "or," and "not." Two things are worth noting: (1) These expressions are used to construct a new proposition from old ones; (2) the newly constructed proposition is always a *truth function* of the original propositions—that is, the truth value of the new proposition is always determined by the truth value of the original propositions. For this reason, these connectives are called *truth-functional connectives*. (Of course, with negation, we start with a *single* proposition, so there are not really two things to connect.) For example, suppose that "*A*" and "*B*" are two true propositions and "*G*" and "*H*" are two false propositions. We can then determine the truth values of more complex propositions built from them using conjunction, disjunction, and negation. Sometimes the correct assignment is obvious at a glance:

A & *B*	True
A & *G*	False
~*A*	False
~*G*	True
A ∨ *H*	True
G ∨ *H*	False
~*A* & *G*	False

As noted earlier, parentheses can be used to distinguish groupings. Sometimes the placement of parentheses can make an important difference, as in the following two expressions:

~*A* & *G*

~(*A* & *G*)

Notice that in the first expression the negation symbol applies only to the proposition "*A*," whereas in the other expression it applies to the entire proposition "*A* & *G*." Thus, the first expression above is false, and the second expression is true. Only the second expression can be translated as "Not both *A* and *G*." Both of these expressions are different from "~*A* & ~*G*," which means "Neither *A* nor *G*."

As expressions become more complex, we reach a point where it is no longer obvious how the truth values of the component propositions determine the truth value of the entire proposition. Here a regular procedure is helpful. The easiest method is to fill in the truth values of the basic propositions and then, step-by-step, make assignments progressively wider, going from the inside out. For example:

$$\sim((A \vee G) \,\&\, \sim(\sim H \,\&\, B))$$
$$\sim((T \vee F) \,\&\, \sim(\sim F \,\&\, T))$$
$$\sim((T \vee F) \,\&\, \sim(T \,\&\, T))$$
$$\sim(T \,\&\, \sim(T))$$
$$\sim(T \,\&\, F)$$
$$\sim(F)$$
$$T$$

With a little practice, you can master this technique in dealing with other very complex examples.

Given that "*A*," "*B*," and "*C*" are true propositions and "*X*," "*Y*," and "*Z*" are false propositions, determine the truth values of the following compound propositions:

1. ~*X* ∨ *Y*
2. ~(*X* ∨ *Y*)
3. ~(*Z* ∨ *Z*)
4. ~(*Z* ∨~*Z*)
5. ~ ~(*A* ∨ *B*)
6. (*A* ∨ *Z*) & *B*
7. (*A* ∨ *X*) & (*B* ∨ *Z*)
8. (*A* & *Z*) ∨ (*B* & *Z*)

9. ~(*A* ∨ (*Z* ∨ *X*))
10. ~(*A* ∨ ~(*Z* ∨ *X*))
11. ~*A* ∨ ~(*Z* ∨ *X*)
12. ~*Z* ∨ (*Z* & *A*)
13. ~(*Z* ∨ (*Z* & *A*))
14. ~((*Z* ∨ *Z*) & *A*)
15. *A* ∨ ((~*B* & *C*) ∨~(~*B* ∨ ~(*Z* ∨ *B*)))
16. *A* & ((~*B* & *C*) n ~(~*B* ∨ ~(*Z* ∨ *B*)))

TESTING FOR VALIDITY

What is the point of all this? In everyday life, we rarely run into an expression as complicated as the one in our example at the end of the previous section. Our purpose here is to sharpen our sensitivity to how truth-functional connectives work and then to express our insights in clear ways. This is important because the validity of many arguments depends on the logical features of these truth-functional connectives. We can now turn directly to this subject.

Earlier we saw that every argument with the form "*p* & *q*; ∴ *p*" will be valid. This is obvious in itself, but we saw that this claim could be justified by an appeal to truth tables. A truth table analysis shows us that an argument with this form can never have an instance in which the premise is true and the conclusion is false. We can now apply this same technique to arguments that are more complex. In the beginning, we will examine arguments that are still easy to follow without the use of technical help. In the end, we will consider some arguments that most people cannot follow without guidance.

Consider the following argument:

> Valerie is either a doctor or a lawyer.
> Valerie is neither a doctor nor a stockbroker.
> ──────────────
> ∴ Valerie is a lawyer.

We can use the following abbreviations:

D = Valerie is a doctor.

L = Valerie is a lawyer.

S = Valerie is a stockbroker.

Using these abbreviations, the argument and its counterpart argument form look like this:

$$D \vee L \qquad\qquad p \vee q$$
$$\underline{\sim(D \vee S)} \qquad\qquad \underline{\sim(p \vee r)}$$
$$\therefore L \qquad\qquad \therefore q$$

The expression on the right gives the argument form of the argument presented on the left. To test the argument for validity, we ask whether the argument form is valid. The procedure is cumbersome, but perfectly mechanical:

p	q	r	PREMISE $(p \vee q)$	PREMISE $(p \vee r)$	$\sim(p \vee r)$	CONCLUSION q	
T	T	T	T	T	F	T	
T	T	F	T	T	F	T	
T	F	T	T	T	F	F	
T	F	F	T	T	F	F	
F	T	T	T	T	F	T	
F	T	F	T	F	T	T	OK
F	F	T	F	T	F	F	
F	F	F	F	F	T	F	

Notice that there is only one combination of truth values for which both premises are true, and in that case the conclusion is true as well. So the original argument is valid because it is an instance of a valid argument form—that is, an argument form with no substitution instances for which true premises are combined with a false conclusion.

This last truth table may need some explaining. First, why do we get eight rows in this truth table where before we got only four? The answer to this is that we need to test the argument form for *every possible combination of truth values* for the component propositions. With two variables, there are four possible combinations: (TT), (TF), (FT), and (FF). With three variables, there are eight possible combinations: (TTT), (TTF), (TFT), (TFF), (FTT), (FTF), (FFT), and (FFF). The general rule is this: If an argument form has n variables, the truth table used in its analysis must have $2n$ rows. For four variables there will be sixteen rows; for five variables, thirty-two rows; for six variables, sixty-four rows; and so on. You can be sure that you capture all possible combinations of truth values by using the following pattern in constructing the columns of your truth table under each individual variable:

First column	Second column	Third column . . .
First half Ts,	First quarter Ts,	First eighth Ts,
second half Fs.	second quarter Fs,	second eighth Fs,
	and so on.	and so on.

A glance at the earlier examples in this chapter will show that we have been using this pattern, and it is the standard way of listing the possibilities.

Of course, as soon as an argument becomes at all complex, these truth tables become very large indeed. But there is no need to worry about this, because we will not consider arguments with many variables. Those who do so turn to a computer for help.

The style of the truth table above is also significant. The premises are plainly labeled, and so is the conclusion. A line is drawn under every row in which the premises are all true. (In this case, there is only one such row—row 6.) If the conclusion on this line is also true, it is marked "OK." If every line in which the premises are all true is OK, then the argument form is valid. Marking all this may seem rather childish, but it is worth doing. First, it helps guard against mistakes. More importantly, it draws one's attention to the purpose of the procedure being used. Cranking out truth tables without understanding what they are about—or even why they might be helpful—does not enlighten the mind or elevate the spirit.

For the sake of contrast, we can next consider an invalid argument:

(1) Valerie is either a doctor or a lawyer.
(2) Valerie is not both a lawyer and a stockbroker.
∴(3) Therefore, Valerie is a doctor.

Using the same abbreviations as earlier, this becomes:

$$D \lor L \qquad\qquad p \lor q$$
$$\underline{\sim(L \,\&\, S)} \qquad\qquad \underline{\sim(q \,\&\, r)}$$
$$\therefore D \qquad\qquad\quad \therefore p$$

The truth table for this argument form looks like this:

p	q	r	Premise $(p \lor q)$	$(q \,\&\, r)$	Premise $\sim(q \,\&\, r)$	Conclusion p	
T	T	T	T	T	F	T	
T	T	F	T	F	T	T	OK
T	F	T	T	F	T	T	OK
T	F	F	T	F	T	T	OK
F	T	T	T	T	F	F	
F	T	F	T	F	T	F	Invalid
F	F	T	F	F	T	F	
F	F	F	F	F	T	F	

This time, we find four rows in which all the premises are true. In three cases the conclusion is true as well, but in one of these cases (row 6), the conclusion is false. This line is marked "Invalid." Notice that every line in which all of the premises are true is marked either as "OK" or as "Invalid." If even one row is marked "Invalid," then the argument form as a whole is invalid. The argument form under consideration is thus invalid, because it is possible for it to have a substitution instance in which all the premises are true and the conclusion is false.

The labeling not only shows *that* the argument form is invalid, it also shows *why* it is invalid. Each line that is marked "Invalid" shows a combination of truth values that makes the premises true and the conclusion false. Row 6 presents the combination in which Valerie is not a doctor, is a lawyer, and is not a stockbroker. With these assignments, it will be true that she is either a doctor or a lawyer (premise 1), and also true that she is not both a lawyer and a stockbroker (premise 2), yet false that she is a doctor (the conclusion). It is this possibility that shows why the argument form is not valid.

In sum, we can test a propositional argument form for validity by following these simple steps:

1. Provide a column for each premise and the conclusion.
2. Fill in truth values in each column.
3. Underline each row where all of the premises are true.
4. Mark each row "OK" if the conclusion is true on that row.
5. Mark each row "Invalid" if the conclusion is false on that row.
6. If any row is marked "Invalid," the argument form is invalid.
7. If no row is marked "Invalid," the argument form is valid.

EXERCISE XIII

Using the truth table technique outlined above, show that argument forms 1–2 in the above section on process of elimination are valid and that argument forms 3–4 in the same section are invalid.

EXERCISE XIV

Is the following argument valid in our technical sense? Explain why or why not. Could it be sound? Explain why or why not.
(1) Frogs are green.
(2) Frogs are not green.
∴ (3) I am president. (from 1–2)

EXERCISE XV

Using the truth table technique outlined above, test the following argument forms for validity:

1. $\sim p \vee q$
   p
   $\therefore \sim q$

2. $\sim (p \vee q)$
   $\therefore \sim q$

(continued)

$$3. \sim(p \lor q)$$
$$\underline{p}$$
$$\therefore q$$
$$4. \sim(p \lor q)$$
$$\underline{p}$$
$$\therefore r$$
$$5. \sim(p \& q)$$
$$\underline{q}$$
$$\therefore \sim p$$
$$6. \sim(p \& q)$$
$$\underline{\sim q}$$
$$\therefore p$$

$$7. (p \& q) \lor (p \& r)$$
$$\therefore \overline{p \& (q \lor r)}$$
$$8. (p \lor q) \& (p \lor r)$$
$$\therefore p \& (q \lor r)$$
$$9. \underline{p \& q}$$
$$\therefore (p \lor r) \& (q \lor r)$$
$$10. \underline{p \lor q}$$
$$\therefore (p \& r) \lor (q \& r)$$

SOME FURTHER CONNECTIVES

We have developed the logic of propositions using only three basic notions corresponding (perhaps roughly) to the English words "and," "or," and "not." Now let us go back to the question of the two possible senses of the word "or": one exclusive and the other inclusive. Sometimes "or" seems to rule out the possibility that both alternatives are true; at other times "or" seems to allow this possibility. This is the difference between exclusive and inclusive disjunction.

Suppose we use the symbol "$\underline{\lor}$" to stand for exclusive disjunction. This is the same as the symbol for inclusive disjunction except that it is underlined. (After this discussion, we will not use it again.) We could then give two truth table definitions, one for each of these symbols:

		Inclusive	Exclusive
p	q	$p \lor q$	$p \underline{\lor} q$
T	T	T	F
T	F	T	T
F	T	T	T
F	F	F	F

We could also define this new connective in the following way:

$$(p \underline{\lor} q) = \text{(by definition) } ((p \lor q) \& \sim(p \& q))$$

It is not hard to see that the expression on the right side of this definition captures the force of exclusive disjunction. Because we can always define exclusive disjunction when we want it, there is no need to introduce it into our system of basic notions.

EXERCISE XVI

Construct a truth table analysis of the expression on the right side of the preceding definition, and compare it with the truth table definition of exclusive disjunction.

EXERCISE XVII

Use truth tables to test the following argument forms for validity:

1. p _____

∴ $p \veebar q$

2. $p \veebar q$

p _____

∴ $\sim q$

3. p & q _____

∴ $\sim(p \veebar q)$

4. $\sim(p$ & $q)$ _____

∴ $p \veebar q$

5. $p \veebar q$ _____

∴ $p \vee q$

6. $p \vee q$ _____

∴ $p \veebar q$

Actually, in analyzing arguments we have been defining new logical connectives without thinking about it much. For example, "not both p and q" was symbolized as "$\sim(p$ & $q)$." "Neither p nor q" was symbolized as "$\sim(p \vee q)$." Let us look more closely at the example "$\sim(p \vee q)$." Perhaps we should have symbolized it as "$\sim p$ & $\sim q$." In fact, we could have used this symbolization, because the two expressions amount to the same thing. Again, this may be obvious, but we can prove it by using a truth table in yet another way. Compare the truth table analysis of these two expressions:

p	q	$\sim p$	$\sim q$	$\sim p$ & $\sim q$	$(p \vee q)$	$\sim(p \vee q)$
T	T	F	F	F	T	F
T	F	F	T	F	T	F
F	T	T	F	F	T	F
F	F	T	T	T	F	T

Under "$\sim p$ & $\sim q$" we find the column (FFFT), and we find the same sequence under "$\sim(p \vee q)$." This shows that, for every possible substitution we make, these two expressions will yield propositions with the same truth value. We will say that these propositional forms are *truth-functionally equivalent*. The above table also shows that the expressions "$\sim q$" and "$\sim p$ & $\sim q$" are *not* truth-functionally equivalent, because the columns underneath these two expressions differ in the second row, so some substitutions into these expressions will not yield propositions with the same truth value.

Given the notion of truth-functional equivalence, the problem of more than one translation can often be solved. If two translations of a sentence are truth-functionally equivalent, then it does not matter which one we use in testing for validity. Of course, some translations will seem more natural than others. For example, "$p \lor q$" is truth-functionally equivalent to

~$((\sim p \And \sim p) \And (\sim q \lor \sim q))$

Despite this equivalence, the first form of expression is obviously more natural than the second when translating sentences, such as "It is either cloudy or sunny."

EXERCISE XVIII

Use truth tables to test which of the following propositional forms are truth-functionally equivalent to each other:

1. ~$(p \lor q)$
2. ~$(\sim p \lor \sim q)$
3. ~$p \And \sim q$
4. $p \And q$

EXERCISE XIX

Use truth tables to determine whether the expressions in each of the following pairs are truth-functionally equivalent:

1. "p" and "$p \And p$"
2. "p" and "$p \lor p$"
3. "$p \lor \sim p$" and "~$(p \And \sim p)$"
4. "p" and "$p \And (q \lor \sim q)$"
5. "p" and "$p \And (q \And \sim q)$"
6. "p" and "$p \lor (q \And \sim q)$"
7. "$p \And (q \lor r)$" and "$p \lor (q \And r)$"
8. "$p \And (q \And r)$" and "$(p \And q) \And r$"

9. "~$(p \lor q)$" and "~$p \lor q$"
10. "~$(p \lor q)$" and "~$p \And \sim q$"
11. "~~$(p \lor q)$" and "~~$p \And \sim\sim q$"
12. "~$(p \And q)$" and "~$p \lor q$"
13. "~~$(p \And q)$" and "~~$p \lor \sim\sim q$"
14. "~~p n ~~q" and "~$(\sim p \And \sim q)$"
15. "~~$p \And \sim\sim q$" and "~$(\sim p \lor \sim q)$"
16. "$p \And \sim\sim q$" and "~~$p \And q$"

CONDITIONALS

So far in this chapter we have seen that by using conjunction, disjunction, and negation, it is possible to construct compound propositions out of simple propositions. A distinctive feature of compound propositions constructed in these three ways is that the truth of the compound proposition is always a function of the truth of its component propositions. Thus, these three notions allow us to construct truth-functionally compound propositions. Some arguments depend for their validity simply on these truth-functional connectives. When this is so, it is possible to test for validity in a purely mechanical way. This can be done through the use of truth tables. Thus, in this area at least, we are able to give a clear account of validity and to specify exact procedures for testing for validity.

This truth-functional approach might seem problematic in another area: *conditionals.* We will argue that an important group of conditionals can be handled in much the same way as negation, conjunction, and disjunction. We separate conditionals from the other connectives only because a truth-functional treatment of conditionals is more controversial and faces problems that are instructive.

Conditionals have the form "If _____, then _____." What goes in the first blank of this pattern is called the *antecedent* of the conditional; what goes in the second blank is called its *consequent.* Sometimes conditionals appear in the indicative mood:

If it rains, then the crop will be saved.

Sometimes they occur in the subjunctive mood:

If it had rained, then the crop would have been saved.

There are also conditional imperatives:

If a fire breaks out, then call the fire department first!

And there are conditional promises:

If you get into trouble, then I promise to help you.

Indeed, conditionals get a great deal of use in our language, often in arguments. It is important, therefore, to understand them.

Unfortunately, there is no general agreement among experts concerning the correct way to analyze conditionals. We will simplify matters and avoid some of these controversies by considering only indicative conditionals. We will not examine conditional imperatives, conditional promises, or subjunctive conditionals. Furthermore, at the start, we will examine only what we will call *propositional conditionals.* We get a propositional conditional by substituting indicative sentences that express propositions—something either true or false— into the schema "If ____, then _____." Or, to use technical language already introduced, a propositional conditional is a substitution instance of "If p, then q" in which "p" and "q" are propositional variables. Of the four conditional sentences listed above, only the first is clearly a propositional conditional.

Even if we restrict our attention to propositional conditionals, this will not avoid all controversy. Several competing theories claim to provide the correct analysis of propositional conditionals, and no consensus has been reached concerning which is right. It may seem surprising that theorists disagree about such a simple and fundamental notion as the if-then construction, but they do. In what follows, we will first describe the most standard treatment of propositional conditionals, and then consider alternatives to it.

TRUTH TABLES FOR CONDITIONALS

For conjunction, disjunction, and negation, the truth table method provides an approach that is at once plausible and effective. A propositional conditional is also compounded from two simpler propositions, and this suggests that we might be able to offer a truth table definition for these conditionals as well. What should the truth table look like? When we try to answer this question, we get stuck almost at once, for it is unclear how we should fill in the table in three out of four cases.

p	q	If p, then q
T	T	?
T	F	F
F	T	?
F	F	?

It seems obvious that a conditional cannot be true if the antecedent is true and the consequent is false. We record this by putting "F" in the second row. But suppose "p" and "q" are replaced by two arbitrary true propositions—say, "Two plus two equals four" and "Chile is in South America." Consider what we shall say about the conditional:

If two plus two equals four, then Chile is in South America.

This is a *very* strange statement, because the arithmetical remark in the antecedent does not seem to have anything to do with the geographical remark in the consequent. So this conditional is odd—indeed, extremely odd—but is it true or false? At this point, a reasonable response is bafflement.

Consider the following argument, which is intended to solve all these problems by providing reasons for assigning truth values in each row of the truth table. First, it seems obvious that, if "If p, then q" is true, then it is not the case that both "p" is true and "q" is false. That in turn means that "$\sim(p \ \& \sim q)$" must be true. The following, then, seems to be a valid argument form:

> If p, then q.
> _____
> $\therefore \sim(p \ \& \sim q)$

Second, we can also reason in the opposite direction. Suppose we know that "$\sim(p \ \& \sim q)$" is true. For this to be true, "$p \ \& \sim q$" must be false. We know this from the truth table definition of negation. Next let us suppose that "p" is true. Then "$\sim q$" must be false. We know this from the truth table definition of conjunction. Finally, if "$\sim q$" is false, then "q" itself must be true. This line of reasoning is supposed to show that the following argument form is valid:

> $\sim(p \ \& \sim q)$
> _____
> $\therefore$ If p, then q.

The first step in the argument was intended to show that we can validly derive "$\sim(p \ \& \sim q)$" from "If p, then q." The second step was intended to show that the derivation can be run in the other direction as well. But if each of these expressions is derivable from the other, this suggests that they are equivalent. We use this background argument as a justification for the following definition:

If p, then q = (by definition) not both p and not q.

We can put this into symbolic notation using "⊃" (called a *horseshoe*) to symbolize the conditional connective:

$p \supset q$ = (by definition) ~(p & ~q)

Given this definition, we can now construct the truth table for propositional conditionals. It is simply the truth table for "~(p & ~q)":

p	q	~(p & ~q)	$p \supset q$	~$p \vee q$
T	T	T	T	T
T	F	F	F	F
F	T	T	T	T
F	F	T	T	T

Notice that "~(p & ~q)" is also truth-functionally equivalent to the expression "~$p \vee q$." We have cited it here because "~$p \vee q$" has traditionally been used to define "$p \supset q$." For reasons that are now obscure, when a conditional is defined in this truth-functional way, it is called a *material conditional*.

Let's suppose, for the moment, that the notion of a material conditional corresponds exactly to our idea of a propositional conditional. What would follow from this? The answer is that we could treat conditionals in the same way in which we have treated conjunction, disjunction, and negation. A propositional conditional would be just one more kind of truth-functionally compound proposition capable of definition by truth tables. Furthermore, the validity of arguments that depend on this notion (together with conjunction, disjunction, and negation) could be settled by appeal to truth table techniques. Let us pause for a moment to examine this.

One of the most common patterns of reasoning is called *modus ponens*. It looks like this:

If p, then q. $p \supset q$
p p
_____   _____
∴ q ∴ q

The truth table definition of a material conditional shows at once that this pattern of argument is valid:

PREMISE		PREMISE	CONCLUSION	
p	q	$p \supset q$	q	
T	T	T	T	OK
T	F	F	F	
F	T	T	T	
F	F	T	F	

EXERCISE XX

The argument form called *modus tollens* looks like this:

$p \supset q$

$\underline{\sim q}$

$\therefore \sim p$

Use truth tables to show that this argument form is valid.

Farcus

by David Waisglass
Gordon Coulthart

WAISGLASS/COULTHART

© 1997 Farcus Cartoons

Farcus/LaughingStock Licensing Inc.

**"So, I say if it's not worth doing well,
it's not worth doing at all."**

These same techniques allow us to show that one of the traditional fallacies is, indeed, a fallacy. It is called the fallacy of *denying the antecedent,* and it has this form:

$p \supset q$

$\underline{\sim p}$

$\therefore \sim q$

The truth table showing the invalidity of this argument form looks like this:

p	q	PREMISE $p \supset q$	PREMISE $\sim p$	CONCLUSION $\sim q$	
T	T	T	F	F	
T	F	F	F	T	
F	T	T	T	F	Invalid
F	F	T	T	T	OK

EXERCISE XXI

A second standard fallacy is called *affirming the consequent*. It looks like this:

$$p \supset q$$

$$q$$

$$\therefore p$$

Use truth tables to show that this argument form is invalid.

EXERCISE XXII

In his radio address to the nation on April 17, 1982, President Ronald Reagan argued that the United States should not accept a treaty with the Soviet Union that would mutually freeze nuclear weapons at current levels, because he believed that the United States had fallen behind. Here is a central part of his argument:

> It would be wonderful if we could restore the balance of power with the Soviet Union without increasing our military power. And, ideally, it would be a long step towards assuring peace if we could have significant and verifiable reductions of arms on both sides. But let's not fool ourselves. The Soviet Union will not come to any conference table bearing gifts. Soviet negotiators will not make unilateral concessions. To achieve parity, we must make it plain that we have the will to achieve parity by our own effort.

Put Reagan's central argument into standard form. Then symbolize it and its form. Does his argument commit any fallacy? If so, identify it.

The relations among these last four argument forms can be seen in this diagram:

	Antecedent	Consequent
Affirming	Affirming the Antecedent = *Modus Ponens* (valid)	Affirming the Consequent (invalid)
Denying	Denying the Antecedent (invalid)	Denying the Consequent = *Modus Tollens* (valid)

Another argument form that has been historically significant is called a *hypothetical syllogism:*

$$p \supset q$$
$$q \supset r$$
$$\therefore p \supset r$$

Because we are dealing with an argument form containing three variables, we must perform the boring task of constructing a truth table with eight rows:

			PREMISE	PREMISE	CONCLUSION	
p	q	r	$p \supset q$	$q \supset r$	$p \supset r$	
T	T	T	T	T	T	OK
T	T	F	T	F	F	
T	F	T	F	T	T	
T	F	F	F	T	F	
F	T	T	T	T	T	OK
F	T	F	T	F	T	
F	F	T	T	T	T	OK
F	F	F	T	T	T	OK

This is fit work for a computer, not for a human being, but it is important to see that it actually works.

Why is it important to see that these techniques work? Most people, after all, could see that hypothetical syllogisms are valid without going through all of this tedious business. We seem only to be piling boredom on top of triviality. This protest deserves an answer. Suppose we ask someone *why* he or she thinks that the conclusion follows from the premises in a hypothetical syllogism. The person might answer that anyone can see that—which, by the way, is false. Beyond this, he or she might say that it all depends on the meanings of the words or that it is all a matter of definition. But if we go on to ask, "which words?" and "what definitions?" then most people will fall silent. We have discovered that the validity of some arguments depends on the meanings of such words as "and," "or," "not," and "if-then." We have then gone on to give explicit definitions of these terms—definitions, by the way, that help us see how these terms function in an argument. Finally, by getting all these *simple* things right, we have produced what is called a *decision procedure* for determining the validity of every argument depending only on conjunctions, disjunctions, negations, and propositional conditionals. Our truth table techniques give us a mechanical procedure for settling questions of validity in this area. In fact, truth table techniques have practical applications, for example, in computer programming. But the important point here is that, through an understanding of how these techniques work, we can gain a deeper insight into the notion of validity.

Two more classic, common, and useful argument forms combine conditionals with disjunction. Using truth tables, test them for validity.

Constructive Dilemma

$p \lor q$
$p \supset r$
$q \supset r$
_____
$\therefore r$

Destructive Dilemma

$\sim p \lor \sim q$
$r \supset p$
$r \supset q$
_____
$\therefore \sim r$

Using the truth table techniques employed above, test the following argument forms for validity. (For your own entertainment, guess whether the argument form is valid or invalid before working it out.)

1. $p \supset q$
   _____
   $\therefore q \supset p$

2. $p \supset q$
   _____
   $\therefore \sim q \supset \sim p$

3. $\sim q \supset \sim p$
   _____
   $\therefore p \supset q$

4. $p \supset q$
   $q \supset r$
   _____
   $\therefore p \supset (q \,\&\, r)$

5. $p \supset q$
   $q \supset r$
   $\sim r$
   _____
   $\therefore \sim p$

6. $p \supset q$
   $q \supset r$
   _____
   $\therefore \sim r \supset \sim p$

7. $p \lor q$
   $p \supset q$
   $q \supset r$
   _____
   $\therefore r$

8. $p \supset (q \lor r)$
   $\sim q$
   $\sim r$
   _____
   $\therefore \sim p$

9. $(p \lor q) \supset r$
   _____
   $\therefore p \supset r$

10. $(p \,\&\, q) \supset r$
    _____
    $\therefore p \supset r$

11. $p \supset (q \supset r)$
    _____
    $\therefore (p \,\&\, q) \supset r$

12. $(p \,\&\, q) \supset r$
    _____
    $\therefore p \supset (q \supset r)$

13. $p \supset (q \supset r)$
    q
    $\sim r$
    _____
    $\therefore \sim p$

14. $p \supset (q \supset r)$
    $p \supset q$
    _____
    $\therefore r$

(continued)

15. $(p \lor q) \,\&\, (p \lor r)$

$\sim r$ _____

$\therefore \sim q$

16. $(p \supset q) \,\&\, (p \supset \sim r)$

$q \,\&\, r$ _____

$\therefore \sim p$

17. $(p \lor q) \supset p$ _____

$\therefore \sim q$

18. $(p \lor q) \supset (p \,\&\, q)$ _____

$\therefore (p \supset q) \,\&\, (q \supset p)$

19. $(p \,\&\, q) \supset (p \text{ n } q)$ _____

$\therefore (p \supset q) \text{ n } (q \supset p)$

20. r _____

$\therefore (p \supset q) \lor (q \supset p)$

LOGICAL LANGUAGE AND EVERYDAY LANGUAGE

Early in this chapter we started out by talking about such common words as "and" and "or," and then we slipped over to talking about *conjunction* and *disjunction*. The transition was a bit sneaky, but intentional. To understand what is going on here, we can ask how closely these logical notions we have defined match their everyday counterparts. We will start with conjunction, and then come back to the more difficult question of conditionals.

At first sight, the match between conjunction as we have defined it and the everyday use of the word "and" may seem fairly bad. To begin with, in everyday discourse, we do not go about conjoining random bits of information. We do not say, for example, "Two plus two equals four and Chile is in South America." We already know why we do not say such things, for unless the context is quite extraordinary, this is bound to violate the conversational rule of Relevance. But if we are interested in validity, the rule of Relevance—like all other conversational (or pragmatic) rules—is simply beside the point. When dealing with validity, we are interested in only one question: If the premises of an argument are true, must the conclusion be true as well? Conversational rules, as we saw in Chapter 2, do not affect truth.

The truth-functional notion of conjunction is also insensitive to another important feature of our everyday discourse: By reducing all conjunctions to their bare truth-functional content, the truth-functional notion often misses the argumentative point of a conjunction. As we saw in Chapter 3, each of the following remarks has a different force in the context of an argument:

The ring is beautiful, but expensive.

The ring is expensive, but beautiful.

These two remarks point in opposite directions in the context of an actual argument, but from a purely truth-functional point of view, we treat them as equivalent. We translate the first sentence as "$B \,\&\, E$" and the second as

"*E & B.*" Their truth-functional equivalence is too obvious to need proof. Similar oddities arise for all discounting terms, such as "although," "whereas," and "however."

It might seem that if formal analysis cannot distinguish an "and" from a "but," then it can hardly be of any use at all. This is not true. A formal analysis of an argument will tell us just one thing: whether the argument is valid or not. If we expect the analysis to tell us more than this, we will be sorely disappointed. It is important to remember two things: (1) We expect deductive arguments to be valid, and (2) usually we expect much more than this from an argument. To elaborate on the second point, we usually expect an argument to be sound as well as valid; we expect the premises to be true. Beyond this, we expect the argument to be informative, intelligible, convincing, and so forth. Validity, then, is an important aspect of an argument, and formal analysis helps us evaluate it. But validity is not the only aspect of an argument that concerns us. In many contexts, it is not even our chief concern.

We can now look at our analysis of conditionals, for here we find some striking differences between the logician's analysis and everyday use. The following argument forms are both valid:

1. p
$\therefore q \supset p$

2. $\sim p$
$\therefore p \supset q$

EXERCISE XXV

Check the validity of the argument forms above using truth tables.

Though valid, both argument forms seem odd—so odd that they have actually been called *paradoxical*. The first argument form seems to say this: If a proposition is true, then it is *implied by* any proposition whatsoever. Here is an example of an argument that satisfies this argument form and is therefore valid:

Lincoln was president.
$\therefore$ If the moon is made of cheese, Lincoln was president.

This is a peculiar argument to call valid. First, we want to know what the moon has to do with Lincoln's having been president. Beyond this, how can his having been president depend on a blatant falsehood? We can give these questions even more force by noticing that even the following argument is valid:

Lincoln was president.
$\therefore$ If Lincoln was not president, then Lincoln was president.

Both arguments are instances of the valid argument form "p; ∴ $q \supset p$."

The other argument form is also paradoxical. It seems to say that a false proposition implies any proposition whatsoever. The following is an instance of this argument form:

Columbus was not president.

∴ If Columbus was president, then the moon is made of cheese.

Here it is hard to see what the falsehood that Columbus was president has to do with the composition of the moon.

At this point, nonphilosophers become impatient, whereas philosophers become worried. We started out with principles that seemed to be both obvious and simple. Now, quite suddenly, we are being overwhelmed with a whole series of peculiar results. What in the world has happened, and what should be done about it? Philosophers remain divided in the answers they give to these questions. The responses fall into two main categories: (1) Simply give up the idea that conditionals can be defined by truth-functional techniques and search for a different and better analysis of conditionals that avoids the difficulties involved in truth-functional analysis; or (2) take the difficult line and argue that there is nothing wrong with calling the aforementioned argument forms valid.

The first approach is highly technical and cannot be pursued in detail in this book, but the general idea is this: Instead of identifying "If p, then q" with "Not both p and not q," identify it with "Not *possibly* both p and not q." This provides a stronger notion of a conditional and avoids some—though not all—of the problems concerning conditionals. This theory is given a systematic development by offering a logical analysis of the notion of possibility. This branch of logic is called *modal* logic, and it has shown remarkable development in recent decades.

The second line has been taken by Paul Grice, whose theories played a prominent part in Chapter 2. He acknowledges—as anyone must—that the two argument forms above are decidedly odd. He denies, however, that this oddness has anything to do with *validity*. Validity concerns one thing and one thing only: a relationship between premises and conclusion. An argument is valid if the premises cannot be true without the conclusion being true as well. The above arguments are valid by this definition of "validity."

Of course, arguments can be defective in all sorts of other ways. Look at the first argument form: (1) p; ∴ $q \supset p$. Because "q" can be replaced by any proposition (true or false), the rule of Relevance will often be violated. It is worth pointing out violations of the rule of Relevance, but, according to Grice, this issue has nothing to do with validity. Beyond this, arguments having this form can also involve violations of the rule of Quantity. A conditional will be true whenever the consequent is true. Given this, it does not matter to the truth of the whole conditional whether the antecedent is true or false. Yet it can be misleading to use a conditional on the basis of this logical feature. For example, it would be misleading for a museum guard to say, "If you give me five dollars, then I will let you into the exhibition," when, in fact, he will admit you in any case. For Grice, this is misleading because it violates the rule of Quantity. Yet strictly speaking, it is not false. Strictly speaking, it is true.

The Grice line is attractive because, among other things, it allows us to accept the truth-functional account of conditionals, with all its simplicity. Yet sometimes it is difficult to swallow. Consider the following remark:

If God exists, then there is evil in the world.

If Grice's analysis is correct, even the most pious person will have to admit that this conditional is true provided only that he or she is willing to admit that there is evil in the world. Yet, this conditional plainly suggests that there is some connection between God's existence and the evil in the world—presumably, that is the point of connecting them in a conditional. The pious will wish to deny this suggestion. All the same, this connection is something that is conversationally implied, not asserted. So, once more, this conditional could be misleading—and therefore is in need of criticism and correction—but it is still, strictly speaking, true.

Philosophers and logicians have had various responses to Grice's position. No consensus has emerged on this issue. The authors of this book find it adequate, at least in most normal cases, and therefore have adopted it. This has two advantages: (1) The appeal to conversational rules fits in well with our previous discussions, and (2) it provides a way of keeping the logic simple and within the range of a beginning student. Other philosophers and logicians continue to work toward a definition superior to the truth table definition for indicative conditionals.

OTHER CONDITIONALS IN ORDINARY LANGUAGE

So far we have considered only one form in which propositional conditionals appear in everyday language: the conditional "If p, then q." But propositional conditionals come in a variety of forms, and some of them demand careful treatment.

We can first consider the contrast between constructions using "if" and those using "only if":

1. I'll clean the barn if Hazel will help me.
2. I'll clean the barn only if Hazel will help me.

Adopting the following abbreviations:

B = I'll clean the barn
H = Hazel will help me

the first sentence is symbolized as follows:

$H \supset B$

Notice that in the prose version of item 1, the antecedent and consequent appear in reverse order; "q if p" means the same thing as "If p, then q."

How shall we translate the second sentence? Here we should move slowly and first notice what seems incontestable: If Hazel does not help me, then I will not clean the barn. This is translated in the following way:

$\sim H \supset \sim B$

And that is equivalent to:

$B \supset H$

If this equivalence is not obvious, it can quickly be established using a truth table.

A more difficult question arises when we ask whether an implication runs the other way. When I say that I will clean the barn only if Hazel will help me, am I committing myself to cleaning the barn if she does help me? There is a strong temptation to answer the question "yes" and then give a fuller translation of item 2 in the following way:

$(B \supset H) \& (H \supset B)$

Logicians call such two-way implications *biconditionals,* and we will discuss them in a moment. But adding this second conjunct is almost surely a mistake, for we can think of parallel cases where we would not be tempted to include it. A government regulation might read as follows:

> A student may receive a New York State Scholarship only if the student attends a New York State school.

From this it does not follow that anyone who attends a New York State school may receive a New York State Scholarship. There may be other requirements as well—for example, being a New York State resident.

Why were we tempted to use a biconditional in translating sentences containing the connective "only if"? Why, that is, are we tempted to think that the statement "I'll clean the barn only if Hazel will help me" implies "If Hazel helps me, then I will clean the barn"? The answer turns on the notion of conversational implication first discussed in Chapter 2. If I am *not* going to clean the barn whether Hazel helps me or not, then it will be misleading—a violation of the rule of Quantity—to say that I will clean the barn only if Hazel helps me. For this reason, in many contexts, the *use* of a sentence of the form "p only if q" will conversationally imply a commitment to "p if and only if q."

To appreciate the complexities of the little word "only," it is useful to notice that it fits at every point in the sentence "I hit him in the eye":

Only I hit him in the eye.

I only hit him in the eye.

I hit only him in the eye.

I hit him only in the eye.

I hit him in only the eye.

I hit him in the only eye.

I hit him in the eye only.

Explain what each of these sentences means.

We can next look at sentences of the form "*p* if and only if *q*"—so-called biconditionals. If I say that I will clean the barn if and only if Hazel will help me, then I am saying that I will clean it if she helps and I will not clean it if she does not. Translated, this becomes:

$(H \supset B) \,\&\, (\sim\!H \supset \sim\!B)$

This is equivalent to:

$(H \supset B) \,\&\, (B \supset H)$

We thus have an implication going both ways—the characteristic form of a biconditional. In fact, constructions containing the expression "if and only if" do not often appear in everyday speech. They appear almost exclusively in technical or legal writing. In ordinary conversation, we capture the force of a biconditional by saying something like this:

I will clean the barn, but only if Hazel helps me.

The decision whether to translate a remark of everyday conversation into a conditional or a biconditional is often subtle and difficult. We have already noticed that the use of sentences of the form "*p* only if *q*" will often conversationally imply a commitment to the biconditional "*p* if and only if *q*." In the same way, the *use* of the conditional "*p* if *q*" will often carry this same implication. If I plan to clean the barn whether Hazel helps me or not, it will certainly be misleading—again, a violation of the rule of Quantity—to say that I will clean the barn *if* Hazel helps me.

We can close this discussion by considering one further, rather difficult case. What is the force of saying "*p unless q*"? Is this a biconditional, or just a conditional? If it is just a conditional, which way does the implication go? There is a strong temptation to treat this as a biconditional, but the following example shows this to be wrong:

McCain will lose the election unless he carries the South.

This sentence clearly indicates that McCain will lose the election if he does not carry the South. Using abbreviations, we get the following:

N = McCain will carry the South.

L = McCain will lose the election.

$\sim N \supset L$

The original statement does not imply—even conversationally—that McCain will win the election if he does carry the South. Thus,

p unless $q = \sim q \supset p$

In short, "unless" means "if not." We can also note that "$\sim p$ unless q" means the same thing as "p only if q," and they both are translated thus:

$p \supset q$

Our results can be diagrammed as follows:

	Translates as	Often Conversationally Implies
p if q	$q \supset p$	$(p \supset q) \,\&\, (q \supset p)$
p only if q	$p \supset q$	$(p \supset q) \,\&\, (q \supset p)$
p unless q	$\sim q \supset p$	$(p \supset \sim q) \,\&\, (\sim q \supset p)$

EXERCISE XXVII

Translate each of the following sentences into symbolic notation, using the suggested symbols as abbreviations.

1. The Reds will win only if the Dodgers collapse. (R, D)
2. The Steelers will win if their defense holds up. (S, D)
3. If it rains or snows, the game will be called off. (R, S, O)
4. If she came home with a trophy and a prize, she must have won the tournament. (T, P, W)
5. If you order the dinner special, you get dessert and coffee. (S, D, C)
6. If you order the dinner special, you get dessert; but you can have coffee whether or not you order the dinner special. (S, D, C)
7. If the house comes up for sale, and if I have the money in hand, I will bid on it. (S, M, B)
8. If you come to dinner, I will cook you a lobster, if you want me to. (D, L, W)
9. You can be a success if only you try. (S, T)
10. You can be a success only if you try. (S, T)
11. Only if you try can you be a success. (S, T)

12. You can be a success if you are the only one who tries. (S, O)
13. Unless there is a panic, stock prices will continue to rise. (P, R)
14. I won't scratch your back unless you scratch mine. (I, Y)
15. You will get a good bargain provided you get there early. (B, E)
16. You cannot lead a happy life without friends. (Let H = You can lead a happy life, and let F = You have friends.)
17. The only way that horse will win the race is if every other horse drops dead. (Let W = That horse will win the race, and let D = Every other horse drops dead.)
18. You should take prescription drugs if, but only if, they are prescribed for you. (T, P)
19. The grass will die without rain. (D, R = It rains.)
20. Given rain, the grass won't die. (R, D = The grass will die.)
21. Unless it doesn't rain, the grass won't die. (R, D = The grass will die.)

EXERCISE XXVIII

(a) Translate each of the following arguments into symbolic notation. Then (b) test each argument for truth-functional validity using truth table techniques, and (c) comment on any violations of conversational rules.

Example: Harold is clever; so, if Harold isn't clever, then Anna isn't clever either. (H, A)

(a) H

∴ $\sim H \supset \sim A$

p

∴ $\sim p \supset \sim q$

(b)

PREMISE			CONCLUSION		
p	q	$\sim p$	$\sim q$	$\sim p \supset \sim q$	
T	T	F	F	T	OK
T	F	F	T	T	OK
F	T	T	F	F	
F	F	T	T	T	

(c) The argument violates the rule of Relevance, because Anna's cleverness is irrelevant to Harold's cleverness.

1. Jones is brave, so Jones is brave or Jones is brave. (J)
2. The Republicans will carry either New Mexico or Arizona; but, since they will carry Arizona, they will not carry New Mexico. (A, N)
3. The Democrats will win the election whether they win Idaho or not. Therefore, they will win the election. (D, I)

(continued)

4. The Democrats will win the election. Therefore, they will win the election whether they win Idaho or not. (*D, I*)

5. The Democrats will win the election. Therefore, they will win the election whether they win a majority or not. (*D, M*)

6. If Bobby moves his queen there, he will lose her. Bobby will not lose his queen. Therefore, Bobby will not move his queen there. (*M, L*)

7. John will play only if the situation is hopeless. But the situation is hopeless. So John will play. (*P, H*)

8. Although Brown will pitch, the Rams will lose. If the Rams lose, their manager will get fired. So their manager will get fired. (*B, L, F*)

9. America will win the Olympics unless China does. China will win the Olympics unless Germany does. So America will win the Olympics unless Germany does. (*A, R, E*)

10. If you dial 0, you will get the operator. So, if you dial 0 and do not get the operator, then there is something wrong with the telephone. (*D, O, W*)

11. The Democrats will run either Jones or Borg. If Borg runs, they will lose the South. If Jones runs, they will lose the North. So the Democrats will lose either the North or the South. (*J, B, S, N*)

12. I am going to order either the fish special or the meat special. Either way, I will get soup. So I'll get soup. (*F, M, S*)

13. The grass will die if it rains too much or it does not rain enough. If it does not rain enough, it won't rain too much. If it rains too much, then it won't not rain enough. So the grass will die. (*D* = The grass will die, *M* = It rains too much, *E* = It rains enough.)

14. If you flip the switch, then the light will go on. But if the light goes on, then the generator is working. So if you flip the switch, then the generator is working. (*F, L, G*) (This example comes from Charles L. Stevenson.)

8

ARGUMENTS TO AND FROM GENERALIZATIONS

This chapter begins our investigation of inductive arguments by distinguishing the inductive standard of strength from the deductive standard of validity. Inductive arguments are defined as arguments that are intended to be strong rather than valid. Two common examples of inductive arguments are discussed next. In statistical generalizations, *a claim is made about a population on the basis of features of a sample of that population. In* statistical applications, *a claim is made about members of a population on the basis of features of the population. Statistical generalizations take us up from samples to general claims, and statistical applications then take us back down to individual cases.*

INDUCTION VERSUS DEDUCTION

The distinction between deductive arguments and inductive arguments can be drawn in a variety of ways, but the fundamental difference concerns the relationship that is claimed to hold between the premises and the conclusion for each type of argument. An argument is *deductive* insofar as it is intended or claimed to be *valid*. As we know from Chapter 5, an argument is valid if and only if it is impossible for the conclusion to be false when its premises are true. The following is a valid deductive argument:

> All ravens are black.
> ∴ If there is a raven on top of Pikes Peak, then it is black.

Because the premise lays down a universal principle governing all ravens, if it's true, then it *must* be true of all ravens (if any) on top of Pikes Peak. This same relationship does not hold for invalid arguments. Nonetheless, arguments that are not valid can still be deductive if they are intended or claimed to be valid.

In contrast, inductive arguments are not intended to be valid, so they should not be criticized for being invalid. The following is an example of an inductive argument:

> All ravens that we have observed so far are black.
> ∴ All ravens are black.

Here we have drawn an inductive inference from the characteristics of *observed* ravens to the characteristics of *all* ravens, most of which we have not observed. Of course, the premise of this argument *could be* true, yet the conclusion turn out to be false. A raven that has not yet been observed might be albino. The obviousness of this possibility suggests that someone who gives this argument does not put it forth as valid, so it is not a deductive argument. Instead, the premise is put forth as a *reason* or *support* for the conclusion. When an argument is not claimed to be valid but is intended only to provide a reason for the conclusion, the argument is *inductive*.

Because inductive arguments are supposed to provide reasons, and reasons vary in strength, inductive arguments can be evaluated as *strong* or *weak*, depending on the strength of the reasons that they provide for their conclusions. If we have seen only ten ravens, and all of them were in our backyard, then the above argument gives at most a very weak reason to believe that all ravens are black. But, if we have traveled around the world and seen over half the ravens that exist, then the above argument gives a strong reason to believe that all ravens are black. Inductive arguments are usually intended to provide strong support for their conclusions, in which case they can be criticized if the support they provide is not strong enough for the purposes at hand.

The most basic distinction, then, is not between two kinds of argument but is instead between two standards for evaluating arguments. The deductive standard is validity. The inductive standard is strength. Arguments themselves are classified as either deductive or inductive in accordance with the standard that they are intended or claimed to meet.

There are several important differences between deductive and inductive standards. One fundamental feature of the deductive standard of validity is that adding premises to a valid argument cannot make it invalid. The definition of validity guarantees this: In a valid argument, it is not possible for the premises to be true without the conclusion being true as well. If any further premises could change this, then it would be possible for this relationship not to hold, so the argument would not be valid after all. Additional information might, of course, lead us to question the truth of one of the premises, but that is another matter.

The situation is strikingly different when we deal with inductive arguments. To cite a famous example, before the time of Captain Cook's voyage to Australia, Europeans had observed a great many swans, and every one of them was white. Thus, up to that time Europeans had very strong inductive evidence to support the claim that all swans are white. Then Captain Cook discovered black swans in Australia. What happens if we add this new piece of information to the premises of the original inductive argument? Provided that we accept Cook's report, we now produce a sound *deductive* argument in behalf of the opposite claim that *not* all swans are white; for, if some swans are black, then not all of them are white. This, then, is a feature of the inductive standard of strength: No matter how strong an inductive argument is, the possibility remains open that further information can undercut, perhaps completely, the strength of the argument and the support that the premises give to the conclusion. Because inductive strength and inductive arguments can always be defeated in this way, they are described as *defeasible*. Valid deductive arguments do not face a similar peril, so they are called *indefeasible*.

A second important difference between inductive and deductive standards is that inductive strength comes in degrees, but deductive validity does not. An argument is either valid or invalid. There is no question of how much validity an argument has. In contrast, inductive arguments can be more or less strong. The more varied ravens or swans we observe, the stronger the inductive arguments above. Some inductive arguments are extremely strong and put their conclusions beyond any reasonable doubt. Other inductive arguments are much weaker, even though they still have some force.

Because of the necessary relationship between the premises and the conclusion of a valid deductive argument, it is often said that the premises of valid deductive arguments (if true) provide *conclusive* support for their conclusions, whereas true premises of strong inductive arguments provide only *partial* support for their conclusions. There is something to this. Because the premises of a valid deductive argument necessitate the truth of the conclusion, if those premises are definitely known to be true, then they do supply conclusive reasons for the conclusion. The same cannot be said for inductive arguments.

It would be altogether misleading, however, to conclude from this that inductive arguments are inherently inferior to deductive arguments in supplying a justification or ground for a conclusion. In the first place, inductive arguments often place matters beyond any reasonable doubt. It is possible that the next pot of water will not boil at any temperature, however high, but this is not something we worry about. We do not take precautions against it, and we shouldn't.

More important, deductive arguments normally enjoy no advantages over their inductive counterparts. We can see this by comparing the two following arguments:

DEDUCTIVE	INDUCTIVE
All ravens are black.	All observed ravens are black.
∴ If there is a raven on top of Pikes Peak, it is black.	∴ If there is a raven on top of Pikes Peak, it is black.

Of course, it is true for the deductive argument (and not true for the inductive argument) that if the premise is true, then the conclusion must be true. This may seem to give an advantage to the deductive argument over the inductive argument. But before we can decide how much support a deductive argument gives its conclusion, we must ask whether its premises are, after all, true. That is not something we can just take for granted. If we examine the premises of these two arguments, we see that it is easier to establish the truth of the premise of the inductive argument than it is to establish the truth of the premise of the deductive argument. If we have observed carefully and kept good records, then we might be fully confident that all *observed* ravens have been black. On the other hand, how can we show that *all* ravens (observed and unobserved—past, present, and future) are black? The most obvious way (though there may be other ways) would be to observe ravens to see whether they are black or not. This, of course, involves producing an inductive argument (called a statistical generalization) for the premise of the deductive argument. Here our confidence in the truth of the premise of the deductive argument should be no greater than our confidence in the strength of the inference in the statistical generalization. In this case—and it is not unusual—the deductive argument provides no stronger grounds in support of its conclusion than does its inductive counterpart, because any reservations we might have about the *strength* of the inductive inference will be paralleled by doubts concerning the *truth* of the premise of the deductive argument.

We will also avoid the common mistake of saying that deductive arguments always move from the general to the particular, whereas inductive arguments always move from the particular to the general. In fact, both sorts of arguments can move in either direction. There are inductive arguments intended to establish particular matters of fact, and there are deductive arguments that involve generalizations from particulars. For example, when scientists assemble empirical evidence to determine whether the extinction of the dinosaurs was caused by the impact of a meteor, their discussions are models of inductive reasoning. Yet they are not trying to establish a generalization or a scientific law. Instead, they are trying to determine whether a particular event occurred some 65 million years ago. Inductive reasoning concerning particular matters of fact occurs constantly in everyday life as well, for example, when we check to see whether our television reception is being messed up by someone using a hair dryer. Deductive arguments from the particular to the general also exist, though they tend to be trivial, and hence boring. Here's one:

> Benjamin Franklin was the first postmaster general; therefore, anyone who is identical with Benjamin Franklin was the first postmaster general.

Of course, many deductive arguments do move from the general to the particular, and many inductive arguments do move from particular premises to a general conclusion. It is important to remember, however, that this is not the *definitive* difference between these two kinds of arguments. What makes deductive arguments deductive is precisely that they are intended to meet the deductive standard of validity, and what makes inductive arguments inductive is just that they are not intended to be deductively valid but are, instead, intended to be inductively strong.

EXERCISE I

Assuming a standard context, label each of the following arguments as deductive or inductive. Explain what it is about the words or form of argument that indicates whether or not each argument is intended or claimed to be valid. If it is not clear whether the argument is inductive or deductive, say why.

1. The sun is coming out, so the rain will probably stop soon.

2. It's going to rain tomorrow, so it will either rain or be clear tomorrow.

3. No woman has ever been elected president. Therefore, no woman will ever be elected president.

4. Diet cola never keeps me awake at night. I know because I drank it just last night without any problems.

5. The house is a mess, so Jeff must be home from college.

6. If Harold were innocent, he would not go into hiding. Since he is hiding, he must not be innocent.

7. Nobody in Paris seems to understand me, so either my French is rotten or Parisians are unfriendly.

8. Because both of our yards are near rivers in Tennessee, and my yard has lots of mosquitoes, there must also be lots of mosquitoes in your yard.

9. Most likely, her new husband speaks English with an accent, because he comes from Germany, and most Germans speak English with an accent.

10. There is no even number smaller than two, so one is not an even number.

STATISTICAL GENERALIZATIONS

One classic example of an inductive argument is an opinion poll. Suppose a candidate wants to know how popular she is with voters. Because it would be practically impossible to survey all voters, she takes a sample of voting opinion and then infers that the opinions of those sampled indicate the overall opinion of voters. Thus, if 60 percent of the voters sampled say that they will vote for her, she concludes that she will get around 60 percent of the vote in the actual election. As we shall see later, inferences of this kind often go wrong, even when made by experts, but the general pattern of this reasoning is quite clear: Statistical features of a sample are used to make statistical claims about the population as a whole.

Basically the same form of reasoning can be used to reach a universal conclusion. An example is the inductive inference discussed at the start of this chapter: All observed ravens are black, so all ravens are black. Again, we sample part of a population to draw a conclusion about the whole. Arguments of this form, whether the conclusion is universal or partial (as when it cites a particular percentage), are called *statistical generalizations*.

How do we assess such inferences? To begin to answer this question, we can consider a simple example of a statistical generalization. On various occasions, Harold has tried to use Canadian quarters in American vending machines and found that they have not worked. From this he draws the conclusion that Canadian quarters do not work in American vending machines. Harold's inductive reasoning looks like this:

> In the past, when I tried to use Canadian quarters in American vending machines, they did not work.
>
> ∴ Canadian quarters do not work in American vending machines.

The force of the conclusion is that Canadian quarters *never* work in American vending machines.

In evaluating this argument, what questions should we ask? We can start with a question that we should ask of any argument.

SHOULD WE ACCEPT THE PREMISES?

Perhaps Harold has a bad memory, has kept bad records, or is a poor observer. For some obscure reason, he may even be lying. It is important to ask this question explicitly, because fairly often the premises, when challenged, will not stand up to scrutiny.

If we decide that the premises are acceptable (that is, true and justified), then we can shift our attention to the relationship between the premises and the conclusion and ask how much support the premises give to the conclusion. One commonsense question is this: "How many times has Harold tried to use Canadian quarters in American vending machines?" If the answer is "Once,"

then our confidence in his argument should drop to almost nothing. So, for statistical generalizations, it is always appropriate to ask about the size of the sample.

IS THE SAMPLE LARGE ENOUGH?

One reason we should be suspicious of small samples is that they can be affected by runs of luck. Suppose Harold flips a Canadian quarter four times and it comes up heads each time. From this, he can hardly conclude that Canadian quarters always come up heads when flipped. He could not even reasonably conclude that *this* Canadian quarter would always come up heads when flipped. The reason for this is obvious enough: If you spend a lot of time flipping coins, runs of four heads in a row are not all that unlikely (the probability is actually one in sixteen), and therefore samples of this size can easily be distorted by chance. On the other hand, if Harold flipped the coin twenty times and it continued to come up heads, he would have strong grounds for saying that this coin, at least, will always come up heads. In fact, he would have strong grounds for thinking that he has a two-headed coin. Because an overly small sample can lead to erroneous conclusions, we need to make sure that our sample includes enough trials.

How many is enough? On the assumption, for the moment, that our sampling has been fair in all other respects, how many samples do we need to provide the basis for a strong inductive argument? This is not always an easy question to answer, and sometimes answering it demands subtle mathematical techniques. Suppose your company is selling 10 million computer chips to the Department of Defense, and you have guaranteed that no more than 0.2 percent of them will be defective. It would be prohibitively expensive to test all the chips, and testing only a dozen would hardly be enough to reasonably guarantee that the total shipment of chips meets the required specifications. Because testing chips is expensive, you want to test as few as possible; but because meeting the specifications is crucial, you want to test enough to guarantee that you have done so. Answering questions of this kind demands sophisticated statistical techniques beyond the scope of this text.

Sometimes, then, it is difficult to decide how many instances are needed to give reasonable support to inductive generalizations; yet many times it is obvious, without going into technical details, that the sample is too small. Drawing an inductive conclusion from a sample that is too small can lead to the fallacy of *hasty generalization*. It is surprising how common this fallacy is. We see a person two or three times and find him cheerful, and we immediately leap to the conclusion that he is a cheerful person. That is, from a few instances of cheerful behavior, we draw a general conclusion about his personality. When we meet him later and find him sad, morose, or grouchy, we then conclude that he has changed—thus swapping one hasty generalization for another.

By making our samples sufficiently large, we can guard against distortions due to "runs of luck," but even very large samples can give us a poor basis for a statistical generalization. Suppose that Harold has tried hundreds of times to use a Canadian quarter in an American vending machine, and it has never worked. This will increase our confidence in his generalization, but size of sample alone is not a sufficient ground for a strong inductive argument. Suppose that Harold has tried the same coin in hundreds of American vending machines, or tried a hundred different Canadian coins in the same vending machine. In the first case, there might be something wrong with this particular coin; in the second case, there might be something wrong with this particular vending machine. In neither case would he have good grounds for making the general claim that *no* Canadian quarters work in *any* American vending machine. This leads us to the third question we should ask of any statistical generalization.

IS THE SAMPLE BIASED?

When the sample, however large, is not representative of the population, then it is said to be unfair or biased. Here we can speak of the fallacy of *biased sampling.*

One of the most famous errors of biased sampling was committed by a magazine named the *Literary Digest.* Before the presidential election of 1936, this magazine sent out 10 million questionnaires asking which candidate the recipient would vote for: Franklin Roosevelt or Alf Landon. It received 2.5 million returns, and on the basis of the results, confidently predicted that Landon would win by a landslide: 56 percent for Landon to only 44 percent for Roosevelt. When the election results came in, Roosevelt had won by an even larger landslide in the opposite direction: 62 percent for Roosevelt to a mere 38 percent for Landon.

What went wrong? The sample was certainly large enough; in fact, by contemporary standards it was much larger than needed. It was the way the sample was selected, not its size, that caused the problem: The sample was randomly drawn from names in telephone books and from club member-ship lists. In 1936 there were only 11 million payphones in the United States, and many of the poor—especially the rural poor—did not have payphones. During the Great Depression there were more than nine million unem-ployed in America; they were almost all poor and thus underrepresented on club membership lists. Finally, a large percentage of these underrepresented groups voted for Roosevelt, the Democratic candidate. As a result of these biases in its sampling, along with some others, the *Literary Digest* underesti-mated Roosevelt's percentage of the vote by a whopping 18 percent.

Looking back, it may be hard to believe that intelligent observers could have done such a ridiculously bad job of sampling opinion, but the story repeats itself, though rarely on the grand scale of the *Literary Digest* fiasco. In 1948, for example, the Gallup poll, which had correctly predicted Roosevelt's victory in 1936, predicted, as did other major polls, a clear victory for Thomas Dewey over Harry Truman. Confidence was so high in this prediction that the *Chicago Tribune* published a banner headline declaring that Dewey had won the election before the votes were actually counted.

What went wrong this time? The answer here is more subtle. The Gallup pollsters (and others) went to great pains to make sure that their sample was representative of the voting population. The interviewers were told to poll a certain number of people from particular social groups—rural poor, suburban middle class, urban middle class, ethnic minorities, and so on—so that the proportions of those interviewed matched, as closely as possible, the proportions of those likely to vote. (The *Literary Digest* went bankrupt after its incorrect prediction, so the pollsters were taking no chances.) Yet somehow bias crept into the sampling; the question was, "How?" One speculation was that a large percentage of those sampled did not tell the truth when they were interviewed; another was that a large number of people changed their minds at the last minute. So perhaps the data collected were not reliable. The explanation generally accepted was more subtle. Although Gallup's workers were told to interview specific numbers of people from particular classes (so many from the suburbs, for example), they were not instructed to choose people randomly from within each group. Without seriously thinking about it, they tended to go to "nicer" neighborhoods and interview "nicer" people. Because of this, they biased the sample in the direction of their own (largely) middle-class preferences and, as a result, under-represented constituencies that would give Truman his unexpected victory.

IS THE SAMPLING PROCEDURE BIASED?

Because professionals using modern techniques can make bad statistical generalizations through biased sampling, it is not surprising that our everyday, informal inductive generalizations are often inaccurate. Sometimes we go astray because of small samples and biased samples. This happens, for example, when we form opinions about what people think or what people are like by asking only our friends. But bias can affect our reasoning in other ways as well.

One of the main sources of bias in everyday life is *prejudice.* Even if we sample a wide enough range of cases, we often reinterpret what we hear or see in light of some preconception. People who are prejudiced will find very little good and a great deal bad in those they despise, no matter how these people actually behave. In fact, most people are a mixture of good and bad qualities. By ignoring the former and dwelling on the latter, it is easy enough for a prejudiced person to confirm negative opinions.

Another common source of bias in sampling arises from phrasing questions in ways that encourage certain answers while discouraging others. Even if a fair sample is asked a question, it is well known that the way a question is phrased can exert a significant influence on how people will answer it. Questions like the following are not intended to elicit information, but instead to push people's answers in one direction rather than another:

Which do you favor: (a) preserving a citizen's constitutional right to bear arms or (b) leaving honest citizens defenseless against armed criminals?

Which do you favor: (a) restricting the sale of assault weapons or (b) knuckling under to the demands of the well-financed gun lobby?

In both cases, one alternative is made to sound attractive, the other unattractive. When questions of this sort are used, it is not surprising that different pollsters can come up with wildly different results.

Now we can summarize and restate our questions. Confronted with inductive generalizations, there are four questions that we should routinely ask:

1. Are the premises acceptable?
2. Is the sample too small?
3. Is the sample biased?
4. Is the sampling procedure biased?

EXERCISE II

By asking the preceding questions, specify what, if anything, is wrong with the following statistical generalizations:

1. This philosophy class is about logic, so most philosophy classes are probably about logic.
2. Most college students like to ski, because I asked a lot of students at several colleges in the Rocky Mountains, and most of them like to ski.
3. K-Mart asked all of their customers throughout the country whether they prefer K-Mart to Walmart, and 90 percent said they did, so 90 percent of all shoppers in the country prefer K-Mart.
4. A Swede stole my bicycle, so most Swedes are thieves.
5. I've never tried it before, but I just put a kiwi fruit in a tub of water. It floated. So most kiwi fruits float in water.
6. I have lots of friends. Most of them think that I would make a great president. So most Americans would probably agree.
7. In exit polls after people had just voted, most people told our candidate that they voted for her, so probably most people did vote for her.
8. Mary told me that all of her older children are geniuses, so her baby will probably be a genius, too.
9. When asked whether they would prefer a tax break or a bloated budget, almost everyone said that they wanted a tax break. So a tax break is overwhelmingly popular with the people.
10. When hundreds of convicted murderers in states without the death penalty were asked whether they would have committed the murder if the state had a death penalty, most of them said that they would not have done it. So most murders can be deterred by the death penalty.

STATISTICAL APPLICATIONS

In a statistical generalization, we draw inferences concerning a population from information concerning a sample of that population. If 60 percent of the population sampled said that they would vote for candidate X, we might draw the conclusion that roughly 60 percent of the population will vote for candidate X. With a *statistical application* (sometimes called a *statistical syllogism*), we reason in the reverse direction: From information concerning a population, we draw a conclusion concerning a member or subset of that population. Here is an example:

> Ninety-seven percent of the Republicans in California voted for Romney.
> Marvin is a Republican from California.
>
> ∴ Marvin voted for Romney.

Such arguments have the following general form:

> X percent of Fs have the feature G.
> a is an F.
>
> ∴ a has the feature G.[1]

Obviously, when we evaluate the strength of a statistical application, the percentage of Fs that have the feature G will be important. As the figure approaches 100 percent, the argument gains strength. Thus, our original argument concerning Marvin is quite strong. We can also get strong statistical applications when the figure approaches 0 percent. The following is a strong inductive argument:

> Three percent of the socialists from California voted for Romney.
> Maureen is a socialist from California.
>
> ∴ Maureen did *not* vote for Romney.

Statistical applications of the kind considered here are strong only if the figures are close to 100 percent or 0 percent. When the percentages are in the middle of this range, such statistical applications are weak.

A more interesting problem in evaluating the strength of a statistical application concerns the *relevance* of the premises to the conclusion. In the above schematic representation, F stands for what is called the *reference class*. In our first example, being a Republican from California is the reference class; in our second example, being a socialist from California is the reference class. A striking feature of statistical applications is that using different reference classes can yield incompatible results. To see this, consider the following example:

> Three percent of Obama's relatives voted for Romney.
> Marvin is a relative of Obama.
>
> ∴ Marvin did not vote for Romney.

We now have a statistical application that gives us strong support for the claim that Marvin did not vote for Romney. This is incompatible with our first statistical application, which gave strong support to the claim that he did. To overlook this conflict between arguments based on different reference classes would be a kind of fallacy. Which statistical application, if either, should we trust? This will depend on which of the reference classes we take to be more relevant. Which counts more, political affiliation or family ties? That might be hard to say.

One way of dealing with competing statistical applications is to combine the reference classes. We could ask, for example, what percentage of Republicans from California who are relatives of Obama voted for Romney? The result might come out this way:

> Forty-two percent of Republicans from California who were relatives of Obama voted for Romney.
>
> Marvin is a Republican from California who is a relative of Obama.
>
> ∴ Marvin voted for Romney.

This statistical application provides very weak support for its conclusion. Indeed, it supplies some weak support for the denial of its conclusion—that is, for the claim that Marvin did *not* vote for Romney.

This situation can be diagrammed with ellipses of varying sizes to represent the percentages of Californians and relatives of Obama who do or do not vote for Romney. First, we draw an ellipse to represent Republicans from California and place a vertical line so that it cuts off roughly (very roughly!) 97 percent of the area of that ellipse to represent the premise that 97 percent of the Republicans from California voted for Romney:

Next, we add a second ellipse to represent Obama's relatives:

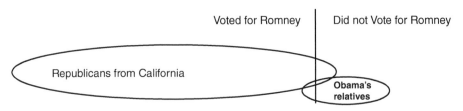

Only about 3 percent of the small ellipse is left of the line to represent the premise that 3 percent of Obama's relatives voted for Romney. The area that lies within both ellipses represents the people who are both Republicans from California and also relatives of Obama. About 42 percent of that area is left of the line to represent the premise that 42 percent of Republicans from California who were relatives of Obama voted for Romney. The whole diagram now shows how all of these premises can be true, even though they lead to conflicting conclusions.

This series of arguments illustrates in a clear way what we earlier called the *defeasibility of inductive inferences:* A strong inductive argument can be made weak by adding further information to the premises. Given that Marvin is a Republican from California, we seemed to have good reason to think that he voted for Romney. But when we added to this the additional piece of information that he was a relative of Obama, the original argument lost most of its force. And new information could produce another reversal. Suppose we discover that Marvin, though a relative of Obama, actively campaigned for Romney. Just about everyone who actively campaigns for a candidate votes for that candidate, so it seems that we again have good reason for thinking that Marvin voted for Romney.

It is clear, then, that the way we select our reference classes will affect the strength of a statistical application. The general idea is that we should define our reference classes in a way that brings all relevant evidence to bear on the subject. But this raises difficulties. It is not always obvious which factors are relevant and which are not. In our example, party affiliation is relevant to how people voted in the 2012 election; shoe size presumably is not. Whether gender is significant, and, if so, how significant, is a matter for further statistical research.

These difficulties concerning the proper way to fix reference classes reflect a feature of all inductive reasoning: To be successful, such reasoning must take place within a broader framework that helps determine which features are significant and which features are not. Without this framework, there would be no reason not to consider shoe size when trying to decide how someone will vote. This shows how statistical applications, like all of the other inductive arguments that we will study, cannot work properly without appropriate background assumptions.

EXERCISE III

Carry the story of Marvin two steps further, producing two more reversals in the strength of the statistical application with the conclusion that Marvin voted for Romney.

EXERCISE IV

For each of the following statistical applications, identify the reference class, and then evaluate the strength of the argument in terms of the percentages or proportions cited and the relevance of the reference class.

1. Less than 1 percent of the people in the world voted for Romney.
   Michelle is a person in the world.

   ∴ Michelle did not vote for Romney.

2. Very few teams repeat as Super Bowl champions.
   New England was the last Super Bowl champion.

   ∴ New England will not repeat as Super Bowl champion.

3. A very high percentage of people in the Senate are men.
   Elizabeth Warren is in the Senate.

   ∴ Elizabeth Warren is a man.

4. Three percent of socialists with blue eyes voted for Romney.
   Maureen is a socialist with blue eyes.

   ∴ Maureen did not vote for Romney.

5. Ninety-eight percent of what John says is true.
   John said that his father is also named John.

   ∴ John's father is named John.

6. Ninety-eight percent of what John says is true.
   John said that the Giants are going to win.

   ∴ The Giants are going to win.

7. Half the time he doesn't know what he is doing.
   He is eating lunch.

   ∴ He does not know that he is eating lunch.

8. Most people do not understand quantum mechanics.
   My physics professor is a person.

   ∴ My physics professor probably does not understand quantum mechanics.

9. Almost all birds can fly.
   This penguin is a bird.

   ∴ This penguin can fly.

10. Most people who claim to be psychic are frauds.
    Mary claims to be psychic.

    ∴ Mary is a fraud.

DISCUSSION QUESTION

Although both in science and in daily life, we rely heavily on the methods of inductive reasoning, this kind of reasoning raises a number of perplexing problems. The most famous problem concerning the legitimacy of induction was formulated by the eighteenth-century philosopher David Hume, first in his *Treatise of Human Nature* and then later in his *Enquiry Concerning Human Understanding*. A simplified version of Hume's skeptical argument goes as follows: Our inductive generalizations seem to rest on the assumption that *unobserved* cases will follow the patterns that we discovered in *observed* cases. That is, our inductive generalizations seem to presuppose that nature operates uniformly: The way things are observed to behave here and now are accurate indicators of how things behave anywhere and at any time. But by what right can we assume that nature is uniform? Because this claim itself asserts a contingent matter of fact, it could only be established by inductive reasoning. But because all inductive reasoning presupposes the principle that nature is uniform, any inductive justification of this principle would seem to be circular. It seems, then, that we have no ultimate justification for our inductive reasoning at all. Is this a good argument or a bad one? Why?

NOTE

[1] We can also have a *probabilistic* version of the statistical syllogism:

Ninety-seven percent of the Republicans from California voted for Romney.
Marvin is a Republican from California.

∴ There is a 97 percent chance that Marvin voted for Romney.

We will discuss arguments concerning probability in Chapter 11.

9

INFERENCE TO THE BEST
EXPLANATION AND FROM ANALOGY

Even if we can generalize from a sample to the conclusion that most women in a country voted for a certain candidate, and even if we can apply that generalization and conclude that Ilina probably voted for that candidate, this generalization and application still might not explain why *Ilina voted for that candidate. Did she like his experience or his policies? Which policies? Or did she just dislike his opponent? As we saw in Chapter 1, generalization is not always enough for explanation. We also saw in Chapter 1 that some arguments can be used to explain a phenomenon when they help us understand why it happened. In contrast, explanations can also play a different role in a new kind of inductive argument. Sometimes we cite the explanatory value of a hypothesis as evidence for that hypothesis. This form of argument, which is described as* inference to the best explanation, *is the first topic in this chapter. It requires us to determine which explanation is best, so we will investigate common standards for assessing explanations, including falsifiability, conservativeness, modesty, simplicity, power, and depth. After explaining these standards, this chapter will turn to a related form of argument called* argument from analogy, *in which the fact that two things have certain features in common is taken as evidence that they have further features in common. The chapter ends by suggesting that many arguments from analogy are ultimately based on implicit inferences to the best explanation.*

INFERENCES TO THE BEST EXPLANATION

One of the most common forms of inductive argument is *inference to the best explanation.*[1] The general idea behind such inferences is that a hypothesis gains inductive support if, when added to our stock of previously accepted beliefs, it enables us to explain something that we observe or believe, and no competing explanation works nearly as well.

To see how inferences to the best explanation work, suppose you return to your home and discover that the lock on your front door is broken and some valuables are missing. In all likelihood, you will immediately conclude that you have been burglarized. Of course, other things *could* have produced the mess. Perhaps the police mistakenly busted into your house looking for drugs and took your valuables as evidence. Perhaps your friends are playing a strange joke on you. Perhaps a meteorite struck the door and then vaporized your valuables. In fact, all of these things *could* have happened (even the last), and further investigation could show that one of them did. Why, then, do we so quickly accept the burglary hypothesis without even considering these competing possibilities? The reason is that the hypothesis that your home was robbed is not highly improbable; and this hypothesis, together with other things we believe, provides the best—the strongest and the most natural—explanation of the phenomenon. The possibility that a meteorite struck your door is so wildly remote that it is not worth taking seriously. The possibility that your house was raided by mistake or that your friends are playing a strange practical joke on you is not wildly remote, but neither fits the overall facts very well. If it was a police raid, then you would expect to find a police officer there or at least a note. If it is a joke, then it is hard to see the point of it. By contrast, burglaries are not very unusual, and that hypothesis fits the facts extremely well. Logically, the situation looks like this:

(1) OBSERVATION: Your lock is broken, and your valuables are missing.
(2) EXPLANATION: The hypothesis that your house has been burglarized, combined with previously accepted facts and principles, provides a suitably strong explanation of observation 1.
(3) COMPARISON: No other hypothesis provides an explanation nearly as good as that in 2.

∴(4) CONCLUSION: Your house was burglarized.

The explanatory power of the conclusion gives us reason to believe it because doing so increases our ability to understand our observations and to make reliable predictions. Explanation is important because it makes sense out of things—makes them more intelligible—and we want to understand the world around us. Prediction is important because it tests our theories with new data and sometimes allows us to anticipate or even control future events. Inference to the best explanation enables us to achieve such goals.

Here it might help to compare inferences to the best explanation with other forms of argument. Prior to any belief about burglars, you were already *justified* in believing *that* your lock was broken and your valuables were missing. You could see that much. What you could not see was *why* your lock was broken. That question is what the explanation answers. Explanations help us understand why things happen, when we are already justified in believing those things did happen. (Recall Chapter 1.)

Explanations often take the form of arguments. In our example, we could argue:

(1) Your house was burglarized.
(2) When houses are burglarized, valuables are missing.

∴(3) Your valuables are missing.

This explanatory argument starts with the hypothesis that was the conclusion of the inference to the best explanation, and it ends with the observation that was the first premise in that inference to the best explanation. The difference is that this new argument *explains* why its conclusion is true—why the valuables are missing—whereas the inference to the best explanation *justified* belief in its conclusion that your house was burglarized.

More generally, in an explanatory use of argument, we try to make sense of something by deriving it (sometimes deductively) from premises that are themselves well established. With an inference to the best explanation, we reason in the opposite direction: Instead of deriving an observation from its explanation, we derive the explanation from the observation. That a hypothesis provides the best explanation of something whose truth is already known provides evidence for the truth of that hypothesis.

Once we grasp the notion of an inference to the best explanation, we can see this pattern of reasoning everywhere. If you see your friend kick the wall, you infer that he must be angry, because there is no other explanation of why he would kick the wall. Then if he turns away when you say, "Hello," you might think that he is angry *at you,* if you cannot imagine any other reason why he would not respond. Similarly, when your car goes dead right after a checkup, you may conclude that it is out of fuel, if that is the best explanation of why your car stopped. Psychologists infer that people care what others think about them, even when they deny it, because that explains why people behave differently in front of others than when they are alone. Linguists argue that the original Indo-European language arose millennia ago in an area that was not next to the sea but did have lakes and rivers, because that is the best explanation of why Indo-European languages have no common word for seas but do share a common root "nav-" that connotes boats or ships. Astronomers believe that our Universe began with a Big Bang, because that hypothesis best explains the background microwave radiation and spreading of galaxies. All of these arguments and many more are basically inferences to the best explanation.

Solutions to murder mysteries almost always have the form of an inference to the best explanation. The facts of the case are laid out and then the clever detective argues that, given these facts, only one person could possibly have committed the crime. In the story "Silver Blaze," Sherlock Holmes concludes that the trainer must have been the dastardly fellow who stole Silver Blaze, the horse favored to win the Wessex Cup, which was to be run the following day. Holmes's reasoning, as usual, was very complex, but the key part of his argument was that the dog kept in the stable did not bark loudly when someone came and took away the horse.

> I had grasped the significance of the silence of the dog, for one true inference invariably suggests others. [I knew that] a dog was kept in the stables, and yet, though someone had been in and fetched out a horse, he had not barked enough to arouse the two lads in the loft. Obviously the midnight visitor was someone whom the dog knew well.[2]

Together with other facts, this was enough to identify the trainer, Straker, as the person who stole Silver Blaze. In this case, it is the fact that something *didn't* occur that provides the basis for an inference to the best explanation.

Of course, Holmes's inference is not absolutely airtight. It is possible that Straker is innocent and Martians with hypnotic powers over dogs committed the crime. But that only goes to show that this inference is neither valid nor deductive in our sense. It does not show anything wrong with Holmes's inference. Since his inference is inductive, it is enough for it to be strong.

Inferences to the best explanation are also defeasible. No matter how strong such an inference might be, it can always be overturned by future experience. Holmes might later find traces of a sedative in the dog's blood or someone else might confess or provide Straker with an alibi. Alternatively, Holmes (or you) might think up some better explanation. Still, unless and until such new evidence or hypothesis comes along, we have adequate reason to believe that Straker stole the horse, because that hypothesis provides the best available explanation of the information that we have now. The fact that future evidence or hypotheses always might defeat inferences to the best explanation does not show that such inferences are all bad. If it did show this, then science and everyday life would be in trouble, because so much of science and our commonsense view of the world depends on inferences to the best explanation.

WHICH EXPLANATION IS BEST?

To assess such inferences, we still need some standards for determining which explanation is the *best*. There is, unfortunately, no simple rule for deciding this, but we can list some factors that go into the evaluation of an explanation.[3]

First, the hypothesis should really *explain the observations*. A good explanation makes sense out of that which it is intended to explain. In our original example, the broken lock can be explained by a burglary but not by the hypothesis that a friend came to see you (unless you have strange friends). Moreover, the hypothesis needs to explain *all* of the relevant observations. The hypothesis of a mistaken police raid might explain the broken lock but not the missing valuables or the lack of any note or police officers when you return home.

The explanation should also be *deep*. An explanation is not deep but shallow when the explanation itself needs to be explained. It does not help to explain something that is obscure by citing something just as obscure. Why did the police raid your house? Because they suspected you. That explanation is shallow if it immediately leads to another question: Why did they suspect you? Because they had the wrong address. If they did not have the wrong address, then we would wonder why they suspected you. Without an explanation of their suspicions, the police raid hypothesis could not adequately explain even the broken lock.

Third, the explanation should be *powerful*. It is a mark of excellence in an explanation that the same kind of explanation can be used successfully over a wide range of cases. Many broken locks can be explained by burglaries.

Explanatory range is especially important in science. One of the main reasons why Einstein's theory of relativity replaced Newtonian physics is that Einstein could explain a wider range of phenomena, including very small particles at very high speeds.

Explanations go too far, however, when they could explain any possible event. Consider the hypothesis that each particle of matter has its own individual spirit that makes it do exactly what it does. This hypothesis might seem to explain some phenomena that even Einstein's theory cannot explain. But the spirit hypothesis really explains nothing, because it does not explain why any particle behaves one way as opposed to another. Either behavior is compatible with the hypothesis, so neither is explained. To succeed, therefore, explanations need to be incompatible with some possible outcome. In short, they need to be *falsifiable*. (See Chapter 16 on self-sealers.)

Moreover, explanations should be *modest* in the sense that they should not claim too much—indeed, any more than is needed to explain the observations. When you find your lock broken and valuables gone, you should not jump to the conclusion that there is a conspiracy against you or that gangs have taken over your neighborhood. Without further information, there is no need to specify that there was more than one burglar in order to explain what you see. There is also no need to hypothesize that there was only one burglar. For this reason, the most modest explanation would not specify any number of burglars, so no inference to the best explanation could justify any claim about the number of burglars, at least until more evidence comes along.

Modesty is related to *simplicity*. One kind of simplicity is captured by the celebrated principle known as *Occam's razor*, which tells us not to multiply entities beyond necessity. Physicists, for example, should not postulate new kinds of subatomic particles or forces unless there is no other way to explain their experimental results. Similar standards apply in everyday life. We should not believe in ghosts unless they really are necessary to explain the noises in our attic or some other phenomenon. Simplicity is not always a matter of new kinds of entities. In comparison with earlier views, the theory that gases are composed of particles too small to see was simpler insofar as the particle theory allowed gas laws to be explained by the standard physical principles governing the motions of larger particles without having to add any new laws. Simplicity is a mark of excellence in an explanation partly because simple explanations are easier to understand and apply, but considerations of plausibility and aesthetics are also at work in judgments of which explanation is simplest.

The tests of modesty and simplicity might seem to be in tension with the test of power. This tension can be resolved only by finding the right balance. The best explanation will not claim any more than is necessary (so it will be modest), but it will claim enough to cover a wide range of phenomena (so it will be powerful). This is tricky, but the best explanations succeed in reconciling and incorporating these conflicting virtues as much as possible.

Finally, an explanation should be *conservative*. Explanations are better when they force us to give up fewer well-established beliefs. We have strong reasons to believe that cats cannot break metal locks. This rules out the hypothesis that your neighbor's cat broke your front-door lock. Explanations should also not contain claims that are themselves too unlikely to be true. A meteorite would be strong enough to break your lock, but it is very unlikely that a meteorite struck your lock. That makes the burglary hypothesis better, at least until we find other evidence (such as meteorite fragments) that cannot be explained except by a meteorite.

In sum, a hypothesis provides the best explanation when it is more explanatory, broad, powerful, falsifiable, modest, simple, and conservative than any competing hypothesis. Each of these standards can be met to varying degrees, and they can conflict. As we saw, the desire for simplicity might have to be sacrificed to gain a more powerful explanation. Conservatism also might have to give way to explain some unexpected observations, and so on. These standards are not always easy to apply, but they can often be used to determine which explanation is best.

Once we determine that one explanation is the best, we still cannot yet infer that it is true. It might turn out that the best explanation out of a group of weak explanations isn't good enough. For centuries people were baffled by the floods that occurred in the Nile river each spring. The Nile, as far as anyone knew, flowed from an endless desert. Where, then, did the flood waters come from? Various wild explanations were suggested—mostly about deities of one kind or another—but none was any good. Looking for the best explanation among these weak explanations would be a waste of time. It was only after it was discovered that central Africa contains a high mountain range covered with snow in the winter that a reasonable explanation became possible. That, in fact, settled the matter. So it must be understood that the best explanation must also be a *good enough* explanation.

Even when an explanation is both good and best, what it explains might be illusory. Many people believe that shark cartilage prevents cancer, because the best explanation of why sharks do not get cancer lies in their cartilage. One serious problem for this inference is that sharks *do* get cancer. They even get cancer in their cartilage. So this inference to the best explanation fails.

When a particular explanation is both good and much better than any competitor, and when the explained observation is accurate, then an inference to the best explanation will provide *strong* inductive support. At other times, no clear winner or even reasonable contender emerges. In such cases, an inference to the best explanation will be correspondingly *weak*.

CONTEXT IS CRUCIAL

Whether an inference to the best explanation is strong *enough* depends on the context. As contexts shift, standards of rigor can change. Evidence that is strong enough to justify my belief that my spouse took our car might not be strong enough to convict our neighbor of stealing our car. Good judgment is often required to determine whether a certain degree of strength is adequate for the purposes at hand.

Context can also affect the rankings of various factors. Many explanations, for example, depend on universal premises. In such cases, compatibility with observation is usually the primary test. The universal principle should not be refuted by counterexamples (see Chapter 17). But sometimes explanatory power will take precedence: If a principle has strong explanatory power, we may accept it even in the face of clear disconfirming evidence. We do not give up good explanations lightly—nor should we. One reason is that we do not test single propositions in isolation from other propositions in our system of beliefs. When faced with counterevidence to our beliefs, we often have a choice between what to give up and what to continue to hold on to. A simple example will illustrate this. Suppose that we believe the following things:

(1) Either John or Joan committed the crime.
(2) Whoever committed the crime must have had a motive for doing so.
(3) Joan had no motive to commit the crime.

From these three premises we can validly infer that John committed the crime. Suppose, however, that we discover that John could not have committed the crime. (Three bishops and two judges swear that John was somewhere else at the time.) Now, from the fact that John did not commit the crime, we could not immediately conclude that Joan committed it, for that would lead to an inconsistency. If she committed the crime, then, according to premise 3, she would have committed a motiveless crime, but that conflicts with premise 2, which says that motiveless crimes do not occur. So the discovery that John did not commit the crime entails that at least one of the premises in the argument must be abandoned, but it does not tell us which one or which ones.

This same phenomenon occurs when we are dealing with counterevidence to a complex system of beliefs. Counterevidence shows that there must be something wrong somewhere in the system, but it does not show exactly where the problem lies. One possibility is that the *supposed* counterevidence is itself in error. Imagine that a student carries out an experiment and gets the result that one of the fundamental laws of physics is false. This will not shake the scientific community even a little, for the best explanation of the student's result is that she messed things up. Given well-established principles, she could not have gotten the result she did if she had run the experiment correctly. Of course, if a great many reputable scientists find difficulties with a supposed law, then the situation is different. The hypothesis that all of these scientists, like the student, simply messed up is itself highly unlikely. But it is surprising how much contrary evidence will be tolerated when dealing with a strong explanatory theory. Scientists often continue to employ a theory in the face of counterevidence. Sometimes this perpetuates errors. For years, instruments reported that the levels of ozone above Antarctica were lower than before, but scientists attributed these measurements to bad equipment, until finally they announced an ozone hole there. Still, there is often good reason to hold on to a useful theory despite counterevidence, as long as its defects do not make serious trouble—that is, give bad results in areas that count. Good judgment is required to determine when it is finally time to shift to a different explanation.

EXERCISE I

Imagine that you offer an explanation, and a critic responds in the following way. Which virtue (explanatoriness, depth, power, falsifiability, modesty, simplicity, or conservativeness) is your critic claiming that your explanation lacks?

1. But that won't explain anything other than this particular case.
2. But that conflicts with everything we know about biology.
3. But you don't have to claim all of that in order to explain what we see.
4. But that just raises new questions that you need to answer.
5. But that explains only a small part of the story.
6. But that would apply whatever happened.

EXERCISE II

For each of the following explanations, specify which standard of a good explanation, if any, it violates. The standards require that a good explanation be explanatory, deep, powerful, falsifiable, modest, simple, and conservative. A single explanation might violate more than one standard.

1. Although we usually have class at this time in this room, I don't see anybody in the classroom, because a wicked witch made them all invisible.
2. Although we usually have class at this time in this room, I don't see anybody in the classroom, because they all decided to skip class today.
3. Although we usually have class at this time in this room, I don't see anybody in the classroom, because it's Columbus Day.
4. My house fell down, because it was painted red.
5. My house fell down, because of a powerful earthquake centered on my property that did not affect anything or anybody else.
6. My house fell down, because its boards were struck by a new kind of subatomic particle.
7. Although I fished here all day, I didn't catch any fish, because there are no fish in this whole river.
8. Although I fished here all day, I didn't catch any fish, because the river gods don't like me.
9. Although I fished here all day, I didn't catch any fish, because I was unlucky today.
10. That light far up in the night sky is moving quickly, because it is the daily United Airlines flight from Boston to Los Angeles.
11. That light far up in the night sky is moving quickly, because it is an alien space ship.
12. That light far up in the night sky looks like it is moving quickly, because there's something wrong with my eyes right now.

EXERCISE III

Give two competing hypotheses that might be offered to explain each of the following phenomena. Which of these hypotheses is better? Why?

1. You follow a recipe carefully, but the bread never rises.
2. Your house begins to shake so violently that pictures fall off your walls.
3. Your key will not open the door of your house.
4. People start putting television cameras on your lawn, and a man with a big smile comes walking up your driveway.
5. Virtually all of the food in markets has suddenly sold out.
6. You put on a shirt and notice that there is no pocket on the front like there used to be.
7. A cave is found containing the bones of both prehistoric humans and now-extinct predators.
8. A cave is found containing the bones of both prehistoric humans and now-extinct herbivores.
9. After being visited by lobbyists for cigarette producers, your senator votes in favor of tobacco price supports, although he opposed them before.
10. Large, mysterious patterns of flattened wheat appear in the fields of Britain. (Some people attribute these patterns to visitors from another planet.)
11. A palm reader foretells that something wonderful will happen to you soon, and it does.
12. A neighbor sprinkles purple powder on his lawn to keep away tigers, and, sure enough, no tigers show up on his lawn.

DISCUSSION QUESTIONS

1. Read a murder mystery or detective story. Is the solution based on an inference to the best explanation? If so, put that inference in standard form, and evaluate it using the tests discussed above.
2. In the Discussion Question at the end of Chapter 1, Colin Powell gives several arguments that in 2003 Saddam Hussein was still trying to obtain fissile material for a nuclear weapons program. Which of Powell's arguments is an inference to the best explanation? How well do these arguments meet the standards for this form of argument?
3. Put the following inference to the best explanation in standard form, and then evaluate it as carefully as you can, using the tests discussed above.

(continued)

[During the Archean Era, which extended from about 3.8 to 2.5 million years before the present,] the sun's luminosity was perhaps 25% less than that of today. . . . This faint young sun has led to a paradox. There is no evidence from the scant rock record of the Archean that the planetary surface was frozen. However, if Earth had no atmosphere or an atmosphere of composition like that of today, the amount of radiant energy received by Earth from the sun would not be enough to keep it from freezing. The way out of this dilemma is to have an atmosphere present during the early Archean that was different in composition that that of today. . . . For a variety of reasons, it has been concluded, although still debated, that the most likely gases present in greater abundance in the Archean atmosphere were carbon dioxide, water vapor (the most important greenhouse gas) and perhaps methane. The presence of these greenhouse gases warmed the atmosphere and planetary surface and prevented the early Archean Earth from being frozen.[4]

4. Find three more inferences to the best explanation in articles about science in a newspaper, magazine, or professional journal. This should be easy because scientists often use this form of argument. Put those inferences in standard form, and then evaluate them using the tests discussed above.

ARGUMENTS FROM ANALOGY

Another very common kind of inductive argument moves from a premise that two things are similar in some respects to a conclusion that they must also be analogous in a further respect. Such arguments from analogy can be found in many areas of everyday life. When we buy a new car, how can we tell whether it is going to be reliable? *Consumer Reports* might help if it is an old model; but if it is a brand-new model with no track record, then all we can go on is its similarities to earlier models. Our reasoning then seems to be that the new model is like the old model in various ways, and the old model was reliable, so the new model is probably reliable, too.

The same form of argument is used in science. Here's an example from geology:

Meteorites composed predominantly of iron provide evidence that parts of other bodies in the solar system, presumably similar in origin to Earth, were composed of metallic iron. The evidence from meteorite compositions and origins lends support to the conclusion that Earth's core is metallic iron.[5]

The argument here is that Earth is analogous to certain meteors in their origins, and those meteors have a large percentage of iron, so the Earth as a whole probably contains about the same percentage of iron. Because a smaller amount of iron is present in the Earth's crust, the rest must lie in the Earth's core.

Similarly, archaeologists might argue that a certain knife was used in ritual sacrifices because it resembles other sacrificial knives in its size, shape, materials, carvings, and so on. The analogy in this case is between the newly discovered knife and the other knives. This analogy is supposed to support a conclusion about the function of the newly discovered knife.

Although such arguments from analogy have diverse contents, they share a common form that can be represented like this:

(1) Object *A* has properties *P, Q, R,* and so on.
(2) Objects *B, C, D,* and so on also have properties *P, Q, R,* and so on.
(3) Objects *B, C, D,* and so on have property *X.*

∴(4) Object *A* probably also has property *X.*

In the archaeological example, object *A* is the newly discovered knife, and objects *B, C, D,* and so on are previously discovered knives that are known to have been used in sacrifices. Properties *P, Q, R,* and so on are the size, shape, materials, and carvings that make *A* analogous to *B, C, D,* and so on. *X* is the property of being used as a sacrificial knife. Premise 3 says that the previously discovered artifacts have this property. The conclusion, on line 4, says that the newly discovered artifact probably also has this property.

Since arguments from analogy are inductive, they normally aren't valid. It is possible that, even though this knife is analogous to other sacrificial knives, this knife was used to shave the king or just to cut bread. These arguments are also defeasible. The argument about knives obviously loses all of its strength if we find "Made in China" printed on the newly discovered knife. Still, none of this shows that arguments from analogy are no good. Despite being invalid and defeasible, some arguments from analogy can still provide reasons—even strong reasons—for their conclusions.

How can we tell whether an argument from analogy is strong or weak? One obvious requirement is that the premises must be *true.* If the previously discovered knives were not really used in sacrifices, or if they do not really have the same carvings on their handles as the newly discovered knife, then this argument from analogy does not provide much, if any, support for its conclusion.

In addition, the cited similarities must be *relevant.* Suppose someone argues that his old car was red with a black interior and had four doors and a sunroof, and his new car also has these properties, so his new car is probably going to be as reliable as his old car. This argument is very weak because the cited similarities are obviously irrelevant to reliability. Such assessments of relevance depend on background beliefs, such as that reliability depends on the drive train and the engine rather than on the color or the sunroof.

The similarities must also be *important.* Similarities are usually more important the more specific they are. Lots of cars with four tires and a motor are reliable, but this is not enough to infer that, because this particular car also has four tires and a motor, it will be reliable, too. The reason is obvious: There are also lots of unreliable cars with four tires and a motor. In general, if many objects have properties *P, Q,* and *R,* and many of those lack property *X,* then arguments from these analogies will be weak. In contrast, if a smaller percentage of objects that have properties P, Q, and R lack property X, then the argument from these analogies will be strong.

If we are not sure which respects *are* important, we still might have some idea of which respects *might* be important. Then we can try to cite objects that are analogous in as many as possible of those respects. By increasing the number of potentially relevant respects for which the analogy holds, we can increase the likelihood that the important respects will be on our list. That shows why arguments from analogy are usually stronger when they cite *more and closer analogies* between the objects.

Another factor that affects the strength of an argument from analogy is the presence of *relevant disanalogies*. Because arguments from analogy are defeasible, as we saw, a strong argument from analogy can become weak if we add a premise that states an important disanalogy. Suppose my new car is like my old cars in many ways, but there is one difference: The new car has an electric motor, whereas the old cars were powered by gasoline. This one difference is enough to weaken any argument to the conclusion that the new car will be reliable. Of course, other disanalogies, such as a different color, won't matter to reliability; and it will often require background knowledge to determine how important a disanalogy is.

We need to be careful here. Some disanalogies that are relevant do not undermine an argument from analogy. If a new engine design was introduced by top engineers to increase reliability, then this disanalogy might not undermine the argument from analogy. Differences that point to more reliability rather than less might even make the argument from analogy stronger.

Other disanalogies can increase the strength of an argument from analogy in a different way. If the same markings are found on very different kinds of sacrificial knives, then the presence of those markings on the newly discovered knife is even stronger evidence that this knife was also used in sacrifices. Differences among the cases cited only in the premises as analogies (that is, B, C, D, and so on) can strengthen an argument from analogy.

Finally, the strength of an argument from analogy depends on its conclusion. Analogies to other kinds of cars provide stronger evidence for a weak conclusion (such as that the new model will probably be pretty reliable) and weaker evidence for a strong conclusion (such as that the new model will definitely be just as reliable as the old model). As with other forms of argument, an argument from analogy becomes stronger as its conclusion becomes weaker and vice versa.

These standards can be summarized by saying that an argument from analogy is stronger when:

1. It cites more and closer analogies that are more important.
2. There are fewer or less important disanalogies between the object in the conclusion and the other objects.
3. The objects cited only in the premises are more diverse.
4. The conclusion is weaker.

ARE ANALOGIES EXPLANATIONS?

After learning about arguments from analogy, it is natural to wonder how they are related to inferences to the best explanation. Although this is sometimes disputed, it seems to us that arguments from analogy are often—if not always—implicit and incomplete inferences to the best explanation. As we pointed out, analogies don't support any conclusion unless they are relevant, and whether they are relevant depends on how they fit into explanations. The color of a car is irrelevant to its reliability, because color plays no role in explaining its reliability. What explains its reliability is its drive train design, materials, care in manufacturing, and so on. That is why analogies in those respects can support a conclusion about reliability. Similarly, the markings on an artifact are relevant to whether it is a sacrificial knife *if* the best explanation of why it has those markings is that it was used in sacrifices. What makes that explanation best is that it also explains similar markings on other sacrificial knives. Thus, such arguments from analogy can be seen as involving an inference to the best explanation of why objects B, C, D, and so on have property X followed by an application of that explanation to the newly discovered object A.

Sometimes the explanation runs in the other direction. Whereas the conclusion about the knife's use (X) is supposed to explain its shared markings (P, Q, R), sometimes it is the shared features (P, Q, R) that are supposed to explain the feature claimed in the conclusion (X). Here is a classic example:

> We may observe a very great [similarity] between this earth which we inhabit, and the other planets, Saturn, Jupiter, Mars, Venus, and Mercury. They all revolve around the sun, as the earth does, although at different distances and in different periods. They borrow all their light from the sun, as the earth does. Several of them are known to revolve around their axis like the earth, and, by that means, must have a like succession of day and night. Some of them have moons that serve to give them light in the absence of the sun, as our moon does to us. They are all, in their motions, subject to the same law of gravitation, as the earth is. From all this similarity it is not unreasonable to think that those planets may, like our earth, be the habitation of various orders of living creatures. There is some probability in this conclusion from analogy.[6]

The argument here seems to be that some other planet probably supports life, because Earth does and other planets are similar to Earth in revolving around the sun and around an axis, getting light from the sun, and so on. What makes certain analogies relevant is not, of course, that the motion of Earth is explained by the presence of life here. Rather, certain features of Earth explain why Earth is habitable. The argument suggests that the best explanation of why there is life on our planet is that certain conditions make life possible. That generalization can then be used to support the conclusion that other planets with the same conditions probably support life as well.

In one way or another, many (or maybe even all) arguments from analogy can be seen as inferences to the best explanation. But they are usually incomplete explanations. The argument for life on other planets did not have to commit itself to any particular theory about the origin of life or about which conditions are needed to support life. Nor did the car argument specify exactly what makes cars reliable. Such arguments from analogy merely list a number of similarities so that the list will be likely to include whatever factors are needed for life or for reliability. In this way, arguments from analogy can avoid depending on any complete theory about what is and what is not relevant.

This incompleteness makes arguments from analogy useful in situations where we do not yet know enough to formulate detailed theories or even to complete an inference to the best explanation. Yet, the incompleteness of arguments from analogy also makes them more vulnerable to refutation, since the analogies that they list might fail to include a crucial respect. This does not mean that arguments from analogy are never any good. They can be strong. However, it does suggest that their strength will increase as they approach or approximate more complete inferences to the best explanation.

EXERCISE IV

For each of the following arguments, state whether the indicated changes would make the argument weaker or stronger, and explain why. The strength of the argument might not be affected at all. If so, say why it is not affected.

1. My friend and I have seen many movies together, and we have always agreed on whether they are good or bad. My friend liked the movie trilogy *The Lord of the Rings*. So I probably will like it as well.

Would this argument be weaker or stronger if:

   a. The only movies that my friend and I have watched together are comedies, and *The Lord of the Rings* is not a comedy.

   b. My friend and I have seen very many, very different movies together.

   c. My friend and I always watched movies together on Wednesdays, but my friend watched *The Lord of the Rings* on a weekend.

   d. The conclusion claims that I definitely will like *The Lord of the Rings* a lot.

   e. The conclusion claims that I probably won't totally dislike *The Lord of the Rings*.

2. All the students from Joe's high school with high grades and high board scores did well in college. Joe also had high grades and board scores. So he will probably do well in college.

Would this argument be weaker or stronger if:

   a. The other students worked hard, but Joe's good grades came easily to him, so he never learned to work hard.

   b. Joe is going to a different college than the students with whom he is being compared.

    c. Joe plans to major in some easy subject, but the other students were pre-med.

    d. Joe recently started taking drugs on a regular basis.

    e. Joe needs to work full-time to pay his college expenses, but the others had their expenses paid by their parents.

3. A new drug cures a serious disease in rats. Rats are similar to humans in many respects. Therefore, the drug will probably cure the same disease in humans.

Would this argument be weaker or stronger if:

    a. The disease affects the liver, and rat livers are very similar to human livers.

    b. The drug does not cure this disease in cats.

    c. The drug has to be injected into the rat's tail to be effective (that is, it does not work if it is injected anywhere else in the rat).

    d. No drug of this general type has been used on humans before.

    e. The effects of the drug are enhanced by eating cooked foods.

EXERCISE V

Using the criteria mentioned above, evaluate each of the following arguments as strong or weak. Explain your answers. Be sure to specify the properties on which the analogy is based, as well as any background beliefs on which your evaluation depends.

1. This landscape by Cézanne is beautiful. He did another painting of a similar scene around the same time. So it is probably beautiful, too.

2. My aunt had a Siamese cat that bit me, so this Siamese cat will probably bite me, too.

3. The students I know who took this course last year got grades of A. I am a lot like them, since I am also smart and hardworking; and the course this year covers very similar material. So I will probably get an A.

4. This politician was caught cheating in his marriage, and he will have to face similarly strong temptations in his public duties, so he will probably cheat in political life as well.

5. A very high minimum wage led to increased unemployment in one country. That country's economy is similar to the economy in a different country. So a very high minimum wage will probably lead to increased unemployment in the other country as well.

6. I feel pain when someone hits me hard on the head with a baseball bat. Your body is a lot like mine. So you would probably feel pain if I hit you hard on the head with a baseball bat. (This is related to the so-called Problem of Other Minds.)

7. It is immoral for a doctor to lie to a patient about a test result, even if the doctor thinks that lying is in the patient's best interest. We know this because even doctors would agree that it would be morally wrong for a financial adviser to lie to them about a potential investment, even if the financial advisor thinks that this lie is in the doctor's best interests.

8. Chrysler was held legally liable for damages due to defects in the suspension of its Corvair. The defects in the Pinto gas tank caused injuries that were just as serious. Thus, Ford should also be held legally liable for damages due to those defects.

DISCUSSION QUESTIONS

1. The following excerpt presents evidence that Neanderthals were cannibals. Put the central argument from analogy, which is italicized here, into standard form. Then reconstruct the argument as an inference to the best explanation. Which representation best captures the force of the argument, or are they equally good?

"A GNAWING QUESTION IS ANSWERED"[7]

Tim White is worried that he may have helped to pin a bad rap on the Neanderthals, the prehistoric Europeans who died out 25,000 years ago. "There is a danger that everyone will think that all Neanderthals were cannibals and that's not necessarily true," he says. White was part of a French-American team of paleoanthropologists who recently found conclusive evidence that at least some Neanderthals ate others about 100,000 years ago. But that doesn't mean they were cannibalistic by nature, he stresses. Most people don't realize that cannibalism is widespread throughout nature, says White, a professor at the University of California at Berkeley and the author of a book on prehistoric cannibalism.

The question of whether the Neanderthals were cannibals had long been a hotly debated topic among anthropologists. No proof had ever been found. That debate ended, however, with the recent analysis by the team of stone tools and bones found in a cave at Moula-Guercy in southern France. The cave is about the size of a living room, perched about 80 metres above the Rhone River. "This one site has all of the evidence right together," says White. "It's as if somebody put a yellow tape around the cave for 100,000 years and kept the scene intact." The bones of deer and other fauna show the clear markings of the nearby stone tools, indicating the deer had been expertly butchered; they were skinned, their body parts cut off and the meat and tendons sliced from

Source: A Gnawing Question is Answered by Michael Downey as appeared in THE TORONTO STAR, October 10, 1999.

the bone. Long bones were bashed open "to get at the fatty marrow inside," says White.

So what does all this have to do with cannibalism? *The bones of the six (so far) humans in the same locations have precisely the same markings made by the same tools. That means these fairly modern humans were skinned and eaten in the same manner as the deer.*

And if you are thinking they were eaten after they just happened to die, they do represent all age groups. Two were children about 6 years old, two were teenagers, and two were adults.

But maybe they were eaten at a time when food was unusually scarce, right? Not so. There is a large number of animal bones at the same dig, indicating that there were options to eating other Neanderthals.

Human bones with similar cut marks have been found throughout Europe, from Spain to Croatia, providing tantalizing hints of Neanderthal cannibalism activity over tens of thousands of years. But finding such clear evidence of the same preparation techniques being used on deer in the same cave site in France, will "necessitate reassessment of earlier finds," always attributed to ritual burial practices or some other explanation, says White.

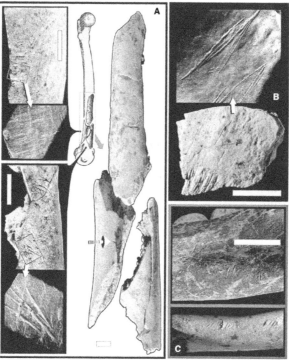

From DEFLEUR ET AL., SCIENCE 286:128 (1999). Reprinted with permission from AAAS.

(continued)

2. In the following passage, William Paley argues for the existence of God on the basis of an analogy to a watch. Reconstruct this argument from analogy and then evaluate it by applying the criteria discussed above. Could Paley's argument also be reconstructed as an inference to the best explanation? If so, would that reconstruction better capture the force of the argument?

"THE WATCH AND THE WATCHMAKER"[8]

In crossing a heath, suppose I pitched my foot against a stone and were asked how the stone came to be there, I might possibly answer that for anything I knew to the contrary it had lain there forever; nor would it, perhaps, be very easy to show the absurdity of this answer. But suppose I had found a watch upon the ground, and it should be inquired how the watch happened to be in that place, I should hardly think of the answer which I had before given, that for anything I knew the watch might have always been there. Yet why should not this answer serve for the watch as well as for the stone? Why is it not as admissible in the second case as in the first? For this reason, and for no other, namely, that when we come to inspect the watch, we perceive—what we could not discover in the stone—that its several parts are framed and put together for a purpose, e.g., that they are so formed and adjusted as to produce motion, and that motion so regulated as to point out the hour of the day; that if the different parts had been differently shaped from what they are, of a different size from what they are, or placed after any other manner or in any other order than that in which they are placed, either no motion at all would have been carried on in the machine, or none which would have answered the use that is now served by it. . . . This mechanism being observed—it requires indeed an examination of the instrument, and perhaps some previous knowledge of the subject, to perceive and understand it; but being once, as we have said, observed and understood—the inference we think is inevitable, that the watch must have had a maker—that there must have existed, at some time and at some place or other, an artificer or artificers who formed it for the purpose which we find it actually to answer, who comprehended its construction and designed its use. . . .

[E]very indication of contrivance, every manifestation of design, which existed in the watch, exists in the works of nature; with the difference, on the side of nature, of being greater and more, and that in a degree which exceeds all computation. I mean that the contrivances of nature surpass the contrivances of art, in the complexity, subtlety, and curiosity of the mechanism; and still more, if possible, do they go beyond them in number and variety; yet in a multitude of cases, are not less evidently mechanical, not less evidently contrivances, not less evidently accommodated to their end, or suited to their office, than are the most perfect productions of human ingenuity.

I know no better method of introducing so large a subject, than that of comparing a single thing with a single thing: an eye, for example, with a telescope. As far as the examination of the instrument goes, there is precisely the same proof that the eye was made for vision, as there is that the telescope was made for assisting it. They are made upon the same principles; both being adjusted to the laws by which the transmission and refraction of rays of light are regulated. I speak not of the origin of the laws themselves; but such laws being fixed, the construction in both cases is adapted to them. . . .

To some it may appear a difference sufficient to destroy all similitude between the eye and the telescope, that the one is a perceiving organ, the other an unperceiving instrument. The fact is that they are both instruments. And as to the mechanism, at least as to mechanism being employed, and even as to the kind of it, this circumstance varies not the analogy at all. . . . The end is the same; the means are the same. The purpose in both is alike; the contrivance for accomplishing that purpose is in both alike. The lenses of the telescopes, and the humors of the eye, bear a complete resemblance to one another, in their figure, their position, and in their power over the rays of light, viz. in bringing each pencil to a point at the right distance from the lens; namely, in the eye, at the exact place where the membrane is spread to receive it. How is it possible, under circumstances of such close affinity, and under the operation of equal evidence, to exclude contrivance from the one; yet to acknowledge the proof of contrivance having been employed, as the plainest and clearest of all propositions, in the other? . . .

Were there no example in the world of contrivance except that of the *eye*, it would be alone sufficient to support the conclusion, which we draw from it, as to the necessity of an intelligent Creator. . . . The proof is not a conclusion that lies at the end of a chain of reasoning, of which chain each instance of contrivance is only a link, and of which, if one link fail, the whole fails; but it is an argument separately supplied by every separate example. An error in stating an example affects only that example. The argument is cumulative in the fullest sense of that term. The eye proves it without the ear; the ear without the eye. The proof in each example is complete; for when the design of the part and the conduciveness of its structure to that design is shown, the mind may set itself at rest; no further consideration can detract anything from the force of the example.

NOTES

[1] Gilbert Harman deserves much credit for calling attention to the importance of inferences to the best explanation; see, for example, his *Thought* (Princeton, NJ: Princeton University Press, 1973). A similar form of argument called abduction was analyzed long ago by Charles Sanders Peirce; see, for example, his *Collected Papers of Charles Sanders Peirce*, Vol. 5 (Cambridge, MA: Harvard University Press, 1931), 189. A wonderful recent discussion is Peter Lipton, *Inference to the Best Explanation* (London: Routledge, 1991).

[2] Sir Arthur Conan Doyle, "Silver Blaze," *The Complete Sherlock Holmes*, Vol. 1 (Garden City, NY: Doubleday, 1930), 349. The stories describe Holmes as a master of deduction, but his arguments are inductive as we define the terms.

[3] This discussion in many ways parallels and is indebted to the fifth chapter of W. V. Quine and J. S. Ullian, *The Web of Belief*, 2nd ed. (New York: Random House, 1978).

[4] From Fred T. Mackenzie, *Our Changing Planet* (Upper Saddle River, NJ: Prentice-Hall, 1998), 192.

[5] Ibid., 42.

[6] Thomas Reid, *Essays on the Intellectual Powers of Man* (Cambridge, MA: MIT Press, 1969), essay I, section 4, 48.

[7] From Michael Downey, *The Toronto Star*, October 10, 1999.

[8] From William Paley, *Natural Theology* (New York: Hopkins, 1836).

10

CAUSAL REASONING

One common way to explain a phenomenon is to cite its cause. You can understand why your clothes shrunk by learning what caused them to shrink. Was the water too hot when you washed them, did you dry them too long, or was it some combination of factors? In order to determine what causes what, we need to engage in a new kind of inductive reasoning—causal reasoning—*which is the topic of this chapter. Causal reasoning is often based on* negative *and* positive *tests for* necessary conditions *and for* sufficient conditions. *After developing these tests and applying them to a concrete example, we will discuss* concomitant variation *as a method of drawing causal conclusions from imperfect correlations. Our goal throughout this chapter is to improve our ability to identify causes so that we can better understand why certain effects happened and also make better predictions about whether similar events will happen in the future.*

REASONING ABOUT CAUSES

If our car goes dead in the middle of rush-hour traffic just after its 20,000-mile checkup, we assume that there must be some reason why this happened. Cars just don't stop for no reason at all. So we ask, "What caused our car to stop?" The answer might be that it ran out of gas. If we find, in fact, that it did run out of gas, then that will usually be the end of the matter. We will think that we have discovered why this particular car stopped running. This reasoning is about a particular car on a particular occasion, but it rests on certain *generalizations:* We are confident that our car stopped running when it ran out of gas, because we believe that all cars stop running when they run out of gas. We probably did not think about this, but our causal reasoning in this particular case appealed to a commonly accepted causal generalization: Lack of fuel causes cars to stop running. Many explanations depend on *causal generalizations.*

Causal generalizations are also used to *predict* the consequences of particular actions or events. A race car driver might wonder, for example, what would happen if he added just a bit of nitroglycerin to his fuel mixture. Would it give him better acceleration, blow him up, do very little, or what?

In fact, the driver may not be in a position to answer this question straight off, but his thinking will be guided by the causal generalization that igniting nitroglycerin can cause a dangerous explosion.

So a similar pattern arises for both causal explanation and causal prediction. These inferences contain two essential elements:

1. The facts in the particular case. (For example, the car stopped and the gas gauge reads empty; or I just put a pint of nitroglycerin in the gas tank of my Maserati, and I am about to turn the ignition key.)

2. Certain causal generalizations. (For example, cars do not run without gas, or nitroglycerin explodes when ignited.)

The basic idea is that causal inferences bring particular facts under causal generalizations.

This shows why causal generalizations are important, but what exactly are they? Although this issue remains controversial, here we will treat them as a kind of *general conditional*. A general conditional has the following form:

For all x, if x has the feature F, then x has the feature G.

We will say that, according to this conditional, x's having the feature F is a *sufficient condition* for its having the feature G; and x's having the feature G is a *necessary condition* for its having the feature F.

Some general conditionals are not *causal*. Neither of these two general conditionals expresses a causal relationship:

If something is a square, then it is a rectangle.

If you are eighteen years old, then you are eligible to vote.

The first conditional tells us that being a square is sufficient for being a rectangle, but this is a *conceptual* (or a priori) relationship, not a causal one. The second conditional tells us that being eighteen years old is a sufficient condition for being eligible to vote. The relationship here is *legal*, not causal.

Although many general conditionals are not causal, all causal conditionals are general, in our view. Consequently, if we are able to show that a causal conditional is false just by virtue of its being a general conditional, we will have refuted it. This will serve our purposes well, for in what follows we will be largely concerned with finding reasons for *rejecting* causal generalizations.

It is important to weed out false causal generalizations, because they can create lots of trouble. Doctors used to think that bloodletting would cure disease. They killed many people in the process of trying to heal them. Thus, although we need causal generalizations for getting along in the world, we also need to get them right. We will be more likely to succeed if we have proper principles for testing and applying such generalizations.

In the past, very elaborate procedures have been developed for this purpose. The most famous set of such procedures was developed by John Stuart Mill and has come to be known as Mill's methods.[1] Though inspired by Mill's methods, the procedures introduced here involve some fundamental simplifications; whereas Mill introduced five methods, we will introduce only three primary rules.

The first two rules are the sufficient condition test (SCT) and the necessary condition test (NCT). We will introduce these tests first at an abstract level. One advantage of formulating these tests abstractly is so that they can be applied to other kinds of sufficient and necessary conditions, for example, those that arise in legal and moral reasoning. Once it is clear how these tests work in general, we will apply them specifically to causal reasoning.

SUFFICIENT CONDITIONS AND NECESSARY CONDITIONS

To keep our discussion as general as possible, we will adopt the following definitions of sufficient conditions and necessary conditions:

Feature F is a *sufficient* condition for feature G if and only if anything that *has* feature F also *has* feature G.

Feature F is a *necessary* condition for feature G if and only if anything that *lacks* feature F also *lacks* feature G.

These definitions are equivalent to those in the previous section, because, if anything that *lacks* feature F also *lacks* feature G, then anything that *has* feature G must also *have* feature F; and if anything that *has* feature G must also *have* feature F, then anything that *lacks* feature F also *lacks* feature G. It follows that feature F is a sufficient condition for feature G if and only if feature G is a necessary condition for feature F.

When F is sufficient for G, the relation between these features can be diagrammed like this:

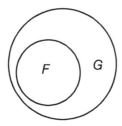

The inside circle represents the sufficient condition, because anything inside that inside circle must also be inside the outside circle. The outside circle represents the necessary condition, for anything outside the outside circle must also be outside the inside circle.

These diagrams, along with the preceding definitions, should make it clear that something can be a sufficient condition for a feature without being a necessary condition for that feature, and vice versa. For example, being the element mercury is a *sufficient* condition for being a metal, but it is not a *necessary* condition for being a metal, since there are other metals. Similarly, being a metal is a *necessary* condition for being mercury, but it is not a *sufficient* condition for being mercury. Of course, some necessary conditions are also sufficient conditions. Being mercury is both necessary and sufficient for being a metallic element that is liquid at twenty degrees Centigrade. Nonetheless, many necessary conditions are not sufficient conditions, and vice versa, so we need to be careful not to confuse the two kinds of conditions.

This distinction becomes complicated when conditions get complex. Our definitions and tests hold for all features, whether positive or negative (such as not having hair) and whether simple or conjunctive (such as having both a beard and a mustache) or disjunctive (such as having either a beard or a mustache). Thus, not having any hair (anywhere) on your head is a sufficient condition of not having a beard, so not having a beard is a necessary condition of not having any hair on your head. But not having any hair on your head is not necessary for not having a beard, because you can have some hair on the top of your head without having a beard. Negation can create confusion, so we need to think carefully about what is being claimed to be necessary or sufficient for what.

Even in simple cases without negation, conjunction, or disjunction, there is a widespread tendency to confuse necessary conditions with sufficient conditions. It is important to keep these concepts straight, for, as we will see, the tests concerning them are fundamentally different.

EXERCISE I

Which of the following claims are true? Which are false?

1. Being a car is a sufficient condition for being a vehicle.
2. Being a car is a necessary condition for being a vehicle.
3. Being a vehicle is a sufficient condition for being a car.
4. Being a vehicle is a necessary condition for being a car.
5. Being an integer is a sufficient condition for being an even number.
6. Being an integer is a necessary condition for being an even number.
7. Being an integer is a sufficient condition for being either an even number or an odd number.
8. Being an integer is a necessary condition for being either an even number or an odd number.
9. Not being an integer is a sufficient condition for not being an odd number.

10. Not being an integer is a sufficient condition for not being an even number.
11. Being both an integer and divisible by 2 without remainder is a sufficient condition for being an even number.
12. Being both an integer and divisible by 2 without remainder is a necessary condition for being an even number.
13. Being an integer divisible by 2 without remainder is a necessary condition for being an even number.
14. Driving seventy-five miles per hour (for fun) is a sufficient condition for violating a legal speed limit of sixty-five miles per hour.
15. Driving seventy-five miles per hour (for fun) is a necessary condition for violating a legal speed limit of sixty-five miles per hour.
16. Cutting off Joe's head is a sufficient condition for killing him.
17. Cutting off Joe's head is a necessary condition for killing him.
18. Cutting off Joe's head and then holding his head under water for ten minutes is a sufficient condition for killing him.

EXERCISE II

Indicate whether the following principles are true or false and why.

1. If having feature *F* is a *sufficient* condition for having feature *G*, then having feature *G* is a *necessary* condition for having feature *F*.
2. If having feature *F* is a *sufficient* condition for having feature *G*, then lacking feature *F* is a *necessary* condition for lacking feature *G*.
3. If lacking feature *F* is a *sufficient* condition for having feature *G*, then having feature *F* is a *necessary* condition for lacking feature *G*.
4. If lacking feature *F* is a *sufficient* condition for having feature *G*, then lacking feature *F* is a *necessary* condition for having feature *G*.
5. If having either feature *F* or feature *G* is a *sufficient* condition for having feature *H*, then having feature *F* is a *sufficient* condition for having feature *H*.
6. If having either feature *F* or feature *G* is a *sufficient* condition for having feature *H*, then having feature *G* is a *sufficient* condition for having feature *H*.
7. If having either feature *F* or feature *G* is a *sufficient* condition for having feature *H*, then not having feature *F* is a *necessary* condition for not having feature *H*.
8. If having both feature *F* and feature *G* is a *necessary* condition for having feature *H*, then lacking feature *F* is a *sufficient* condition for lacking feature *H*.
9. If not having both feature *F* and feature *G* is a *sufficient* condition for having feature *H*, then lacking feature *F* is a *sufficient* condition for having feature *H*.
10. If having either feature *F* or feature *G* is a *sufficient* condition for having feature *H*, then having both feature *F* and feature *G* is a *sufficient* condition for having feature *H*.

THE SUFFICIENT CONDITION TEST

We can now formulate tests to determine when something meets our definitions of sufficient conditions and necessary conditions. It will simplify matters if we first state these tests formally using letters. We will also begin with a simple case where we consider only four *candidates*—A, B, C, and D—for sufficient conditions for a *target* feature, G. A will indicate that the feature is present; ~A will indicate that this feature is absent. Using these conventions, suppose that we are trying to decide whether any of the four features—A, B, C, or D—could be a sufficient condition for G. To this end, we collect data of the following kind:

TABLE 1

Case 1:	A	B	C	D	G
Case 2:	~A	B	C	~D	~G
Case 3:	A	~B	~C	~D	~G

We know by definition that, for something to be a sufficient condition of something else, when the former is present, the latter must be present as well. Thus, to test whether a candidate really is a sufficient condition of G, we only have to examine cases in which the target feature, G, is absent, and then check to see whether any of the candidate features are present. The sufficient condition test (SCT) can be stated as follows:

SCT: Any candidate that is present when G is absent is eliminated as a possible sufficient condition of G.

The test applies to Table 1 as follows: Case 1 need not be examined because G is present, so there can be no violation of SCT in Case 1. Case 2 eliminates two of the candidates, B and C, for both are present in a situation in which G is absent. Finally, Case 3 eliminates A for the same reason. We are thus left with D as our only remaining candidate for a sufficient condition for G.

Now let's consider feature D. Having survived the application of the SCT, does it follow that D is a sufficient condition for G? No! On the basis of what we have been told so far, it remains entirely possible that the discovery of a further case will reveal an instance where D is present and G absent, thus showing that D is also not a sufficient condition for G.

Case 4:	~A	B	C	D	~G

In this way, it is always possible for new cases to refute any inference from a limited group of cases to the conclusion that a certain candidate is a sufficient condition. In contrast, no further case can change the fact that A, B, and C are not sufficient conditions, because they fail the SCT.

This observation shows that, when we apply the SCT to rule out a candidate as a sufficient condition, our argument is *deductive*. We simply find a counterexample to the universal claim that a certain feature is sufficient. (See Chapter 17 on counterexamples.) However, when a candidate is not ruled out and we draw the positive conclusion that that candidate *is* a sufficient condition, then our argument is *inductive*. Inductive inferences, however well confirmed, are always defeasible. (Recall Captain Cook's discovery of black swans at the start of Chapter 8.) That is why our inductive inference to the conclusion that D is a sufficient condition could be refuted by the new data in Case 4.

THE NECESSARY CONDITION TEST

The necessary condition test (NCT) is like the SCT, but it works in the reverse fashion. With the SCT, we eliminated a candidate F from being the sufficient condition for G, if F was ever present when G was absent. With the NCT, we eliminate a candidate F from being a necessary condition for G if we can find a case where G is present, but F is not. This makes sense, because if G can be present when F is not, then F cannot be necessary for the occurrence of G. Thus, in applying the necessary condition test, we only have to examine cases in which the target feature, G, is present, and then check to see whether any of the candidate features are absent.

NCT: Any candidate that is absent when G is present is eliminated as a possible necessary condition of G.

The following table gives an example of an application of this test:

TABLE 2

Case 1:	A	B	C	D	$\sim G$
Case 2:	$\sim A$	B	C	D	G
Case 3:	A	$\sim B$	C	$\sim D$	G

Because Case 1 does not provide an instance where G is present, it cannot eliminate any candidate as a necessary condition of G. Case 2 eliminates A as a necessary condition of G, since it shows that G can be present without A being present. Case 3 then eliminates both B and D, leaving C as the only possible candidate for being a necessary condition for G.

From this, of course, it does not follow that C *is* a necessary condition for G, for, as always, new cases might eliminate it as well. The situation is the same as with the SCT. An argument for a negative conclusion that a candidate is not a necessary condition, because that candidate fails the NCT, is a deductive argument that cannot be overturned by any further cases. In contrast, an argument for a positive conclusion that a candidate is a necessary condition, because that candidate passes the NCT, is an inductive argument that can be overturned by a further case where this candidate fails the NCT. For example, suppose we find:

Case 4:	$\sim A$	$\sim B$	$\sim C$	$\sim D$	G

The information in this new Case 4 is enough to show that C cannot be a necessary condition of the target feature G, regardless of what we found in Cases 1–3.

In applying both the SCT and the NCT, it is crucial to specify the target feature. Case 4 shows that candidate C is not a necessary condition for target feature G. Nonetheless, candidate C still might be necessary for the opposite target feature, ~G. It also might be necessary for features A, B, and D. Nothing in Cases 1–4 rules out these possibilities. Thus, even after Case 4, we cannot say simply that C is not a necessary condition. Case 4 shows that candidate feature C is not a necessary condition *for target feature G*, but C still might be necessary *for something else*. The same point applies to sufficient conditions as well. In Table 1, Case 2 ruled out the possibility that candidate feature B is sufficient for target feature G, but none of the cases in Table 1 show that B is not sufficient for target feature C. To avoid confusion, then, it is always important to specify the target feature when talking about what is or is not a necessary or sufficient condition.

THE JOINT TEST

It is also possible to apply these rules simultaneously in the search for possible conditions that are both sufficient and necessary. Any candidate cannot be both sufficient and necessary if it fails either the SCT or the NCT. In Table 2, C is the only possible necessary condition for G, and it is not also a possible sufficient condition for G, since C fails the SCT in Case 1, where C is present and G is absent. In Table 1, however, D is a possible sufficient condition of G, because D is never present when G is absent; and D might also be a necessary condition for G, since G is never present when D is absent. Thus, none of Cases 1–3 in Table 1 eliminates D as a candidate for a condition that is both sufficient and necessary for G. As before, this possibility still might be refuted by Case 4, so any inference to a positive conclusion that some candidate is a necessary and sufficient condition must be defeasible and, hence, inductive.

EXERCISE III

For each of the following tables determine

a. Which, if any, of the candidates—A, B, C, or D—is not eliminated by the *sufficient* condition test as a sufficient condition for target feature G?

b. Which, if any, of the candidates—A, B, C, or D—is not eliminated by the *necessary* condition test as a necessary condition for target feature G?

c. Which, if any, of the candidates—A, B, C, or D—is not eliminated by *either* test?

EXAMPLE:	Case 1:	A	B	~C	D	~G
	Case 2:	~A	B	C	D	G
	Case 3:	A	~B	C	D	G

a. Only C passes the SCT.

b. Only C and D pass the NCT.

c. Only C passes both tests.

1. Case 1:	A	B	C	D	G
Case 2:	~A	B	~C	D	~G
Case 3:	A	~B	C	~D	G
2. Case 1:	A	B	C	D	G
Case 2:	~A	B	C	D	G
Case 3:	A	~B	C	D	G
3. Case 1:	A	B	C	D	~G
Case 2:	~A	B	C	D	G
Case 3:	A	~B	C	~D	G
4. Case 1:	A	B	C	D	G
Case 2:	~A	~B	C	D	G
Case 3:	A	B	~C	~D	~G
5. Case 1:	A	B	C	D	~G
Case 2:	~A	B	C	~D	~G
Case 3:	A	~B	~C	D	G
6. Case 1:	A	B	~C	D	G
Case 2:	~A	~B	C	D	~G
Case 3:	A	~B	C	~D	~G
7. Case 1:	A	B	~C	D	~G
Case 2:	~A	B	~C	D	~G
Case 3:	A	B	~C	~D	~G
8. Case 1:	A	B	C	D	G
Case 2:	~A	~B	C	D	G
Case 3:	A	~B	~C	D	~G

EXERCISE IV

Imagine that your desktop computer system won't work, and you want to find out why. After checking to make sure that it is plugged in, you experiment with a new central processing unit (CPU), a new monitor (MO), and new system software (SW) in the combinations on the table below. The candidates for necessary conditions and sufficient conditions of failure are the plug position (in or out), the CPU (old or new), the monitor (old or new), and the software (old or new). For each candidate, say (1) which cases, if any, eliminate it as a sufficient condition of your computer's failure and (2) which cases, if any, eliminate it as a necessary condition of your computer's failure. Which candidates, if any, are not eliminated as a sufficient condition of failure? As a necessary condition of failure? Does it follow that these candidates are necessary conditions or sufficient conditions of failure? Why or why not?

(continued)

	Plug	CPU	Monitor	Software	Result
Case 1	In	Old CPU	Old MO	Old SW	Works
Case 2	In	Old CPU	Old MO	New SW	Works
Case 3	In	Old CPU	New MO	Old SW	Fails
Case 4	In	Old CPU	New MO	New SW	Works
Case 5	In	Old CPU	Old MO	Old SW	Works
Case 6	In	Old CPU	Old MO	New SW	Works
Case 7	In	Old CPU	New MO	Old SW	Fails
Case 8	In	Old CPU	New MO	New SW	Works
Case 9	In	New CPU	Old MO	Old SW	Fails
Case 10	In	New CPU	Old MO	New SW	Works
Case 11	In	New CPU	New MO	Old SW	Fails
Case 12	In	New CPU	New MO	New SW	Works

EXERCISE V

After a banquet, several diners get sick and die. You suspect that something they ate or drank caused their deaths. The following table records their meals and fates. The target feature is death. The candidates for necessary conditions and sufficient conditions of death are the soup, entrée, wine, and dessert. For each candidate, say (1) which cases, if any, eliminate it as a sufficient condition of death and (2) which cases, if any, eliminate it as a necessary condition of death. Which candidates, if any, are not eliminated as a sufficient condition of death? Which candidates, if any, are not eliminated as a necessary condition of death? Does it follow that these candidates are necessary conditions or sufficient conditions of death? Why or why not?

Diners	Soup	Entrée	Wine	Dessert	Result
Ann	Tomato	Chicken	White	Pie	Alive
Barney	Tomato	Fish	Red	Cake	Alive
Cathy	Tomato	Beef	Red	Ice Cream	Dead
Doug	Tomato	Beef	Red	Cake	Alive
Emily	Tomato	Fish	Red	Pie	Alive
Fred	Tomato	Fish	Red	Cake	Alive
Gertrude	Leek	Fish	White	Pie	Alive
Harold	Tomato	Beef	White	Cake	Alive
Irma	Leek	Fish	Red	Pie	Alive
Jack	Leek	Beef	Red	Ice Cream	Dead
Ken	Leek	Chicken	Red	Ice Cream	Alive
Leslie	Tomato	Chicken	White	Cake	Alive

RIGOROUS TESTING

Going back to Table 1, it is easy to see that candidates A, B, C, and D are not eliminated by the NCT as necessary conditions of target G, as G is present in only one case (Case 1) and A, B, C, and D are present there as well. So far, so good. But if we wanted to test these features more rigorously, it would be important to find more cases in which target G was present and see whether these candidates are also present and thus continue to survive the NCT.

The following table gives a more extreme example of nonrigorous testing:

TABLE 3

Case 1:	A	$\sim B$	C	D	G
Case 2:	A	$\sim B$	$\sim C$	$\sim D$	$\sim G$
Case 3:	A	$\sim B$	C	$\sim D$	$\sim G$
Case 4:	A	$\sim B$	$\sim C$	D	G

Here candidate feature A is eliminated by SCT (in Cases 2 and 3) but is not eliminated by NCT, so it is a possible necessary condition but not a possible sufficient condition for target feature G. B is not eliminated by SCT but is eliminated by NCT (in Cases 1 and 4), so it is a possible sufficient condition but not a possible necessary condition for target feature G. C is eliminated by both rules (in Cases 3 and 4). Only D is not eliminated by either test, so it is the only candidate for being both a necessary and a sufficient condition for G.

The peculiarity of this example is that candidate A is always present whether target G is present or not, and candidate B is always absent whether target G is absent or not. Now if something is always present, as A is, then it cannot possibly fail the NCT; for there cannot be a case where the target is present and the candidate is absent if the candidate is *always* present. If we want to test candidate A rigorously under the NCT, then we should try to find cases in which A is absent and then check to see whether G is absent as well.

In reverse fashion, but for similar reasons, if we want to test candidate B rigorously under the SCT, then we should try to find cases in which B is present and then check to see if G is present as well. If we restrict our attention to cases where B is always absent, as in Table 3, then B cannot possibly fail the SCT, but passing that test will be trivial for B and so will not even begin to show that B is a sufficient condition for G.

Now consider two more sets of data just like Table 2, except with regard to the target feature, G:

TABLE 4

Case 1:	A	B	C	D	G
Case 2:	$\sim A$	B	C	D	G
Case 3:	A	$\sim B$	C	$\sim D$	G

TABLE 5

Case 1:	A	B	C	D	~G
Case 2:	~A	B	C	D	~G
Case 3:	A	~B	C	~D	~G

Because G is present in all of the cases in Table 4, no candidate can be eliminated by the SCT as a sufficient condition for target feature G. This result is trivial, however. Table 4 does not provide rigorous testing for a sufficient condition of G, because our attention is restricted to a range of cases that is too narrow. Nothing could possibly be eliminated as a sufficient condition of G as long as G is always present.

Similarly, G is absent in all of the cases in Table 5, so no candidate can be eliminated by the NCT as a necessary condition of target feature G. Still, because this data is so limited, its failure to eliminate candidates does not even begin to show that anything is a necessary condition of G.

For both rules, then, rigorous testing involves seeking out cases in which failing the test is a live possibility. For the SCT, this requires looking both at cases in which the candidates are present and also at cases in which the target is absent. For the NCT, rigorous testing requires looking both at cases in which the candidates are absent and also at cases in which the target is present. Without cases like these, passing the tests is rather like a person bragging that he has never struck out when, in fact, he has never come up to bat.

REACHING POSITIVE CONCLUSIONS

Suppose that we performed rigorous testing on candidate C, and it passed the SCT with flying colors. Can we now draw the positive conclusion that C is a sufficient condition for the target G? That depends on which kinds of candidates and cases have been considered. Since rigorous testing was passed, these three conditions are met:

1. We have tested some cases in which the candidate, C, is present.
2. We have tested some cases in which the target, G, is absent.
3. We have not found any case in which the candidate, C, is present and the target, G, is absent.

In cases that meet these three conditions, we sometimes face a dilemma. More than one candidate might pass this rigorous testing. It is possible that both of these candidates is sufficient for the target feature, but there is often some reason to worry that only one of them is really causing the effect. In order to test this hypothesis, we can add another restriction:

4. If there is any other candidate, D, that is never present where the target, G, is absent, then we have tested cases where C is present and D is absent.

The target, G, must also be present in these cases, since C is present and Condition 3 has already been met. Testing this group of cases can reassure us that it is not only candidate D that is sufficient for the target, G.

Finally, for it to be reasonable to reach a positive conclusion that C is sufficient for G, this further condition must also be met:

5. We have tested enough cases of the various kinds that are likely to include a case in which C is present and G is absent if there is any such case.

This new condition cannot be applied in the mechanical way that conditions 1–4 could be applied. To determine whether condition 5 is met, we need to rely on *background information* about how many cases are "enough" and about which kinds of cases "are likely to include a case in which C is present and G is absent, if there is any such case." For example, if we are trying to figure out whether our new software is causing our computer to crash, we do not need to try the same kind of computer in different colors. What we need to try are different kinds of CPUs, monitors, software, and so on, because we know that these are the kinds of factors that can affect performance. Background information like this is what tells us when we have tested enough cases of the right kinds.

Of course, our background assumptions might turn out to be wrong. Even if we have tested many variations of every feature that we think might be relevant, we still might be surprised and find a further case in which C and ~G are present. All that shows, however, is that our inference is defeasible, like all inductive arguments. Despite the possibility that future discoveries might undermine it, our inductive inference can still be strong if our background beliefs are justified and if we have looked long and hard without finding any case in which C is present and G is absent.

Similar rules apply in reverse to positive conclusions about necessary conditions. We have good reason to suppose that candidate C is a necessary condition for target G, if the following conditions are met:

1. We have tested some cases in which the candidate, C, is absent.

2. We have tested some cases in which the target, G, is present.

3. We have not found any case in which the candidate, C, is absent and the target, G, is present.

4. If there is any other candidate, D, that is never absent where the target, G, is present, then we have tested cases where C is absent and D is present.

5. We have tested enough cases of the various kinds that are likely to include a case in which C is absent and G is present, if there is any such case.

This argument again depends on background assumptions in determining whether condition 5 is met. This argument is also defeasible, as before.

Nonetheless, if our background assumptions are justified, the fact that conditions 1–5 are all met can still provide a strong reason for the positive conclusion that candidate C is a necessary condition for target G.

The SCT and NCT themselves are still negative and deductive; but that does not make them better than the positive tests encapsulated in conditions 1–5. The negative SCT and NCT are of no use when we need to argue that some condition *is* sufficient or *is* necessary. Such positive conclusions can be reached only by applying something like condition 5, which will require background information. These inductive arguments might not be as clear-cut or secure as the negative ones, but they can still be inductively strong under the right circumstances. That is all they claim to be.

APPLYING THESE METHODS TO FIND CAUSES

In stating the SCT and NCT and applying these tests to abstract patterns of conditions to eliminate candidates, our procedure was fairly mechanical. We cannot be so mechanical when we try to reach positive conclusions that certain conditions are necessary, sufficient, or both. Applying these rules to actual concrete situations introduces a number of further complications, especially when using our tests to determine causes.

NORMALITY

First, it is important to keep in mind that, in our ordinary understanding of causal conditions, we usually take it for granted that the setting is normal. It is part of common knowledge that if you strike a match, then it will light. Thus, we consider striking a match sufficient to make it light. But if someone has filled the room with carbon dioxide, then the match will not light, no matter how it is struck. Here one may be inclined to say that, after all, striking a match is not sufficient to light it. We might try to be more careful and say that if a match is struck *and* the room is not filled with carbon dioxide, then it will light. But this new conditional overlooks other possibilities—for example, that the room has been filled with nitrogen, that the match has been fireproofed, that the wrong end of the match was struck, that the match has already been lit, and so forth. It now seems that the antecedent of our conditional will have to be endlessly long in order to specify a true or genuine sufficient condition. In fact, however, we usually feel quite happy with saying that if you strike a match, then it will light. We simply do not worry about the possibility that the room has been filled with carbon dioxide, the match has been fireproofed, and so on. Normally we think that things are normal, and give up this assumption only when some good reason appears for doing so.

These reflections suggest the following *contextualized* restatement of our original definitions of sufficient conditions and necessary conditions:

F is a sufficient condition for G if and only if, whenever F is present in a normal context, G is present there as well.

F is a necessary condition for G if and only if, whenever F is absent from a normal context, G is absent from it as well.

What will count as a normal context will vary with the type and the aim of an investigation, but all investigations into causally sufficient conditions and causally necessary conditions take place against the background of many factors that are taken as fixed.

BACKGROUND ASSUMPTIONS

If we are going to subject a causal hypothesis to rigorous testing with the SCT and the NCT, we have to seek out a wide range of cases that might refute that hypothesis. In general, the wider the range of possible refuters the better. Still, some limit must be put on this activity or else testing will get hopelessly bogged down. If we are testing a drug to see whether it will cure a disease, we should try it on a variety of people of various ages, medical histories, body types, and so on, but we will not check to see whether it works on people named Edmund or check to see whether it works on people who drive Volvos. Such factors, we want to say, are plainly irrelevant. But what makes them irrelevant? How do we distinguish relevant from irrelevant considerations?

The answer to this question is that our reasoning about causes occurs within a framework of beliefs that we take to be established as true. This framework contains a great deal of what is called *common knowledge*— knowledge we expect almost every sane adult to possess. We all know, for example, that human beings cannot breathe underwater, cannot walk through walls, cannot be in two places at once, and so on. The stock of these commonplace beliefs is almost endless. Because they are commonplace beliefs, they tend not to be mentioned; yet, they play an important role in distinguishing relevant factors from irrelevant ones.

Specialized knowledge also contains its own principles that are largely taken for granted by experts. Doctors, for example, know a great deal about the detailed structure of the human body, and this background knowledge constantly guides their thought in dealing with specific illnesses. Even if someone claimed to discover that blood does not circulate, no doctor would take the time to refute that claim.

It might seem close-minded to refuse to consider a possibility that someone else suggests. However, giving up our basic beliefs can be very costly. A doctor who took seriously the suggestion that blood does not circulate, for example, would have to abandon our whole way of viewing humans and other animals, along with the rest of biology and science. It is not clear how this doctor could go on practicing medicine. Moreover, there is usually no practical alternative in real life. When faced with time pressure and limited information, we have no way to judge new ideas without taking some background assumptions for granted.

A Detailed Example

To get a clearer idea of the complex interplay between our tests and the reliance on background information, it will be helpful to look in some detail at actual applications of these tests. For this purpose, we will examine an attempt to find the cause of a particular phenomenon, an outbreak of what came to be known as Legionnaires' disease. The example not only shows how causal reasoning relies on background assumptions, it has another interesting feature as well: In the process of discovering the cause of Legionnaires' disease, the investigators were forced to *abandon* what was previously taken to be a well-established causal generalization. In fact, until it was discarded, this false background principle gave them no end of trouble.

The story began at an otherwise boring convention:

> The 58th convention of the American Legion's Pennsylvania Department was held at the Bellevue-Stratford Hotel in Philadelphia from July 21 through 24, 1976. . . . Between July 22 and August 3, 149 of the conventioneers developed what appeared to be the same puzzling illness, characterized by fever, coughing and pneumonia. This, however, was an unusual, explosive outbreak of pneumonia with no apparent cause. . . . Legionnaires' disease, as the illness was quickly named by the press, was to prove a formidable challenge to epidemiologists and laboratory investigators alike.[2]

Notice that at this stage the researchers begin with the assumption that they are dealing with a single illness and not a collection of similar but different illnesses. That assumption could turn out to be wrong; but, if the symptoms of the various patients are sufficiently similar, this is a natural starting assumption. Another reasonable starting assumption is that this illness had a single causative agent. This assumption, too, could turn out to be false, though it did not. The assumption that they were dealing with a single disease with a single cause was at least a good simplifying assumption, one to be held onto until there was good reason to give it up. In any case, we now have a clear specification of our target feature, G: the occurrence of a carefully described illness that came to be known as Legionnaires' disease. The situation concerning it was puzzling because people had contracted a disease with symptoms much like those of pneumonia, yet they had not tested positive for any of the known agents that cause such diseases.

The narrative continues as follows:

> The initial step in the investigation of any epidemic is to determine the character of the illness, who has become ill and just where and when. The next step is to

find out what was unique about the people who became ill: where they were and what they did that was different from other people who stayed well. Knowing such things may indicate how the disease agent was spread and thereby suggest the identity of the agent and where it came from.[3]

Part of this procedure involves a straightforward application of the NCT: Was there any interesting feature that was always present in the history of people who came down with the illness? Progress was made almost at once on this front:

> We quickly learned that the illness was not confined to Legionnaires. An additional 72 cases were discovered among people who had not been directly associated with the convention. They had one thing in common with the sick conventioneers: for one reason or another they had been in or near the Bellevue-Stratford Hotel.[4]

Strictly speaking, of course, all these people who had contracted the disease had more than one thing in common. They were, for example, all alive at the time they were in Philadelphia, and being alive is, in fact, a necessary condition for getting Legionnaires' disease. But the researchers were not interested in this necessary condition because it is a normal background condition for the contraction of any disease. Furthermore, it did not provide a condition that distinguished those who contracted the disease from those who did not. The overwhelming majority of people who were alive at the time did not contract Legionnaires' disease. Thus, the researchers were not interested in this necessary condition because it would fail so badly when tested by the SCT as a sufficient condition. On the basis of common knowledge and specialized medical knowledge, a great many other conditions were also kept off the candidate list.

One prime candidate on the list was presence at the Bellevue-Stratford Hotel. The application of the NCT to this candidate was straightforward. Everyone who had contracted the disease had spent time in or near that hotel. Thus, presence at the Bellevue-Stratford could not be eliminated as a necessary condition of Legionnaires' disease.

The application of the SCT was more complicated, because not everyone who stayed at the Bellevue-Stratford contracted the disease. Other factors made a difference: "Older conventioneers had been affected at a higher rate than younger ones, men at three times the rate for women." Since some young women (among others) who were present at the Bellevue-Stratford did not get Legionnaires' disease, presence at that hotel could be eliminated as a sufficient condition of Legionnaires' disease. Nonetheless, it is part of medical background knowledge that susceptibility to disease often varies with age and gender. Given these differences, some people who spent time at the Bellevue-Stratford were at higher risk for contracting the disease than others. The investigation so far suggested that, for some people, being at the Bellevue-Stratford was connected with a sufficient condition for contracting Legionnaires' disease. Indeed, the conjunction of spending time at the

Bellevue-Stratford and being susceptible to the disease could not be ruled out by the SCT as a sufficient condition of getting the disease.

As soon as spending time at the Bellevue-Stratford became the focus of attention, other hypotheses naturally suggested themselves. Food poisoning was a reasonable suggestion, since it is part of medical knowledge that diseases are sometimes spread by food. It was put on the list of possible candidates, but failed. Investigators checked each local restaurant and each function where food and drink were served. Some of the people who ate in each place did not get Legionnaires' disease, so the food at these locations was eliminated by the SCT as a sufficient condition of Legionnaires' disease. These candidates were also eliminated by the NCT as necessary conditions because some people who did get Legionnaires' disease did not eat at each of these restaurants and functions. Thus, the food and drink could not be the cause.

Further investigation turned up another important clue to the cause of the illness.

> Certain observations suggested that the disease might have been spread through the air. Legionnaires who became ill had spent on the average about 60 percent more time in the lobby of the Bellevue-Stratford than those who remained well; the sick Legionnaires had also spent more time on the sidewalk in front of the hotel than their unaffected fellow conventioneers. . . . It appeared, therefore, that the most likely mode of transmission was airborne.[5]

Merely breathing air in the lobby of the Bellevue-Stratford Hotel still could not be a necessary or sufficient condition, but the investigators reasoned that something in the lobby air probably caused Legionnaires' disease, since the rate of the disease varied up or down in proportion to the time spent in the lobby (or near it on the sidewalk in front). This is an application of the method of concomitant variation, which will be discussed soon.

Now that the focus was on the lobby air, the next step was to pinpoint a specific cause in that air. Again appealing to background medical knowledge, there seemed to be three main candidates for the airborne agents that could have caused the illness: "heavy metals, toxic organic substances, and infectious organisms." Examination of tissues taken from patients who had died from the disease revealed "no unusual levels of metallic or toxic organic substances that might be related to the epidemic," so this left an infectious organism as the remaining candidate. Once more we have an application of NCT. If the disease had been caused by heavy metals or toxic organic substances, then there would have been unusually high levels of these substances in the tissues of those who had contracted the disease. Because this was not always so, these candidates were eliminated as necessary conditions of the disease.

Appealing to background knowledge once more, it seemed that a bacterium would be the most likely source of an airborne disease with the symptoms of Legionnaires' disease. But researchers had already made a routine check for bacteria that cause pneumonia-like diseases, and they had found none. For this reason, attention was directed to the possibility that some previously unknown organism had been responsible but had somehow escaped detection.

It turned out that an undetected and previously unknown bacterium *had* caused the illness, but it took more than four months to find this out. The difficulties encountered in this effort show another important fact about the reliance on a background assumption: Sometimes it turns out to be false. To simplify, the standard way to test for the presence of bacteria is to try to grow them in culture dishes—flat dishes containing nutrients that bacteria can live on. If, after a reasonable number of tries, a colony of a particular kind of bacterium does not appear, then it is concluded that the bacterium is not present. As it turned out, the bacterium that caused Legionnaires' disease would not grow in the cultures commonly used to detect the presence of bacteria. Thus, an important background assumption turned out to be false.

After a great deal of work, a suspicious bacterium was detected using a live-tissue culture rather than the standard synthetic culture. The task, then, was to show that this particular bacterium in fact caused the disease. Again to simplify, when people are infected by a particular organism, they often develop antibodies that are specifically aimed at this organism. In the case of Legionnaires' disease, these antibodies were easier to detect than the bacterium itself. They also remained in the patients' bodies after the infection had run its course. We thus have another chance to apply the NCT: If Legionnaires' disease was caused by this particular bacterium, then whenever the disease was present, this antibody should be present as well. The suspicious bacterium passed this test with flying colors and was named, appropriately enough, *Legionella pneumophila*. Because the investigators had worked so hard to test such a wide variety of candidates, they assumed that the disease must have some cause among the candidates that they checked. So, since only one candidate remained, they felt justified in reaching a positive conclusion that the bacterium was a necessary condition of Legionnaires' disease.

The story of the search for the cause of Legionnaires' disease brings out two important features of the use of inductive methods in the sciences. First, it involves a complicated interplay between what is already established and what is being tested. Confronted with a new problem, established principles can be used to suggest theoretically significant hypotheses to be tested. The tests then eliminate some hypotheses and leave others. If, at the end of the investigation, a survivor remains that fits in well with our previously established principles, then the stock of established principles is increased. The second thing that this example shows is that the inductive method is fallible. Without the background of established principles, the application of inductive principles like the NCT and the SCT would be undirected; yet sometimes these established principles let us down, for they can turn out to be false. The discovery of the false background principle that hindered the search for the cause of Legionnaires' disease led to important revisions in laboratory techniques. The discovery that certain fundamental background principles are false can lead to revolutionary changes in science.

DISCUSSION QUESTIONS

1. Sometimes we describe necessary conditions as causes, but at other times we describe sufficient conditions as causes. Why? Be sure to give at least two different examples of each pattern.

2. *Legionella pneumophila* is necessary for Legionnaire's disease, but so are being alive, having blood, and so on. Why do we think that Legionnaire's disease is caused by *Legionella pneumophila* instead of being caused by being alive, having blood, and other necessary conditions?

CONCOMITANT VARIATION

The use of the sufficient condition test and the necessary condition test depends on certain features of the world being sometimes present and sometimes absent. Some features of the world, however, are always present to some degree. Because they are always present, the NCT will never eliminate them as possible necessary conditions of any event, and the SCT will never eliminate anything as a sufficient condition for them. Yet, the *extent* or *degree* to which a feature exists in the world is often a significant phenomenon that demands causal explanation.

An example should make this clear. In recent decades, a controversy has raged over the impact of acid rain on the environment of the northeastern United States and Canada. Part of the controversy involves the proper interpretation of the data that have been collected. The controversy has arisen for the following reason: The atmosphere always contains a certain amount of acid, much of it from natural sources. It is also known that an excess of acid in the environment can have severe effects on both plants and animals. Lakes are particularly vulnerable to the effects of acid rain. Finally, it is also acknowledged that industries, mostly in the Midwest, discharge large quantities of sulfur dioxide (SO_2) into the air, and this increases the acidity of water in the atmosphere. The question—and here the controversy begins—is whether the contribution of acid from these industries is the cause of the environmental damage downwind of them.

How can we settle such a dispute? The two rules we have introduced provide no immediate help, for, as we have seen, they provide a rigorous test of a causal hypothesis only when we can find contrasting cases with the presence or the absence of a given feature. The NCT provides a rigorous test for a necessary condition only if we can find cases in which the feature does not occur and then check to make sure that the target feature does not occur either. The SCT provides a rigorous test for a sufficient condition only when we can find cases in which the target phenomenon is absent and then check whether the candidate sufficient condition is absent as well. In this case, however, neither check applies, for there is always a certain amount of acid in the atmosphere, so it is not possible to check what happens when atmospheric acid is completely absent. Similarly, environmental damage, which is the target phenomenon under investigation, is so widespread in our modern industrial society that it is also hard to find a case in which it is completely absent.

So, if there is always acid in the atmosphere, and environmental damage always exists at least to some extent, how can we determine whether the SO_2 released into the atmosphere is *significantly* responsible for the environmental damage in the affected areas? Here we use what John Stuart Mill called the *Method of Concomitant Variation*. We ask whether the amount of environmental damage varies directly in proportion to the amount of SO_2 released into the environment. If environmental damage increases with the amount of SO_2 released into the environment and drops when the amount of SO_2 is lowered, this means that the level of SO_2 in the atmosphere is *positively correlated* with environmental damage. We would then have good reason to believe that lowering SO_2 emissions would lower the level of environmental damage, at least to some extent.

Arguments relying on the method of concomitant variation are difficult to evaluate, especially when there is no generally accepted background theory that makes sense of the concomitant variation. Some such variations are well understood. For example, most people know that the faster you drive, the more gasoline you consume. (Gasoline consumption varies *directly* with speed.) Why? There is a good theory here: It takes more energy to drive at a high speed than at a low speed, and this energy is derived from the gasoline consumed in the car's engine. Other correlations are less well understood. Reportedly, there seems to be a correlation between how much a woman smokes during pregnancy and how happy her children are when they reach age thirty. The correlation here is not nearly as good as the correlation between gasoline consumption and speed, for many people are very happy at age thirty even though their mothers smoked a lot during pregnancy, and many others are very unhappy at age thirty even though their mothers never smoked. Furthermore, no generally accepted background theory has been found to explain the correlation that does exist.

This reference to background theory is important, because two sets of phenomena can be correlated to a very high degree, even with no direct causal relationship between them. A favorite example that appears in many statistics texts is the discovered positive correlation in boys between foot size and quality of handwriting. It is hard to imagine a causal relation holding in either direction. Having big feet should not make you write better and, just as obviously, writing well should not give you big feet. The correct explanation is that both foot size and handwriting ability are positively correlated with age. Here, a noncausal correlation between two phenomena (foot size and handwriting ability) is explained by a third common correlation (maturation) that *is* causal.

At times, it is possible to get causal correlations *backward*. For example, a few years ago, sports statisticians discovered a negative correlation between forward passes thrown and winning in football. That is, the more forward passes a team threw, the less chance it had of winning. This suggested that passing is not a good strategy, since the more you do it, the more likely you are to lose. Closer examination showed, however, that the causal relationship, in fact, went in the other direction. Toward the end of a game, losing teams tend to throw a great many passes in an effort to catch up. In other words, teams throw a lot of passes because they are losing, rather than the other way around.

Finally, some correlations seem inexplicable. For example, a strong positive correlation reportedly holds between the birth rate in Holland and the number of storks nesting in chimneys. There is, of course, a background theory that would explain this—storks bring babies—but that theory is not favored by modern science. For the lack of any better background theory, the phenomenon just seems weird.

Courtesy of Randall Munroe

So, given a strong correlation between phenomena of types *A* and *B*, four possibilities exist:

1. *A* is the cause of *B*.
2. *B* is the cause of *A*.
3. Some third thing is the cause of both.
4. The correlation is simply accidental.

Before we accept any one of these possibilities, we must have good reasons for preferring it over the other three.

One way to produce such a reason is to manipulate *A* or *B*. If we vary factor *A* up and down, but *B* does not change at all, this finding provides some reason against possibility 1, since *B* would normally change along with *A* if *A* did cause *B*. Similarly, if we manipulate *B* up and down, but *A* does not vary at all, this result provides some reason against alternative 2 and for the hypothesis that B does not cause A. Together these manipulations can reduce the live options to items 3 and 4.

Many scientific experiments work this way. When scientists first discovered the correlation between smoking and lung cancer, some cigarette manufacturers responded that lung cancer might cause the desire to smoke or there might be a third cause of both smoking and lung cancer that explains the correlation. Possibly, it was suggested, smoking relieves discomfort due to early lung cancer or due to a third factor that itself causes lung cancer. To test these hypotheses, scientists manipulated the amount of smoking by lab animals. When all other factors were held as constant as possible, but smoking was increased, lung cancer increased; and when smoking went down, lung cancer went down. These results would not have occurred if some third factor had caused both smoking and lung cancer but remained stable as smoking was manipulated. The findings would also have been different if incipient lung cancer caused smoking, but had remained constant as scientists manipulated smoking levels. Such experiments can, thus, help us rule out at least some of the options 1–4.

Direct manipulation like this is not always possible or ethically permissible. The data would probably be more reliable if the test subjects were human beings rather than lab animals, but that is not an ethical option. Perhaps more complicated statistical methods could produce more reliable results, but they often require large amounts and special kinds of data. Such data is, unfortunately, often unavailable.

EXERCISE VI

In each of the following examples a strong correlation, either negative or positive, holds between two sets of phenomena, A and B. Try to decide whether A is the cause of B, B is the cause of A, both are caused by some third factor, C, or the correlation is simply accidental. Explain your choice.

1. For a particular United States president, there is a negative correlation between the number of hairs on his head (A) and the population of China (B).

2. My son's height (A) increases along with the height of the tree outside my front door (B).

3. It has been claimed that there is a strong positive correlation between those students who take sex education courses (A) and those who contract venereal disease (B).

4. At one time there was a strong negative correlation between the number of mules in a state (A) and the salaries paid to professors at the state university (B). In other words, the more mules, the lower professional salaries.[6]

5. There is a high positive correlation between the number of fire engines in a particular borough in New York City (A) and the number of fires that occur there (B).[7]

6. "Washington (UPI)—Rural Americans with locked doors, watchdogs or guns may face as much risk of burglary as neighbors who leave doors unlocked, a federally financed study says. The study, financed in part by a three-year $170,000 grant from the Law Enforcement Assistance Administration, was based on a survey of nearly 900 families in rural Ohio. Sixty percent of the rural residents surveyed regularly locked doors [A], but were burglarized more often than residents who left doors unlocked [B]."[8]

7. The speed of a car (A) is exactly the same as the speed of its shadow (B).

8. The length of a runner's ring finger minus the length of the runner's index finger (A) is correlated with the runner's speed in the one-hundred-yard dash (B).

DISCUSSION QUESTIONS

1. After it became beyond doubt that smoking is dangerous to people's health, a new debate arose concerning the possible health hazards of secondhand smoke on nonsmokers. Collect statements pro and con on this issue and evaluate the strength of the inductive arguments on each side.

2. The high positive correlation between CO_2 concentrations in the atmosphere and the Earth's mean surface temperatures is often cited as evidence that increases in atmospheric CO_2 cause global warming. This argument is illustrated by the famous "hockey stick" diagram in Al Gore's *An Inconvenient Truth*. Is this argument persuasive? How could skeptics about global warming respond?

NOTES

[1] Mill's "methods of experimental inquiry" are found in book 3, chap. 8 of his *A System of Logic* (London: John W. Parker, 1843). Mill's method of difference, method of agreement, and joint method parallel our SCT, NCT, and Joint Test, respectively. Our simplification of Mill's methods derives from Brian Skyrms, *Choice and Chance*, 3rd ed. (Belmont, CA: Wadsworth, 1986), chap. 4.

[2] These excerpts are drawn from David W. Fraser and Joseph E. McDade, "Legionellosis," *Scientific American*, October 1979, 82–99.

[3] Ibid.

[4] Ibid.

[5] Ibid.

[6] From Gregory A. Kimble, *How to Use (and Misuse) Statistics* (Englewood Cliffs, NJ: Prentice-Hall, 1978), 182.

[7] Ibid.

[8] "Locked Doors No Bar to Crime, Study Says," *Santa Barbara* [California] *Newspress*, Wednesday, February 16, 1977. This title suggests that locking your doors will not increase safety. Is that a reasonable lesson to draw from this study?

11

Chances

The kinds of arguments discussed in the preceding three chapters are inductive, so they need not meet the deductive standard of validity. They are, instead, intended to meet the inductive standard of strength. Whereas deductive validity hinges on what is possible, inductive strength hinges on what is probable. Roughly, an argument is inductively strong to the extent that its premises make its conclusion more likely or probable. Hence, just as we can get a better theoretical understanding of deductive validity by studying formal logic, as we did in Chapters 6 and 7, so we can get a better theoretical understanding of inductive strength by studying probability, as we will do in this chapter. To complete our survey of inductive arguments, this chapter offers an elementary discussion of probability. It begins by illustrating several common mistakes about probability. To help avoid these fallacies, we need to approach probability more carefully, so formal laws of probability are presented along with Bayes's theorem.

SOME FALLACIES OF PROBABILITY

Probability is pervasive. We all assume or make probability judgments throughout our lives. We do so whenever we form a belief about which we are not certain, as in all of the kinds of inductive arguments studied in Chapters 8–10. Such arguments do not pretend to reach their conclusions with certainty, even if their premises are true. They merely try to show that a conclusion is likely or probable. Judgments about probability are, thus, assumed in assessing such arguments and beliefs. Probability also plays a crucial role in our most important decisions. Mistakes about probability can then lead to disasters. Doctors lose patients' lives, stockbrokers lose clients' money, and coaches lose games because they overestimate or underestimate probabilities. Such mistakes are common and fall into several regular patterns. It is useful to understand these fallacies, so that we can learn to avoid them.

THE GAMBLER'S FALLACY

Casinos thrive partly because so many gamblers misunderstand probability. One mistake is so common that it has been dubbed *the gambler's fallacy*. When people have a run of bad luck, they often increase their bets because they assume that they are due for a run of good luck to even things out. Gambling systems are sometimes based on this fallacious idea. People keep track of the numbers that come up on a roulette wheel, trying to discover a number that has not come up for a long time. They then pile their money on that number on the assumption that it is due. They usually end up losing a bundle.

These gamblers seem to assume, "In the long run, things will even out (or average out)." Interpreted one way, this amounts to what mathematicians call *the law of large numbers,* and it is perfectly correct. When flipping a coin, we expect it to come up heads half the time, so it should come up heads five times in ten flips. If we actually check this out, however, we discover that the number of times it comes up heads in ten flips varies significantly from this predicted value—sometimes coming up heads more than five times, sometimes coming up fewer. What the law of large numbers tells us is that the actual percentage of heads will tend to come closer to the theoretically predicted percentage of heads the more trials we make. If you flipped a coin a million times, it would be very surprising if the percentage of heads were more than 1 percent away from the predicted 50 percent.

This law of large numbers is often misunderstood in a way that leads to the gambler's fallacy. Some people assume that each possible outcome will occur the average number of times in each series of trials. To see that this is a fallacy, we can go back to flipping coins. Toss a coin until it comes up heads three times in a row. (This will take less time than you might imagine.) What is the probability that it will come up heads a fourth time? Put crudely, some people think that the probability of it coming up heads again must be very small, because it is unlikely that a fair coin will come up heads four times in a row, so a tails is needed to even things out. That is wrong. The chances of getting heads on any given toss are the same, regardless of what happened on previous tosses. Previous results cannot affect the probabilities on this new toss.

HEURISTICS

In daily life, we often have to make decisions quickly without full information. To deal with this overload of decisions, we commonly employ what cognitive psychologists call *heuristics*. Technically, a heuristic is a general strategy for solving a problem or coming to a decision. For example, a good heuristic for solving geometry problems is to start with the conclusion you are trying to reach and then work backward.

Recent research in cognitive psychology has shown, first, that human beings rely very heavily on heuristics and, second, that we often have too much confidence in them. The result is that our probability judgments often go very wrong, and sometimes our thinking gets utterly mixed up. In this regard, two heuristics are particularly instructive: the representativeness heuristic and the availability heuristic.

THE REPRESENTATIVENESS HEURISTIC. A simple example illustrates how errors can arise from the representativeness heuristic. Imagine that you are randomly dealt five-card hands from a standard deck. Which of the following two hands is more likely to come up?

HAND #1	HAND #2
Three of clubs	Ace of spades
Seven of diamonds	Ace of hearts
Nine of diamonds	Ace of clubs
Queen of hearts	Ace of diamonds
King of spades	King of spades

A surprisingly large number of people will automatically say that the second hand is much less likely than the first. Actually, if you think about it a little, it should be obvious that any two specific hands have exactly the same likelihood of being dealt in a fair game. Here people get confused because the first hand is unimpressive; and, because unimpressive hands come up all the time, it strikes us as a representative hand. In many card games, however, the second hand is very impressive—something worth talking about—and thus looks unrepresentative. Our reliance on representativeness blinds us to a simple and obvious point about probabilities: Any specific hand is as likely to occur as any other.

DISCUSSION QUESTION

Linda is thirty-one years old, single, outspoken, and very bright. As a student, she majored in philosophy, was deeply concerned with issues of discrimination and social justice, and also participated in antinuclear demonstrations. Rank the following statements with respect to the probability that they are also true of Linda, then explain your rankings:

Linda is a teacher in elementary school.
Linda works in a bookstore and takes yoga classes.
Linda is active in the feminist movement.
Linda is a psychiatric social worker.
Linda is a bank teller.
Linda is an insurance salesperson.
Linda is a bank teller and is active in the feminist movement.[1]

THE AVAILABILITY HEURISTIC. Because sampling and taking surveys is costly, we often do it imaginatively, that is, in our heads. If you ask a baseball fan which team has the better batting average, Detroit or San Diego, that person might just remember, might go look it up, or might think about each team and try to decide which has the most good batters. The latter approach, needless to say, would be a risky business, but many baseball fans have remarkable knowledge of the batting averages of top hitters. Even with this knowledge, however, it is easy to go wrong. The players that naturally come to mind are the stars on each team. They are more available to our memory, and we are likely to make our judgment on the basis of them alone. Yet such a sample can easily be biased because all the batters contribute to the team average, not just the stars. The fact that the weak batters on one team are much better than the weak batters on the other can swing the balance.

DISCUSSION QUESTION

In four pages of a novel (about 2,000 words), how many words would you expect to find that have the form _ _ _ _ _n_ (seven-letter words with "n" in the sixth place)? Write down your answer. Now, how many words would you expect to find that have the form _ _ _ _ing (seven-letter words that end with "ing")? Explain your answers.[2]

The point of examining these heuristics and noting the errors that they produce is not to suggest that we should cease relying on them. First, there is a good chance that this would be psychologically impossible, because the use of such heuristics seems to be built into our psychological makeup. Second, over a wide range of standard cases, these heuristics give quick and largely accurate estimates. Difficulties typically arise in using these heuristics when the situation is nonstandard—that is, when the situation is complex or out of the ordinary.

To avoid such mistakes when making important judgments about probabilities, we need to ask, "Is the situation sufficiently standard to allow the use of heuristics?" Because this is a mouthful, we might simply ask, "Is this the sort of thing that people can figure out in their heads?" When the answer to that question is "No," as it often is, then we need to turn to more formal procedures for determining probabilities.

DISCUSSION QUESTION

In a remarkable study,[3] Thomas Gilovich, Robert Vallone, and Amos Tversky found a striking instance of people's tendency to treat things as statistically significant when they are not. In professional basketball, certain players have the reputation of being streak shooters. Streak shooters seem to score points in batches, then go cold and are not able to buy a basket. Stated more precisely, in streak shooting, "the performance of a player during a particular period is significantly better than expected on the basis of the player's overall record." To test whether streak shooting really exists, the authors made detailed study of a year's shooting record for the players on the Philadelphia 76ers. This team included Andrew Toney, noted around the league as being streak shooter. The authors found no evidence for streak shooting, not even for Andrew Toney. How would you go about deciding whether streak shooting exists or not? If, as Gilovich, Vallone, and Tversky have argued, belief in streak shooting is a "cognitive illusion," why do so many people, including most professional athletes, believe that it does exist?

THE LANGUAGE OF PROBABILITY

The first step in figuring out probabilities is to adopt a more precise way of talking. Our common language includes various ways of expressing probabilities. Some of the guarding terms discussed in Chapter 3 provide examples of informal ways of expressing probability commitments. Thus, someone might say that it is unlikely that the New England Patriots will win the Super Bowl this year without saying how unlikely it is. We can also specify various degrees of probability. Looking out the window, we might say that there is a fifty-fifty chance of rain. More vividly, someone might have remarked that Ron Paul does not have a snowball's chance in hell of ever winning a presidential election. In each case, the speaker is indicating the relative strength of the evidence for the occurrence or nonoccurrence of some event. To say that there is a fifty-fifty chance that it will rain indicates that we hold that the evidence is equally strong that it will rain rather than not rain. The metaphor in the third statement indicates that the person who uttered it believed that the probability of Ron Paul winning a presidential election is essentially nonexistent.

We can make our probability claims more precise by using numbers. Sometimes we use percentages. For example, the weather bureau might say that there is a 75 percent chance of snow tomorrow. This can naturally be changed to a fraction: The probability is 3/4 that it will snow tomorrow. Finally, this fraction can be changed to a decimal expression: There is a 0.75 probability that it will snow tomorrow.

The probability scale has two end points: the absolute certainty that the event will occur and the absolute certainty that it will not occur. Because you cannot do better than absolute certainty, a probability can neither rise above 100 percent nor drop below 0 percent (neither above 1, nor below 0). (This should sound fairly obvious, but it is possible to become confused when combining percentages and fractions, as when Yogi Berra was supposed to have said that success is one-third talent and 75 percent hard work.) Of course, what we normally call probability claims usually fall between these two end points. For this reason, it sounds somewhat peculiar to say that there is a 100 percent chance of rain and just plain weird to say the chance of rain is 1 out of 1. Even so, these peculiar ways of speaking cause no procedural difficulties and rarely come up in practice.

A PRIORI PROBABILITY

When people make probability claims, we have a right to ask why they assign the probability they do. In Chapter 8, we saw how statistical procedures can be used for establishing probability claims. Here we will examine the so-called *a priori* approach to probabilities. A simple example will bring out the differences between these two approaches. We might wonder what the probability is of drawing an ace from a standard deck of fifty-two cards. Using the procedure discussed in Chapter 8, we could make a great many random draws from the deck (replacing the card each time) and then form a statistical generalization concerning the results. We would discover that an ace tends to come up roughly one-thirteenth of the time. From this we could draw the conclusion that the chance of drawing an ace is one in thirteen.

But we do not have to go to all this trouble. We can assume that each of the fifty-two cards has an equal chance of being selected. Given this assumption, an obvious line of reasoning runs as follows: There are four aces in a standard fifty-two-card deck, so the probability of selecting one randomly is four in fifty-two. That reduces to one chance in thirteen. Here the set of favorable outcomes is a subset of the total number of equally likely outcomes, and to compute the probability that the favorable outcome will occur, we merely divide the number of favorable outcomes by the total number of possible outcomes. This fraction gives us the probability that the event will occur on a random draw. Since all outcomes here are equally likely,

$$\text{Probability of drawing an ace} = \frac{\text{number of aces}}{\text{total number of cards}} = \frac{4}{52} = \frac{1}{13}$$

Notice that in coming to our conclusion that there is one chance in thirteen of randomly drawing an ace from a fifty-two-card deck, we used only mathematical reasoning. This illustrates the a priori approach to probabilities. It is called the a priori approach because we arrive at the result simply by reasoning about the circumstances.

In calculating the probability of drawing an ace from a fifty-two-card deck, we took the ratio of favorable equally likely outcomes to total equally likely outcomes. Generally, then, the probability of a hypothesis h, symbolized "Pr(h)," when all outcomes are equally likely, is expressed as follows:

$$\text{Pr}(h) = \frac{\text{favorable outcomes}}{\text{total outcomes}}$$

We can illustrate this principle with a slightly more complicated example. What is the probability of throwing an eight on the cast of two dice? The following table lists all of the equally likely ways in which two dice can turn up on a single cast. Notice that five of the thirty-six possible outcomes produce an eight. Hence, the probability of throwing an eight is 5/36.

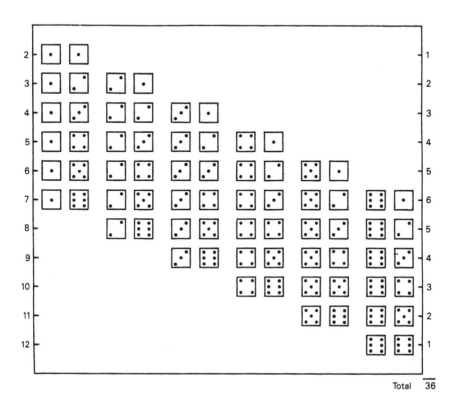

Total   36

EXERCISE I

Using the above chart, answer the following questions about the total on throw of two dice:

1. What is the probability of throwing a five?
2. Which number has the highest probability of being thrown? What is its probability?
3. What is the probability of throwing an eleven?
4. What is the probability of throwing either a seven or an eleven?
5. Which is more likely: throwing either a five or an eight?
6. Which is more likely: throwing a five or an eight, or throwing a two or a seven?
7. What is the probability of throwing a ten or above?
8. What is the probability of throwing an even number?
9. What is the probability of throwing an odd number?
10. What is the probability of throwing a value from four to six?
11. What is the probability of throwing either a two or a twelve?
12. What is the probability of throwing a value from two to twelve?

SOME RULES OF PROBABILITY

Suppose you have determined the probability that certain simple events will occur; how do you go about applying this information to combinations of events? This is a complex question and one that can be touched on only lightly in this text. There are, however, some simple rules of probability that are worth knowing because they can guide us in making choices when outcomes are uncertain.

PROBABILITIES OF NEGATIONS

By convention, events are assigned probabilities between 0 and 1 (inclusive). An event is going to either occur or not occur; that, at least, is certain (that is, it has a probability of 1). From this it is easy to see how to calculate the probability that the event will *not* occur, given the probability that it will occur: We simply subtract the probability that it will occur from 1. This is our first rule:

RULE 1: NEGATION. The probability that an event will *not* occur is 1 minus the probability that it will occur. Symbolically:

$$\Pr(\text{not } h) = 1 - \Pr(h)$$

For example, the probability of drawing an ace from a standard deck is one in thirteen, so the probability of *not* drawing an ace is twelve in thirteen.

This makes sense because there are forty-eight out of fifty-two ways of not drawing an ace, and this reduces to twelve chances in thirteen.

PROBABILITIES OF CONJUNCTIONS

We often want to know not just how likely it is that one single event will occur but, instead, how likely it is that two events will occur together in a certain order. Here's a simple rule for calculating probabilities in some such cases:

RULE 2: CONJUNCTION WITH INDEPENDENCE. Given two independent events, the probability of their *both* occurring is the product of their individual probabilities. Symbolically (where h_1 and h_2 are independent):

$$Pr(h_1 \ \& \ h_2) = Pr(h_1) \times Pr(h_2)$$

Here the word "independent" needs explanation. Suppose you randomly draw a card from the deck, then put it back, shuffle, and draw again. In this case, the outcome of the first draw provides no information about the outcome of the second draw, so it is *independent* of it. What is the probability of drawing two aces in a row using this system? Using Rule 2, we see that the answer is $1/13 \times 1/13$, or 1 chance in 169.

The situation is different if we do *not* replace the card after the first draw. Rule 2 does not apply to this case because the two events are no longer independent. The chances of getting an ace on the first draw are still one in thirteen, but if an ace is drawn and not returned to the pack, then there is one less ace in the deck, so the chances of drawing an ace on the next draw are reduced to three in fifty-one. Thus, the probability of drawing two consecutive aces without returning the first draw to the deck is $4/52 \times 3/51$, or 1 in 221, which is considerably lower than 1 in 169.

If we want to extend Rule 2 to cover cases in which the events are *not* independent, then we will have to speak of the probability of one event occurring, given that another has occurred. The probability that h_2 will occur given that h_1 has occurred is called the *conditional* probability of h_2 on h_1 and is usually symbolized thus: $Pr(h_2 | h_1)$. This probability is calculated by considering only those cases where h_1 is true and then dividing the number of cases within that group where h_2 is also true by the total number of cases in that group. Symbolically:

$$Pr(h_2 | h_1) = \frac{\text{favorable outcomes where } h_1}{\text{total outcomes where } h_1} = \frac{\text{outcomes where } h_1 \text{ and } h_2}{\text{total outcomes where } h_1}$$

Using this notion of conditional probability, Rule 2 can be modified as follows to deal with cases in which events need not be independent:

RULE 2G: CONJUNCTION IN GENERAL. Given two events, the probability of their both occurring is the probability of the first occurring times the probability of the second occurring, given that the first has occurred. Symbolically:

$$Pr(h_1 \ \& \ h_2) = Pr(h_1) \times Pr(h_2 \,|\, h_1)$$

Notice that, in the event that h_1 and h_2 are independent, the probability of h_2 is not related to the occurrence of h_1, so the probability of h_2 on h_1 is simply the probability of h_2. Thus, Rule 2 is simply a special case of the more general Rule 2G.

We can extend these rules to cover more than two events. For example, with Rule 2, regardless of the number of events we might consider, provided that they are independent of each other, the probability of all of them occurring is the product of each one of them occurring. For example, the chances of flipping a coin and having it come up heads is one chance in two. What are the chances of flipping a coin eight times and having it come up heads every time? The answer is:

$$1/2 \times 1/2 \times 1/2 \times 1/2 \times 1/2 \times 1/2 \times 1/2 \times 1/2$$

which equals 1 chance in 256.

PROBABILITIES OF DISJUNCTIONS

Our next rule allows us to answer questions of the following kind: What are the chances of *either* an eight *or* a two coming up on a single throw of the dice? Going back to the chart, we saw that we could answer this question by counting the number of ways in which a two can come up (which is one) and adding this to the number of ways in which an eight can come up (which is five). We could then conclude that the chances of one or the other of them coming up are six in thirty-six, or 1/6. The principle involved in this calculation can be stated as follows:

RULE 3: DISJUNCTION WITH EXCLUSIVITY. The probability that at least one of two mutually exclusive events will occur is the sum of the probabilities that each of them will occur. Symbolically (where h_1 and h_2 are mutually exclusive):

$$Pr(h_1 \ or \ h_2) = Pr(h_1) + Pr(h_2)$$

To say that events are *mutually exclusive* means that they cannot both occur together. You cannot, for example, get both a two and an eight on the same cast of two dice. You might, however, throw neither a two nor an eight, since you might throw some other number.

When events are not mutually exclusive, the rule for calculating disjunctive probabilities becomes more complicated. Suppose, for example, that exactly half the class is female and exactly half the class is over nineteen and the age distribution is the same for females and males. What is the probability that a randomly selected student will be either a female or over nineteen? If we simply add the probabilities $(1/2 + 1/2 = 1)$, we would get the result that we are certain to pick someone who is either female or over nineteen. But that answer is wrong, because a quarter of the class is male and not over nineteen, and one of them might have been randomly selected. The correct answer is that the chances are 3/4 of randomly selecting someone who is either female or over nineteen.

We can see that this is the correct answer by examining the following table:

	Over Nineteen	Not over Nineteen
Female	25%	25%
Male	25%	25%

It is easy to see that in 75 percent of the cases, a randomly selected student will be either female or over nineteen. The table also shows what went wrong with our initial calculation. The top row shows that 50 percent of the students are female. The left column shows that 50 percent of the students are over nineteen. But we cannot simply add these figures to get the probability of a randomly selected student being either female or over nineteen. Why? Because that would double-count the females over nineteen. We would count them once in the top row and then again in the left column. To compensate for such double-counting, we need to subtract the students who are both female and over nineteen. The upper left figure shows that this is 25%. So the correct way to calculate the answer is $50\% + 50\% - 25\% = 75\%$.

This pattern is reflected in the general rule governing the calculation of disjunctive probabilities:

RULE 3G: DISJUNCTION IN GENERAL. The probability that at least one of two events will occur is the sum of the probabilities that each of them will occur, minus the probability that they will both occur. Symbolically:

$$\Pr(h_1 \text{ or } h_2) = \Pr(h_1) + \Pr(h_2) - \Pr(h_1 \& h_2)$$

If h_1 and h_2 are mutually exclusive, then $\Pr(h_1 \& h_2) = 0$, and Rule 3G reduces to Rule 3. Thus, as with Rules 2 and 2G, Rule 3 is simply a special case of the more general Rule 3G.

PROBABILITIES IN A SERIES

Before stating Rule 4, we can think about a particular example. What is the probability of tossing heads at least once in eight tosses of a coin? Here it is tempting to reason in the following way: There is a 50 percent chance of getting heads on the first toss and a 50 percent chance of getting heads on the second toss, so after two tosses it is already certain that we will toss

heads at least once, and thus after eight tosses there should be a 400 percent chance. In other words, you cannot miss. There are two good reasons
for thinking that this argument is fishy. First, probability can never exceed
100 percent. Second, there must be some chance, however small, that we
could toss a coin eight times and not have it come up heads.

The best way to look at this question is to restate it so that the first two
rules can be used. Instead of asking what the probability is that heads will
come up at least once, we can ask what the probability is that heads will *not*
come up at least once. To say that heads will not come up even once is equivalent to saying that tails will come up eight times in a row. By Rule 2, we know
how to compute that probability: It is $1/2$ multiplied by itself eight times,
and that, as we saw, is $1/256$. Finally, by Rule 1 we know that the probability
that this will not happen (that heads will come up at least once) is $1 - (1/256)$.
In other words, the probability of tossing heads at least once in eight tosses is
$255/256$. That comes close to a certainty, but it is not quite a certainty.

We can generalize these results as follows:

Rule 4: Series with Independence. The probability that an event will
occur at least once in a series of independent trials is 1 minus
the probability that it will not occur in that number of trials.
Symbolically (where n is the number of independent trials):

$$\Pr(h \text{ at least once in } n \text{ trials}) = 1 - \Pr(\text{not } h)^n$$

Strictly speaking, Rule 4 is unnecessary, since it can be derived from Rules 1
and 2, but it is important to know because it blocks a common misunderstanding about probabilities: People often think that something is a sure
thing when it is not.

PERMUTATIONS AND COMBINATIONS

Another common confusion is between permutations and combinations. A
permutation is a set of items whose order is specified. A *combination* is a set of
items whose order is not specified. Imagine, for example, that three cards—
the jack, queen, and king of spades—are facedown in front of you. If you
pick two of these cards in turn, there are three possible combinations: jack
and queen, jack and king, and queen and king. In contrast, there are six possible permutations: jack then queen, queen then jack, jack then king, king
then jack, queen then king, and king then queen.

Rule 2 is used to calculate probabilities of permutations—of conjunctions
of events in a particular order. For example, if you flip a fair coin twice, what
is the probability of its coming up heads and tails in that order (that is, heads
on the first flip and tails on the second flip)? Since the flips are independent,
Rule 2 tells us that the answer is $1/2 \times 1/2 = 1/4$. This answer is easily confirmed by counting the possible permutations (heads then heads, heads then
tails, tails then heads, tails then tails). Only one of these four permutations
(heads then tails) is a favorable outcome.

We need to calculate probabilities of combinations in a different way. For example, if you flip a fair coin twice, what is the probability of its landing heads and tails in *any* order? There are two ways for this to happen. The coin could come up either heads then tails or tails then heads. These alternatives are mutually exclusive, so the probability of this disjunction by Rule 3 is $1/4 + 1/4 = 1/2$. This is confirmed by counting two possibilities (heads then tails, tails then heads) out of four (heads then heads, heads then tails, tails then heads, tails then tails). Another way to calculate this probability is to realize that the first flip doesn't matter. Whatever you get on the first flip (heads or tails), you need the opposite on the second flip. You are certain to get either heads or tails on the first flip, so this probability is 1. Then, regardless of what happens on the first flip, the probability of getting the opposite on the second flip is $1/2$. These results are independent, so the probability of their conjunction by Rule 2 is the product $1 \times 1/2 = 1/2$.

We can also use our rules to calculate probabilities of combinations without independence. Rule 2G tells us that the probability of drawing an ace, not putting this card back in the deck, and then drawing a king is $4/52 \times 4/51 = 16/2{,}652$. But what is the probability of drawing an ace and a king in any order? It is the probability of drawing either an ace or a king and then drawing the other one, given that you drew the first one. That probability by Rule 2G is $8/52 \times 4/51 = 32/2{,}652$. The difference between this result and the previous one, where the order was specified, shows why we need to determine whether we are dealing with permutations or combinations.

EXERCISE II

Use the rules of probability to calculate these probabilities:

1. What is the probability of rolling a five on one throw of a fair six-sided die?
2. What is the probability of *not* rolling a five on one throw of a fair six-sided die?
3. If you roll a five on your first throw of a fair six-sided die, what is probability of rolling *another* five on a second throw of that die?
4. If you roll two fair six-sided dice one time, what are the chances that *both* of the dice will come up a five?
5. If you roll two fair six-sided dice one time, what are the chances that *one or the other* (or both) of the dice will come up a five?
6. If you roll two fair six-sided dice one time, what are the chances that *one and only one* of the dice will come up a five?
7. If you roll two fair six-sided dice one time, what are the chances that *at least one* of the dice will come up a five?
8. If you roll two fair six-sided dice one time, what are the chances that *at least one* of the dice will *not* come up a five?
9. If you roll six fair six-sided dice one time, what are the chances that *at least one* of the dice will come up a five?
10. If you roll six fair six-sided dice one time, what are the chances that *at least one* of the dice will *not* come up a five?

Compute the probability of making the following draws from a standard fifty-two-card deck:

1. Drawing either a seven or a five on a single draw.

2. Drawing neither a seven nor a five on a single draw.

3. Drawing a seven and then, without returning the first card to the deck, drawing a five on the next draw.

4. Same as 3, but the first card is returned to the deck and the deck is shuffled after the first draw.

5. Drawing at least one spade in a series of three consecutive draws, when the card drawn is not returned to the deck.

6. Drawing at least one spade in a series of four consecutive draws, when the card drawn is not returned to the deck.

7. Same as 6, but the card is returned to the deck after each draw and the deck is reshuffled.

8. Drawing a heart and a diamond in that order in two consecutive draws, when the first card is returned to the deck and the deck is reshuffled the first draw.

9. Drawing a heart and a diamond in any order in two consecutive draws, when the first card is returned to the deck and the deck is reshuffled the first draw.

10. Drawing a heart and a diamond in any order in two consecutive draws, when the first card is not returned to the deck after the first draw.

Suppose there are two little lotteries in town, each of which sells exactly one hundred tickets.

1. If each lottery has only one winning ticket, and you buy two tickets to the *same* lottery, what is the probability that you will have a winning ticket?

2. If each lottery has only one winning ticket, and you buy one ticket to *each* of the two lotteries, what is the probability that you will have at least one winning ticket?

3. If each lottery has only one winning ticket, and you buy one ticket to each of the two lotteries, what is the probability that you will have *two* winning tickets?

4. If each lottery has two winning tickets, and you buy one ticket to each of the two lotteries, what is the probability that you will have at least one winning ticket?

5. If each lottery has two winning tickets, and you buy two tickets to the same lottery, what is the probability that you will have two winning tickets?

6. If each lottery has two winning tickets, and you buy two tickets to the same lottery, what is the probability that you will have at least one winning ticket?

1. You are presented with two bags, one containing two ham sandwiches and the other containing a ham sandwich and a cheese sandwich. You reach in one bag and draw out a ham sandwich. What is the probability that the other sandwich in the bag is also a ham sandwich?

2. You are presented with three bags: two contain a chicken-fat sandwich and one contains a cheese sandwich. You are asked to guess which bag contains the cheese sandwich. You do so, and the bag you selected is set aside. (You obviously have one chance in three of guessing correctly.) From the two remaining bags, one containing a chicken-fat sandwich is then removed. You are now given the opportunity to switch your selection to the remaining bag. Will such a switch increase, decrease, or leave unaffected your chances of correctly ending up with the bag with the cheese sandwich in it?

BAYES'S THEOREM

Although dice and cards provide nice, simple models for learning how to calculate probabilities, real life is usually more complicated. One particularly interesting and important form of problem arises often in medicine. Suppose that Wendy tests positive for colon cancer. The treatment for colon cancer is painful and dangerous, so, before subjecting Wendy to that treatment, her doctor wants to determine how likely it is that Wendy really has colon cancer. After all, no test is perfect. Regarding the test that was used on Wendy, previous studies have revealed the following probabilities:

The probability that a person in the general population has colon cancer is 0.3 percent (or 0.003).

If a person has colon cancer, then the probability that the test is positive is 90 percent (or 0.9).

If a person does not have colon cancer, then the probability that the test is positive is 3 percent (or 0.03).

On these assumptions, what is the probability that Wendy actually has colon cancer, given that she tested positive? Most people guess that this probability is fairly high. Even most trained physicians would say that Wendy probably has colon cancer.[4]

What is the correct answer? To calculate the probability that a person who tests positive actually has colon cancer, we need to divide the number of favorable outcomes by the number of total outcomes. The favorable outcomes include everyone who tests positive and really has colon cancer. This outcome is not "favorable" to Wendy, so we will describe this group as *true positives*. The total outcomes include everyone who tests positive. This includes the true positives plus the *false positives*, which are those who test positive but do not have colon cancer. Given the stipulated probabilities, in a normal population of 100,000 people, there will be 270 true positives (100,000 × 0.003 × 0.9) and 2,991 false positives [(100,000 – 300) × 0.03]. Thus, the probability that Wendy has colon cancer is about 270/(270 + 2,991). That is only about 8.3 percent, when most people estimate above 50 percent!

Why do people, including doctors, overestimate these probabilities so badly? Part of the answer seems to be that they focus on the rate of true positives (90 percent) and forget that, because there are so many people without colon cancer (99.7 percent of the total population), even a small rate of false positives (3 percent) will yield a large number of false positives (2,991) that swamps the much smaller number of true positives (270). (When the question about probability was reformulated in terms of the number of people in each group, most doctors come up with the correct answer.) For whatever reason, people have a strong tendency to make mistakes in cases like these, so we need to be careful, especially when so much is at stake.

One way to calculate probabilities like these uses a famous theorem that was first presented by an English clergyman named Thomas Bayes (1702–1761). A simple proof of this theorem applies the laws of probability from the preceding section. We want to figure out $\Pr(h \,|\, e)$, that is, the probability of the hypothesis h (for example, Wendy has colon cancer), given the evidence e (for example, Wendy tested positive for colon cancer). To get there, we start from Rule 2G:

1. $\Pr(e \,\&\, h) = \Pr(e) \times \Pr(h \,|\, e)$

Dividing both sides by $\Pr(e)$ gives us:

2. $\Pr(h|e) = \dfrac{\Pr(e \,\&\, h)}{\Pr(e)}$

If two formulas are logically equivalent, they must have the same probability. We can establish by truth tables (as in Chapter 6) that "e" is logically equivalent to "$(e \,\&\, h) \lor (e \,\&\, {\sim}h)$." Consequently, we may replace "e" in the denominator of item 2 with "$(e \,\&\, h) \lor (e \,\&\, {\sim}h)$" to get:

3. $\Pr(h|e) = \dfrac{\Pr(e \,\&\, h)}{\Pr[(e \,\&\, h) \lor (e \,\&\, {\sim}h)]}$

Since "$e \,\&\, h$" and "$e \,\&\, {\sim}h$" are mutually exclusive, we can apply Rule 3 to the denominator of item 3 to get:

4. $\Pr(h|e) = \dfrac{\Pr(e \,\&\, h)}{\Pr(e \,\&\, h) + \Pr(e \,\&\, {\sim}h)}$

Finally, we apply Rule 2G to item 4 and get:

$$\text{BT: } \Pr(h \mid e) = \frac{\Pr(h) \times \Pr(e \mid h)}{[\Pr(h) \times \Pr(e \mid h)] + \Pr(\sim h) \times \Pr(e \mid \sim h)]}$$

This is a simplified version of Bayes's theorem.

This theorem enables us to calculate the desired probability in our original example:

h = the patient has colon cancer

e = the patient tests positive for colon cancer

$\Pr(h) = 0.003$

$\Pr(\sim h) = 1 - \Pr(h) = 0.997$

$\Pr(e \mid h) = 0.9$

$\Pr(e \mid \sim h) = 0.03$

If we substitute these values into Bayes's theorem, we get:

$$\Pr(h \mid e) = \frac{0.003 \times 0.9}{[0.003 \times 0.9] + [0.997 \times 0.03]} = \text{about } 0.083$$

In this way, we can calculate the conditional probability of the hypothesis given the evidence from its reverse, that is, from the conditional probability of the evidence given the hypothesis. That is what makes Bayes's theorem so useful.

Many people find a different method more intuitive. The first step is to set up a table. The two factors to be related are: (1) whether the patient has colon cancer and (2) whether the patient tests positive for colon cancer. To chart all possible combinations of these two factors, we need a table like this:

	Colon Cancer	Not Colon Cancer	Total
Test Positive			
Do Not Test Positive			
Total			

Next, we need to enter a population size in the lower right box. The probabilities will not be affected by the population size, but it is cleaner to pick a population that is large enough to get whole numbers when the population is multiplied by the given probabilities. To determine the right size population, add the number of places to the right of the decimal point in the two most specific probabilities, then pick a population of 10 to the power of that sum. In our example, the most specific probabilities are 0.003 and 0.03, and $3 + 2 = 5$, so we can enter 10^5:

	Colon Cancer	Not Colon Cancer	Total
Test Positive			
Do Not Test Positive			
Total			100,000

This population size represents the total number of people who are tested. We have no information about the ones who are not tested, so they cannot figure into our calculations.

The bottom row can now be filled in by dividing the total population into those who have colon cancer and those who do not have colon cancer. Just multiply the population size by the probability of colon cancer in the general population [$\Pr(h)$] to get a number for the second box on the bottom row. This figure represents the total number of people with colon cancer in this population. Then subtract that product from the population size and put the remainder in the remaining box. This represents the total number of people without colon cancer in this population. Since these two groups exhaust the population, they must add up to the total population size. In our case, we were given that the probability that a person in the general population has colon cancer is 0.003. On this basis, we can fill in the bottom row of the table:

	Colon Cancer	Not Colon Cancer	Total
Test Positive			
Do Not Test Positive			
Total	300	99,700	100,000

Next, fill out the second column by dividing the total number of people with colon cancer into those who test positive and those who do not test positive. These numbers can be calculated with the given conditional probability of testing positive, given colon cancer [$\Pr(e \mid h)$]. In our example, if a person has colon cancer, the probability that the test is positive is 0.9. Thus, 270 (= 0.9 × 300) of the people in the colon cancer column will test positive and the rest (300 − 270 = 30) will not, so we get these figures:

	Colon Cancer	Not Colon Cancer	Total
Test Positive	270		
Do Not Test Positive	30		
Total	300	99,700	100,000

Similarly, we can fill out the third column by dividing the total number of people without colon cancer into those who test positive and those who do not test positive. Here we use the conditional probability of a positive test, given that a person does not have colon cancer [$Pr(e|\sim h)$]. This probability was given as 0.03, and $0.03 \times 99{,}700 = 2{,}991$. This number means that, out of a normal population of 99,700 without colon cancer, 2,991 will test positive. Since the figures in this column must add up to a total of 99,700, the remaining figure is $99{,}700 - 2{,}991 = 96{,}709$:

	Colon Cancer	Not Colon Cancer	Total
Test Positive	270	2,991	
Do Not Test Positive	30	96,709	
Total	300	99,700	100,000

Finally, we can fill out the fourth column by calculating total numbers of people who test positive or do not test positive. Simply add across the rows:

	Colon Cancer	Not Colon Cancer	Total
Test Positive	270	2,991	3,261
Do Not Test Positive	30	96,709	96,739
Total	300	99,700	100,000

Check your calculations by adding the right column: $3{,}261 + 96{,}739 = 100{,}000$.

Now that our population is divided up, the solution is staring you in the face. This table shows us that, in a normal population of 100,000 tested people distributed according to the given probabilities, a total of 3,261 will test positive. Out of those, 270 will have colon cancer. Thus, the probability that the patient has colon cancer, given that this patient tested positive, is 270/3,261, which is about 0.083 or 8.3 percent, just as before.

You can also read off other conditional probabilities. If you want to know the conditional probability of *not* having colon cancer, given that your test did *not* come out positive, then you need to look at the row for those who do *not* test positive. The figure at the right of this row tells you that a total of 96,739 out of the total population do not test positive. The column under "Not Colon Cancer" then tells you that 96,709 of these do not have colon cancer. Thus, the conditional probability of not having colon cancer given your test did not come out positive is 96,709/96,739 or about 0.9997. That means that, if you test negative, the odds are extremely high that you do not have colon cancer.

Tables like these work by dividing the population into groups. We already learned some names for these groups:

	Hypothesis (h)	Not Hypothesis (~h)	
Evidence (e)	True Positives	False positives	
Not Evidence (~e)	False Negatives	True Negatives	
			Population

False positives are sometimes also called *false alarms,* and false negatives are sometimes called *misses.* A little more terminology is also common:

Pr(*h*) = base rate or prevalence or prior probability

Pr(*h* | *e*) = solution or posterior probability

Pr(*e* | *h*) = sensitivity of the test

Pr(~*e* | ~*h*) = specificity of the test

$1 - \Pr(e\,|\,h) = 1 - \text{sensitivity} = \text{false negative rate}$

$1 - \Pr(\sim e\,|\,\sim h) = 1 - \text{specificity} = \text{false positive rate}$

You don't need to use these terms in order to calculate the probabilities, but it is useful to learn them so that you will be able to understand people who discuss these issues.

One of the most important lessons of Bayes's theorem is that the base rate has big effects. To see how much it matters, let's recalculate the solution [Pr(*h* | *e*)] in our colon cancer example for different values of the base rate [Pr(*h*)] using the same test with the same sensitivity (Pr(*e* | *h*) = 0.9) and specificity [Pr(~*e* | ~*h*) = 0.97]:

If Pr(*h*) = 0.003, then Pr(*h* | *e*) = 0.083

If Pr(*h*) = 0.03, then Pr(*h* | *e*) = 0.48

If Pr(*h*) = 0.3, then Pr(*h* | *e*) = 0.93

EXERCISE VI

Construct tables to confirm these calculations of Pr(*h* | *e*) for base rates of 0.03 and 0.3.

These calculations show that a positive test result for a given test means a lot more when the base rate is high than when it is low. Thus, if doctors use the specified test as a *screening test* in the general population, and if the rate of colon cancer in that general population is only 0.003, then a positive test result by itself does not show that the patient has cancer. In contrast, if doctors use the specified test as a *diagnostic test* only for people with certain symptoms, and if the rate of colon cancer among people with those symptoms is 0.3, then a positive test result does show that the patient probably has cancer, though the test still might be mistaken. Bayes's theorem, thus, reveals the right ways and the wrong ways to use and interpret such tests.

Notice also what happens to the probabilities when additional tests are performed. In our original example, one positive test result raises the probability of cancer from the base rate of 0.003 to our solution of 0.083. Now suppose that the doctor orders an additional independent test, and the result is again positive. To apply Bayes's theorem at this point, we can take the probability after the original positive test result (0.083) as the prior probability or base rate in calculating the probability after the second positive test result. This method makes sense because we are now interested not in the general population but only in the subpopulation that already tested positive on the first test. The solution after two tests [$Pr(h \mid e)$], where "e" is now two independent positive test results in a row, is 0.731. Next, if the doctor orders a third independent test, and if the result is positive yet again, then $Pr(h \mid e)$ increases to 0.988. Bayes's theorem, thus, reveals the technical rationale behind the commonsense practice of ordering additional tests. Problems arise only when doctors put too much faith in a single positive test result without doing any additional tests.

EXERCISE VII

Construct tables to confirm the above calculations of probabilities after a second and third positive test result.

EXERCISE VIII

1. What would Wendy's chances of having colon cancer be if the other probabilities remained the same as in the original example, except that the probability that a person in the general population has colon cancer only 0.1 percent (or 0.001)?

2. What would Wendy's chances of having colon cancer be if the other probabilities remained the same as in the original example, except that the probability that a person in the general population has colon cancer 1 percent (0.01)?

3. What would Wendy's chances of having colon cancer be if the other probabilities remained the same as in the original example, except that the conditional probability that the test is positive, given that the patient has colon cancer, is only 50 percent (or 0.5)?

4. What would Wendy's chances of having colon cancer be if the other probabilities remained the same as in the original example, except that the conditional probability that the test is positive, given that the patient has colon cancer, is 99 percent (or 0.99)?

(continued)

5. What would Wendy's chances of having colon cancer be if the other probabilities remained the same as in the original example, except that the conditional probability that the test is positive, given that the patient does not have colon cancer, is 1 percent (or 0.01)?

6. What would Wendy's chances of having colon cancer be if the other probabilities remained the same as in the original example, except that the conditional probability that the test is positive, given that the patient does not have colon cancer, is 10 percent (0.1)?

7. Chris tested positive for cocaine once in a random screening test. This test has a sensitivity and specificity of 95 percent, and 20 percent of the students in Chris's school use cocaine. What is the probability that Chris really did use cocaine?

8. As in problem 7, 20 percent of the students in Chris's school use cocaine, but this time Chris tests positive for cocaine on two independent tests, both of which have a sensitivity and specificity of 95 percent. Now what is the probability that Chris really did use cocaine?

9. In your neighborhood, 20 percent of the houses have high levels of radon gas in their basements, so you ask an expert to test your basement. An inexpensive test comes out positive in 80 percent of the basements that actually have high levels of radon, but it also comes out positive in 10 percent of the basements that do not have high levels of radon. If this inexpensive test comes out positive in your basement, what is the probability that there is a high level of radon gas in your basement?

10. A more expensive test for radon is also more accurate. It comes out positive in 99 percent of the basements that actually have high levels of radon. It also tests positive in 2 percent of the basements that do not high levels of radon. As in problem 7, 20 percent of the houses in your neighborhood have radon in their basement. If the expensive test comes out positive in your basement, what is the probability that there is a high level of radon gas in your basement?

11. Late last night a car ran into your neighbor and drove away. In your town, there are 500 cars, and 2 percent of them are Porsches. The only eyewitness to the hit-and-run says the car that hit your neighbor was a Porsche. Tested under similar conditions, the eyewitness mistakenly classifies cars of other makes as Porsches 10 percent of the time, and correctly classifies Porsches as such 80 percent of the time. What are the chances that the car that hit your neighbor really was a Porsche?

12. Late last night a dog bit your neighbor. In your town, there are 400 dogs, 95 percent of them are black Labrador retrievers, and the rest are pit bulls. The only eyewitness to the event, a veteran dog breeder, says that the dog who bit your neighbor was a pit bull. Tested under similar low-light conditions, the eyewitness mistakenly classifies black Labs as pit bulls only 2 percent of the time, and correctly classifies pit bulls as pit bulls 90 percent of the time. What are the chances that dog who bit your neighbor really was a pit bull?

13. In a certain school, the probability that a student reads the assigned pages before a lecture is 80 percent (or 0.8). If a student does the assigned reading in advance, then the probability that the student will understand the lecture is 90 percent (or 0.9). If a student does not do the assigned reading in advance, then the probability that the student will understand the lecture is 10 percent (or 0.1). What is the probability that a student did the reading in advance, given that she did understand the lecture? What is the probability that a student did *not* do the reading in advance, given that she did *not* understand the lecture?

14. In a different school, the probability that a student reads the assigned pages before a lecture is 60 percent (or 0.6). If a student does the assigned reading in advance, then the probability that, when asked, the student will tell the professor that he did the reading is 100 percent (or 1.0). If a student does not do the assigned reading in advance, then the probability that, when asked, the student will tell the professor that he did the reading is 70 percent (or 0.7). What is the probability that a student did the reading in advance, given that, when asked, he told the professor that he did the reading? What is the probability that a student did not do the reading in advance, given that, when asked, he told the professor that he did not do the reading?

NOTES

[1] Amos Tversky and Daniel Kahneman, "Extensional Versus Intuitive Reasoning: The Conjunction Fallacy in Probability Judgment," *Psychological Review* 90 (1983): 297.

[2] Ibid.

[3] Thomas Gilovich, Robert Vallone, and Amos Tversky, "The Hot Hand in Basketball: The Misperception of Random Sequences," *Cognitive Psychology* 17 (1985): 295–314. The quotation is from pages 295 to 296.

[4] See Gerd Gigerenzer, *Calculated Risk: How to Know When Numbers Deceive You* (New York: Simon & Schuster, 2003).

12

CHOICES

Probabilities are used not only when we determine what to believe but also when we choose what to do. Although we sometimes assume that we know how our actions will turn out, we often have to make decisions in the face of risk, when we do not know what the outcomes of our options will be, but we do know the probabilities of those outcomes. To help us assess reasoning about choices involving risk, this chapter will explain the notions of expected monetary value and expected overall value. Our most difficult choices arise, however, when we do not know even the probabilities of various outcomes. Such decisions under ignorance or uncertainty pose special problems, for which a number of rules have been proposed. Although these rules are useful in many situations, their limitations will also be noted.

EXPECTED MONETARY VALUE

It is obvious that having some sense of probable outcomes is important for running our lives. If we hear that there is a 95 percent chance of rain, this usually provides a good enough reason to call off a picnic. But the exact relationship between probabilities and decisions is complex and often misunderstood.

The best way to illustrate these misunderstandings is to look at lotteries in which the numbers are fixed and clear. A $1 bet in a lottery might make you as much as $10 million. That sounds good. Why not take a shot at $10 million for only a dollar? Of course, there is not much chance of winning the lottery—say, only 1 chance in 20 million—and that sounds bad. Why throw $1 away on nothing? So we are pulled in two directions. What we want to know is just how good the bet is. Is it, for example, better or worse than a wager in some other lottery? To answer questions of this kind, we need to introduce the notion of expected monetary value.

The idea of expected monetary value takes into account three features that determine whether a bet is financially good or bad: the probability of winning, the net amount you gain if you win, and the net amount you lose if you lose. Suppose that on a $1 ticket there is 1 chance in 20 million of winning the New York State Lottery, and you will get $10 million from the state if you do. First, it is worth noticing that, if the state pays you $10 million, your net gain on your $1 ticket is only $9,999,999. The state, after all, still has your original $1. So the net gain equals the payoff minus the cost of betting. This is not something that those who win huge lotteries worry about, but taking into account the cost of betting becomes important when this cost becomes high relative to the size of the payoff. There is nothing complicated about the net amount that you lose when you lose on a $1 ticket: It is $1.[1]

We can now compute the expected monetary value or financial worth of a bet in the following way:

Expected monetary value =

(the probability of winning times the net gain in money of winning) minus

(the probability of losing times the net loss in money of losing)

In our example, a person who buys a $1 ticket in the lottery has 1 chance in 20 million of a net gain of $9,999,999 and 19,999,999 chances in 20 million of a net loss of a dollar. So the expected monetary value of this wager equals:

$$(1/20,000,000 \times \$9,999,999) - (19,999,999/20,000,000 \times \$1)$$

That comes out to −$0.50.

What does this mean? One way of looking at it is as follows: If you could somehow buy up all the lottery tickets and thus ensure that you would win, your $20 million investment would net you $10 million, or $0.50 on the dollar—certainly a bad investment. Another way of looking at the situation is as follows: If you invested a great deal of money in the lottery over many millions of years, you could expect to win eventually, but, in the long run, you would be losing fifty cents on every ticket you bought. One last way of looking at the situation is this: You go down to your local drugstore and buy a blank lottery ticket for $0.50. Since it is blank, you have no chance of winning, with the result that you lose $0.50 every time you bet. Although almost no one looks at the matter in this way, this is, in effect, what you are doing financially over the long run when you buy lottery tickets.

We are now in a position to distinguish favorable and unfavorable expected monetary values. The expected monetary value is favorable when it is greater than zero. Changing our example, suppose the chances of hitting a $20 million payoff on a $1 bet are 1 in 10 million. In this case, the state still has the $1 you paid for the ticket, so your gain is actually $19,999,999. The expected monetary value is calculated as follows:

$$(1/10,000,000 \times \$19,999,999) - (9,999,999/10,000,000 \times \$1)$$

That comes to $1. Financially, this is a good bet, for in the long run you will gain $1 for every $1 you bet in such a lottery.

The rule, then, has three parts: (1) If the expected monetary value of the bet is more than zero, then the expected monetary value is *favorable*. (2) If the expected monetary value of the bet is less than zero, then the expected monetary value is *unfavorable*. (3) If the expected monetary value of the bet is zero, then the bet is *neutral*—a waste of time as far as money is concerned.

EXERCISE I

Compute the probability and the expected monetary value for the following bets. Each time, you lay down $1 to bet that a certain kind of card will appear from a standard fifty-two-card deck. If you win, you collect the amount indicated, so your net gain is $1 less. If you lose, of course, you lose your $1.

> Example: Draw a seven of spades. Win: $26.
> Probability of winning = 1/52
> Expected value: [1/52 × $(26−1)] − (51/52 × $1) = −$0.50

1. Draw a seven of spades or a seven of clubs. Win: $26.
2. Draw a seven of any suit. Win: $26.
3. Draw a face card (jack, queen, or king). Win: $4.
4. Do *not* draw a face card (jack, queen, or king). Win: $2.
5. On two consecutive draws without returning the first card to the deck, draw a seven of spades and then a seven of clubs. Win: $1,989.
6. Same as in problem 5, but this time the card is returned to the deck and the deck is shuffled before the second draw. Win: $1,989.
7. On two consecutive draws without returning the first card to the deck, do not draw a club. Win: $1.78.
8. Same as in problem 7, but this time the card is returned to the deck and the deck is shuffled before the second draw. Win: $1.78.
9. On four consecutive draws without returning any cards to the deck, a seven of spades, then a seven of clubs, then a seven of hearts, and then seven of diamonds. Win: $1,000,001.
10. On four consecutive draws without returning any cards to the deck, draw four sevens in any order. Win: $1,000,001.

EXERCISE II

Fogelin's Palace in Border, Nevada, offers the following unusual bet. If you win, you make a 50 percent profit on your bet; if you lose, you take a 40 percent loss. That is, if you bet $1 and win, then you get back $1.50; if you bet $1 and lose, you get back $0.60. The chances of winning are fifty-fifty. This sounds like a marvelous opportunity, but there is one hitch: To play, you must let your bet ride with its winnings, or losses, for four plays. For example, with $100, a four-bet sequence might look like this:

	Win	Win	Lose	Win
Total	$150	$225	$135	$202.50

At the end of this sequence, you can pick up $202.50, and thus make a $102.50 profit. It seems that Fogelin's Palace is a good place to gamble, but consider

(continued)

the following argument on the other side. Because the chances of winning are fifty-fifty, you will, on the average, win half the time. But notice what happens in such a case:

	Win	**Lose**	**Lose**	**Win**
Total	$150	$90	$54	$81

So, even though you have won half the time, you have come out $19 behind.

Surprisingly, it does not matter what order the wins and losses come in; if two are wins and two are losses, you come out behind. (You can check this.) So, because you are only going to win roughly half the time, and when you win half the time you actually lose money, it now seems to be a bad idea to gamble at Fogelin's Palace.

What should you do: gamble at Fogelin's Palace or not? Why?

EXPECTED OVERALL VALUE

Given that lotteries usually have an extremely unfavorable expected monetary value, why do millions of people invest billions of dollars in them each year? Part of the answer is that some people are stupid, superstitious, or both. People will sometimes reason, "Somebody has to win; why not me?" They can also convince themselves that their lucky day has come. But that is not the whole story, for most people who put down money on lottery tickets realize that the bet is a bad bet, but think that it is worth doing anyway. People fantasize about what they will do with the money if they win, and fantasies are fun. Furthermore, if the bet is only $1, and the person making the bet is not desperately poor, losing is not going to hurt much. Even if the expected monetary value on the lottery ticket is the loss of fifty cents, this might strike someone as a reasonable price for the fun of thinking about winning. (After all, you accept a sure loss of $8 every time you pay $8 to see a movie.) So a bet that is bad from a purely monetary point of view might be acceptable when other factors are considered.

The reverse situation can also arise: A bet may be unreasonable, even though it has a positive expected monetary value. Suppose, for example, that you are allowed to participate in a lottery in which a $1 ticket gives you 1 chance in 10 million of getting a payoff of $20 million. Here, as noted above, the expected monetary value of a $1 bet is a profit of $1, so from the point of view of expected monetary value, it is a good bet. This makes it sound reasonable to bet in this lottery, and a small bet probably is reasonable. But under these circumstances, would it be reasonable for you to sell everything you owned to buy lottery tickets? The answer to this is almost certainly no, for, even though the expected monetary value is positive, the odds of winning are still low, and the loss of your total resources would be personally catastrophic.

When we examine the effects that success or failure will have on a particular person relative to his or her own needs, resources, preferences, and so on, we are then examining what we shall call the *expected overall value* or *expected utility* of a choice. Considerations of this kind often force us to make adjustments in weighing the significance of costs and payoffs. In the examples we just examined, the immediate catastrophic consequences of a loss outweigh the long-term gains one can expect from participating in the lottery.

Another factor that typically affects the expected overall value of a bet is the phenomenon known as the *diminishing marginal value* or *diminishing marginal utility* of a payoff as it gets larger. Suppose someone offers to pay a debt by buying you a hamburger. Provided that the debt matches the cost of a hamburger and you feel like having one, you might go along with this. But suppose this person offers to pay off a debt ten times larger by buying you ten hamburgers. The chances are that you will reject the offer, for even though ten hamburgers cost ten times as much as one hamburger, they are not worth ten times as much to you. At some point you will get stuffed and not want any more. After one or two hamburgers, the marginal value of one more hamburger becomes pretty low. The notion of marginal value applies to money as well. If you are starving, $10 will mean a lot to you. You might be willing to work hard to get it. If you are wealthy, $10 more or less makes little difference; losing $10 might only be an annoyance.

Because of this phenomenon of diminishing marginal value, betting on lotteries is an even worse bet than most people suppose. A lottery with a payoff of $20 million sounds attractive, but it does not seem to be twenty times more attractive than a payoff of $1 million. So even if the expected monetary value of your $1 bet in a lottery is the loss of $0.50, the actual value to you is really something less than this, and so the bet is even worse than it seemed at first.

In general, then, when payoffs are large, the expected overall value of the payoff to someone is reduced because of the effects of diminishing marginal value. But not always. It is possible to think of exotic cases in which expected overall value increases with the size of the payoff. Suppose a witch told you that she would turn you into a toad if you did not give her $10 million by tomorrow. You believe her, because you know for a fact that she has turned others into toads when they did not pay up. You have only $1 to your name, but you are given the opportunity to participate in the first lottery described above, where a $1 ticket gives you 1 chance in 20 million of hitting a $10 million payoff. We saw that the expected monetary value of that wager was an unfavorable negative $0.50. But now consider the overall value of $1 to you if you are turned into a toad. Toads have no use for money, so to you, as a toad, the value of the dollar would drop to nothing. Thus, unless some other, more attractive alternatives are available, it would be reasonable to buy a lottery ticket, despite the unfavorable expected monetary value of the wager.

1. Though the situation is somewhat far-fetched, suppose you are going to the drugstore to buy medicine for a friend who will die without it. You have only $10—exactly what the medicine costs. Outside the drugstore a young man is playing three-card monte, a simple game in which the dealer shows you three cards, turns them over, shifts them briefly from hand to hand, and then lays them out, face down, on the top of a box. You are supposed to identify a particular card (usually the ace of spades); and, if you do, you are paid even money. You yourself are a magician and know the sleight-of-hand trick that fools most people, and you are sure that you can guess the card correctly nine times out of ten. First, what is the expected monetary value of a bet of $10? In this context, would it be reasonable to make this bet? Why or why not?

2. Provide an example of your own where a bet can be reasonable even though the expected monetary value is unfavorable. Then provide another example where the bet is unreasonable even though the expected monetary value is favorable. Explain what makes these bets reasonable or unreasonable.

Consider the following game: You flip a coin continuously until you get tails once. If you get no heads (tails on the first flip), then you are paid nothing. If you get one heads (tails on the second flip), then you are paid $2. If you get two heads (tails on the third flip), then you are paid $4. If you get three heads, then you are paid $8. And so on. The general rule is that for any number n, if you get n heads, then you are paid 2^n. What is the expected monetary value of this game? What would you pay to play this game? Why that amount rather than more or less?

DECISIONS UNDER IGNORANCE

So far we have discussed choices where the outcomes of the various options are not certain, but we know their probabilities. Decisions of this kind are called *decisions under risk*. In other cases, however, we do not know the probabilities of various outcomes. Decisions of this kind are called *decisions under ignorance* (or, sometimes, *decisions under uncertainty*). If we do not have any idea where the probabilities of various outcomes lie, the ignorance is complete. If we know that these probabilities lie within some general range, the ignorance is partial.

As an example of partial ignorance, suppose that, just after graduating from college, you are offered three jobs. First, the Exe Company offers you a salary of $20,000. Exe is well established and secure. The next offer comes from the Wye Company. Here the salary is $30,000, but Wye is a new company, so it is less secure. You think that this new company will probably do well, but you don't know how likely it is to last or for how long. Wye might go bankrupt, and then you will be left without a job. The final offer comes from the Zee Company, which is as stable as Exe and offers you a salary of $40,000 per year. These offers are summarized in the following table:

	Wye does not go bankrupt	Wye goes bankrupt
Take job at Exe	$20,000	$20,000
Take job at Wye	$30,000	$0
Take job at Zee	$40,000	$40,000

Let's assume that other factors (such as benefits, vacations, location, interest, working conditions, bonuses, raises, and promotions) are all equally desirable in the three jobs. Which job should you take?

The answer is clear: Take the job from the Zee Company. This decision is easy because you end up better off regardless of whether or not Wye goes bankrupt, so it doesn't matter how likely Wye's bankruptcy is. Everyone agrees that you should choose any option that is best whatever happens. This is called the *rule of dominance.*

The problem with the rule of dominance is that it can't help you make choices when no option is better regardless of what happens. Suppose you discover that the letter from the Zee Company is a forgery—part of a cruel joke by your roommate. Now your only options are Exe and Wye. The job with Wye will be better if Wye does not go bankrupt, but the job with Exe will be better if Wye does go bankrupt. Neither job is better no matter what happens, so the rule of dominance no longer applies.

To help you choose between Exe and Wye, you might look for a rational way to assign probabilities despite your ignorance of which assignments are correct. One approach of this kind uses the *rule of insufficient reason:* When you have no reason to think that any outcome is more likely than any other, assume that the outcomes are equally probable. This assumption enables us to calculate expected monetary value or utility, as in the preceding sections, and then we can choose the option with the highest expected utility. In our example, this rule of insufficient reason favors the job at Exe, because your expected income in that job is $20,000, whereas your expected income in the job at Wye is only $15,000 (= 0.5 × $30,000), assuming that the Wye company has as much chance of going bankrupt as of staying in business.

The problem with the rule of insufficient reason is that it may seem arbitrary to assume that unknown probabilities are equal. Often we suspect that the probabilities of various outcomes are not equal, even while we do not know what the probabilities are. Moreover, the rule of insufficient reason yields different results when the options are described differently. We can distinguish four possibilities: Wye goes bankrupt, Wye stays the same size, Wye increases in size, and Wye decreases in size but stays in business. If we do not have any reason to see any of these outcomes as more likely than any other, then the rule of insufficient reason tells us to assign them equal probabilities. On that assumption, and if you will keep your job as long as Wye stays in business, then you have only one chance in four of losing your job; so your expected income in the job at Wye is now $22,500 (= 0.75 × $30,000). Thus, if we stick with the rule of insufficient reason, the expected value of the job at Wye and whether you should take that job seem to depend on how the options are divided. That seems crazy in this case.

Another approach tries to work without any assumptions about probability in cases of ignorance. Within this approach, several rules might be adopted. One possibility is the *maximax rule,* which tells you to choose the option whose best outcome is better than the best outcome of any other option. If you follow the maximax rule, then you will accept the job with the Wye Company, because the best outcome of that job is a salary of $30,000 when this new company does not go bankrupt, and this is better than any outcome with the Exe Company. Optimists and risk takers will favor this rule.

Other people are more pessimistic and tend to avoid risks. They will favor a rule more like the *maximin rule,* which says to choose the option whose worst outcome is better than the worst outcome of any other option. If you follow the maximin rule, you will accept the job with the Exe Company, because the worst outcome in that job is a steady salary of $20,000, whereas the worst outcome is unemployment if you accept the job with the Wye Company.

Each of these rules works by focusing exclusively on part of your information and disregarding other things that you know. The maximax rule considers only the best outcomes for each option—the best-case scenario. The maximin rule pays attention to only the worst outcome for each option—the worst-case scenario. Because they ignore other outcomes, the maximax rule strikes many people as too risky (since it does not consider how much you could lose by taking a chance), and the maximin rule strikes many people as too conservative (since it does not consider how much you could have gained if you had taken a small risk).

Another problem is that the maximax and maximin rules do not take probabilities into account at all. This makes sense when you know nothing about the probabilities. But when some (even if limited) information about probabilities is available, then it seems better to use as much information as you have. Suppose, for example, that each of two options might lead to disaster, and you do not know how likely a disaster is after either option, but you do know that one option is more likely to lead to disaster than another. In such situations, some decision theorists argue that you should choose the option that minimizes the chance that any disaster will occur. This is called the *disaster avoidance rule*.

To illustrate this rule, consider a different kind of case:

> A forty-year-old man is diagnosed as having a rare disease and consults the world's leading expert on the disease. He is informed that the disease is almost certainly not fatal but often causes serious paralysis that leaves its victims bedridden for life. (In other cases it has no lasting effects.) The disease is so rare that the expert can offer only a vague estimate of the probability of paralysis: 20 to 60 percent. There is an experimental drug that, if administered now, would almost certainly cure the disease. However, it kills a significant but not accurately known percentage of those who take it. The expert guesses that the probability of the drug being fatal is less than 20 percent, and the patient thus assumes that he is definitely less likely to die if he takes the drug than he is to be paralyzed if he lets the disease run its course. The patient would regard bedridden life as preferable to death, but he considers both outcomes as totally disastrous compared to continuing his life in good health. Should he take the drug?[2]

Since the worst outcome is death, and this outcome will not occur unless he takes the drug, the maximin rule would tell him not to take the drug. In contrast, the disaster avoidance rule would tell him to take the drug, because both death and paralysis are disasters and taking the drug minimizes his chances that any disaster will occur. Thus, although the disaster avoidance rule opposes risk taking, it does so in a different way than the maximin rule.

We are left, then, with a plethora of rules: dominance, insufficient reason, maximax, maximin, and disaster avoidance. Other rules have been proposed as well. With all of these rules in the offing, it is natural to ask which is correct. Unfortunately, there is no consensus on this issue. Each rule applies and seems plausible in some cases but not in others. Many people conclude that each rule is appropriate to different kinds of situations. It is still not clear, however, which rule should govern decisions in which circumstances. The important problem of decision under ignorance remains unsolved.

◿ DISCUSSION QUESTIONS ◺

1. In the game of ignorance, you draw one card from a deck, but you do not know how many cards or which kinds of cards are in the deck. It might be a normal deck or it might contain only diamonds or only aces of spades or any other combination of cards. It costs nothing to play. If you bet that the card you draw will be a spade, and it is a spade, then you win $100. If you bet that the card you draw will not be a spade, and it is not a spade, then you win $90. You may make only one bet. Which bet would you make if you followed the maximax rule? The maximin rule? The disaster avoidance rule? The rule of insufficient reason? Which rule seems most plausible this case? Which bet should you make? Why?

2. In which circumstances do you think it is appropriate to use the dominance rule? The rule of insufficient reason? The maximax rule? The maximin rule? The disaster avoidance rule? Why?

3. Suppose that you may choose either of two envelopes. You know that one envelope contains twice as much money as the other, but you do not know the amount of money in either envelope. You choose an envelope, open it, and see that it contains $100. Now you know that the other envelope must contain either $50 or $200. At this point, you are given a choice: You may exchange your envelope for the other envelope. Should you switch envelopes, according to the rule of insufficient reason? Is this result plausible? Why or why not?

NOTES

[1] If the lottery gave a consolation prize of a shiny new quarter to all losers, their net loss would be only seventy-five cents. Since most lotteries do not give consolation prizes, the net loss equals the cost of playing such lotteries.

[2] Gregory Kavka, "Deterrence, Utility, and Rational Choice," reprinted in *Moral Paradoxes of Nuclear Deterrence* (New York: Cambridge University Press, 1987), 65–66. Kavka uses this medical example to argue for his disaster avoidance rule and, by analogy, to defend the rationality of nuclear deterrence.